OECD Reviews of Migrant Education

Immigrant Students at School

EASING THE JOURNEY TOWARDS INTEGRATION

Please cite this publication as:
OECD (2015), *Immigrant Students at School: Easing the Journey towards Integration*, OECD Publishing.
http://dx.doi.org/10.1787/9789264249509-en

ISBN (print) 978-92-64-24949-3
ISBN (PDF) 978-92-64-24950-9

Series: OECD Reviews of Migrant Education
ISSN: 20776802 (print)
ISSN: 20776829 (online)

Photo credit:
© Jazzmany/Shutterstock.com

Corrigenda to OECD publications may be found on line at: www.oecd.org/publishing/corrigenda.

Foreword

How school systems respond to migration has an enormous impact on the economic and social well-being of all members of the communities they serve, whether they have an immigrant background or not. This begins with ensuring that immigrant children succeed academically. It extends to preparing all students for a world in which people are willing and able to collaborate with others of diverse cultural origins and appreciate different ideas, perspectives and values. And it ends with making school a place where all children feel they belong.

Some systems need to integrate large numbers of school-age immigrants and asylum seekers quickly; some need to accommodate students whose mother tongue is different from the language spoken in the host community or whose families are socio-economically disadvantaged; some systems are confronted with all three challenges at once.

The difficulties can seem insurmountable, but the fact that the educational, social and emotional success of immigrant students differs so widely across countries and school settings, and that countries pursue such different policies and practices in leveraging the potential of immigrant children, underlines that there is much that countries can learn from each other.

This report pulls together available data and policy pointers in this area to establish the foundation for a much wider set of activities. The OECD offers its support to countries who want to build on this foundation to meet the needs of immigrants and refugees and to give their children the best chance of fulfilling their potential.

The report draws on analyses of the OECD Programme for International Student Assessment (PISA) and was drafted by the OECD Directorate for Education and Skills, principally Francesca Borgonovi and Mario Piacentini. Rowena Phair contributed material for Chapter 6 and Ann Scowcroft from UNHCR contributed material for the special section on refugee education in Chapter 3. Marilyn Achiron edited the publication, Judit Pál and Giannina Rech provided statistical support, and Sophie Limoges co-ordinated production of the publication. Thomas Liebig, from the Directorate for Employment, Labour and Social Affairs, provided comments on the report.

Editorial

by **Andreas Schleicher**

Over the past several months, tens of thousands of migrants and asylum-seekers – including an unprecedented number of children – have braved rough seas and barbed-wire barricades to find safety and a better life in Europe. Are our schools prepared to help immigrant students integrate into their new communities? And will they succeed in preparing all students for a world in which people are willing and able to collaborate with others of diverse cultural origins; appreciate different ideas, perspectives and values; and join others in life, work and citizenship?

Even before this latest influx, the population of immigrant students in OECD countries had been growing. In 2012, 12% of 15-year-old students had an immigrant background, on average across OECD countries. Between 2003 and 2012, the share of immigrant students had grown by between 4 and 6 percentage points in Ireland, Italy and Spain. And such averages mask important variations, not just across countries but also within countries, as immigrant children are often concentrated in schools and classrooms, amplifying the challenge of diversity for teachers and school leaders.

What has been the result? This report shows that the increase in the share of immigrant students between 2003 and 2012 did not lead to a decline in the education standards in host communities. More generally, the OECD Programme for International Student Assessment (PISA) shows no relationship between the share of immigrant students in a school system and the performance of that system. That may be surprising only at a first look. While it is true that migrants often endure economic hardship and precarious living conditions, many immigrants bring to their host countries valuable skills and human capital: on average across OECD countries, the majority of the first-generation immigrants taking part in the PISA 2012 assessment had at least one parent who had attended school for as many years as the average parent in the host country.

High aspirations

Many immigrants are determined to make the most of any opportunity that arises from the sacrifices they made by migrating. Most immigrant students – and their parents – hold an ambition to succeed that in most cases matches, and in some cases surpasses, the aspirations of families in their host country. For example, parents of immigrant students in Belgium, Germany and Hungary are more likely to expect that their children will earn a university-level degree than are the parents of students without an immigrant background. That is remarkable, given that immigrant students in these countries do not perform as well as, and their families are more disadvantaged than, students without an immigrant background.

When comparing students of similar socio-economic status, the difference between immigrant and non-immigrant students in their parents' educational expectations for them grows even larger. In Belgium, Germany, Hong Kong-China and Hungary, the parents of immigrant students hold much higher educational expectations for their children than the parents of similarly disadvantaged non-immigrant students. And this is true even when comparing students who perform similarly at school. In 14 countries in 2012, immigrant students themselves held more ambitious career expectations than students without an immigrant background. Students who hold ambitious – yet realistic – expectations about their educational prospects are more likely to put effort into their learning and make better use of the education opportunities available to them to achieve their goals.

The analysis shows that in Australia, Israel and the United States, the share of socio-economically disadvantaged students who perform among the top quarter of all PISA students is larger among immigrant students than among non-immigrant students (Figure 5.4). These highly motivated students, who managed to overcome the double disadvantage of poverty and an immigrant background, have the potential to make exceptional contributions to their host countries and the communities that helped them thrive.

The importance of sound policies

A second striking finding of this analysis is the remarkable cross-country variation in performance between students with and students without an immigrant background, even after accounting for socio-economic status (Figure 2.1). This suggests that policy has an important role to play in reducing the disadvantage that accompanies displacement.

But designing education policies to address the needs of students with an immigrant background – particularly language instruction – is not easy; and education policy alone is insufficient. For example, the performance of students in PISA is more strongly (and negatively) associated with the concentration of socio-economic disadvantage in schools than with the concentration of immigrants or of students who speak a different language at home from the language in which they are taught. Reducing the concentration of disadvantage in schools may require changes in other social policy, such as housing or welfare, to encourage a more balanced social mix in schools.

A third important finding is that, even if the culture and the education acquired before migrating have an impact on student performance, the country where immigrant students settle matters more. For example, students from Arabic-speaking countries who settled in the Netherlands score 100 points higher in mathematics than students from the same countries who settled in Qatar, even after accounting for socio-economic differences – that's about the achievement gap between Greece and Korea (Figure 2.3). Albanian students in Greece score 50 points higher in mathematics than Albanian students of similar socio-economic status in Montenegro, a difference that is very close to the average performance difference between Greece and Montenegro. And while students born in China do better than their native peers in virtually any country, that advantage varies across countries too. These findings indicate how much public policy can contribute to integrating the children of immigrants.

Feeling part of a new community

Beyond performance in school, an important indication of how well immigrant students are integrating into their new community is whether, and to what extent, they feel they belong to their new surroundings – and, for 15-year-olds, one of the most important social environments is school. PISA asked students about their sense of belonging and the results varied widely, not only overall, but also in the extent to which first- and second-generation immigrant students were more or less likely than students without an immigrant background to feel that they belong at school.

The well-being of immigrant students is affected not just by cultural differences between the country of origin and the host country, but also by how schools and communities help immigrant students to deal with daily problems of living, learning and communicating. For example, when it comes to academic performance, immigrant students from the Arab-speaking world do better in the Netherlands than they do in Finland, but they express a stronger sense of belonging in Finland than they do in the Netherlands. In France, immigrant students have both academic difficulties and report the weakest sense of belonging.

In Belgium, Ireland, Luxembourg and Portugal, first-generation immigrant students expressed the most alienation from education systems as compared to students without an immigrant background. Integration unfolds over time in Luxembourg, Norway and Spain, where second-generation immigrant students expressed a stronger sense of belonging at school than first-generation immigrant students. In Australia, Canada, New Zealand and Qatar, the percentages of both first- and second-generation immigrant students who reported that that feel they belong at school were higher than the percentage of non-immigrant students who so reported. All four of these countries adopt highly selective immigration policies (Figure 2.8).

What the hosts think

Despite the important role immigrants can play in host countries, particularly in light of falling fertility rates and lack of qualified workers in key sectors of the economy, perceptions on the potential short- and long-term value of immigration often clash with concerns over increasing cultural and linguistic diversity. Given the economic hardship that many host-country nationals have faced as a consequence of the recent economic crisis and related cuts in social welfare and protection programmes, new immigrants are often perceived as an economic and social burden.

The analysis shows that, on average, residents in the Czech Republic, Hungary and Israel tended to indicate that they preferred their country to allow few people from poorer countries outside Europe to settle in their country, while residents in Germany, Norway, Poland and Sweden expressed stronger support for allowing many immigrants to settle in their countries.

On average, attitudes towards migration changed little between 2000 and 2012, a period preceding the current migration wave. If anything, between 2000 and 2012 there was a small increase in support for allowing more immigrants from poorer countries outside of Europe to settle in respondents' countries. However, attitudes seem to have grown more polarised over time. Support for migrants appears to have grown stronger in Germany and Sweden, where, in 2000, residents had already expressed comparatively positive attitudes towards allowing many migrants to settle. But support diminished in those countries whose citizens had comparatively negative attitudes towards allowing migrants to settle, such as the Czech Republic and Israel.

During the same period, Poland and Spain saw considerable increases in citizens' willingness to allow more migrants from poorer countries to settle in their country. Even in countries where increases in favourable attitudes towards migration are observed, such as Germany, Norway and Sweden, residents are more likely to express support for allowing entry to more migrants who are similar to themselves than to migrants who differ considerably in their racial and ethnic profile. Conversely, the strong negative attitudes towards migration expressed in Hungary and Israel are primarily directed towards migrants from different ethnic and racial groups than resident populations. Obviously, all of these data come from the period before the latest influx of refugees.

Narrowing the performance gap

While immigrant students, in general, perform worse in school than their non-immigrant peers, the analysis finds that narrowing the performance gap between immigrant students and students without an immigrant background is not only possible, but it can be accomplished at a remarkable pace. Across OECD countries, the performance gap between these two groups narrowed by around 10 score points between 2003 and 2012 – the equivalent of around a semester of school. Some countries saw even more striking progress. In less than one decade, Germany managed to improve the mathematics performance of second-generation immigrant students by 46 score points – the equivalent of more than one year of formal schooling, even when taking composition effects into account. In Portugal, first-generation immigrant students performed much better in 2012 than in 2003, and that improvement was greater than the improvement observed among students without an immigrant background (Figures 2.4 and 2.5).

Various school- and system-related factors are shown to be associated with the performance disadvantage among immigrant students.

First, low performance among immigrant students can be partly linked to the fact that these students tend to be concentrated in disadvantaged schools. A high concentration of socio-economic disadvantage tends to be associated with a larger gap in test scores between immigrant and non-immigrant students. Across OECD countries, the concentration of immigrants in "enclave schools" is particularly high in Canada, Greece and Italy (Figure 4.1).

In most countries, students who attend schools where the concentration of immigrants is high (i.e. where more than a quarter of students are immigrants) tend to perform worse than those in schools with no immigrant students (Figure 4.2), even after accounting for socio-economic status. Here, PISA results mirror evidence from other studies indicating that it is primarily the concentration of disadvantage, not the concentration of immigrant students, that has detrimental effects on learning.

The need to dismantle language barriers

Long-term, successful integration requires social and welfare systems that can reduce rates of poverty among immigrants and provide adequate labour market participation. Education systems can act as an important socialisation mechanisms, both for immigrants and host communities, to foster mutual understanding, respect and trust. But many education systems struggle to provide the language training necessary for immigrants to succeed in their new communities while ensuring that those migrants who want to maintain their heritage language also have the opportunity to do so.

Many students with an immigrant background are also blocked by a language barrier. Those students who were not born in the country and who migrated at a relatively late age face a particular set of difficulties: they need to learn in a language in which they are not proficient – and nor, most likely, are their parents.

The analysis shows that the language profile of students with an immigrant background varies markedly across countries (Figure 4.4). On average, 64% of first-generation immigrant students and 41% of second-generation students speak a language at home that is different from the language of instruction. Indeed, in the Czech Republic, Finland, Iceland, Israel, Slovenia and Sweden, over 80% of first-generation immigrants speak a different language at home from the language of instruction.

Interestingly, the analysis shows no marked differences in reading proficiency between those who arrived before the age of five and those who arrived between the ages of 6 and 11 (Figure 4.8). By contrast, in most OECD countries, immigrant students who arrived at age 12 or later – and therefore spent at most 4 years in their new country – lag farther behind students in the same grade in reading proficiency than immigrants who arrived at younger ages. These students have to quickly acquire language skills and catch up with the higher levels of attainment achieved by their peers, all while coping with the difficulties of adjusting to a new school and social environment. But here too, countries vary markedly in the magnitude of this "late-arrival penalty" for immigrant students. The largest penalties are found in Germany, Israel and Slovenia.

The importance of early learning

One of the ways in which education systems can help to integrate immigrant children into their new communities is to encourage their enrolment in pre-primary education programmes. Across OECD countries, immigrant students who reported that they had attended pre-primary education programmes score 49 points higher in the PISA reading assessment than immigrant students who reported that they had not participated in such programmes (Figure 4.15). But in most countries, participation in pre-primary programmes among immigrant students is considerably lower than it is among students without an immigrant background (Figure 4.14). In some countries, this may be due to a resistance to pre-primary education programmes on the part of immigrant parents, possibly because they had little or no experience of these types of programmes in their country of origin. In other countries, these differences reflect a broader socio-economic divide. PISA finds that disadvantaged 15-year-old students are considerably less likely than their more advantaged peers to have attended pre-primary education.

The analysis also shows that immigrant students are much less familiar than non-immigrant students with the mathematics concepts that they are expected to learn in secondary education. And immigrant students are also likely to have spent considerable time out of school as they were making their way from their country of origin to their host country. More than one in six immigrant students who attend school in an OECD country lost more than two months of school at least once in their life (Figure 4.17).

The pernicious effects of ability grouping

Early tracking of students into academic or vocational programmes tends to increase inequality, because students from disadvantaged backgrounds are more likely to end up in tracks with lower performance expectations. The analysis shows that early tracking has particularly adverse effects on immigrant students, even after accounting for their prior academic achievement. That may be because immigrant parents are unlikely to be familiar with the education system of the host country and thus may not know how to choose the programme that would best suit their child. Even fully informed parents might fail to have their children enrolled in academic tracks if negative expectations or stereotypes about immigrant students are deeply entrenched in the host society.

For example, research has shown that children of immigrants in Germany are less likely to receive a teacher recommendation for an academic track, and this difference cannot be attributed to differences in test scores or general intelligence alone. The tracking of disadvantaged immigrants into less-demanding programmes not only limits their educational development, but also creates barriers to entry into high-status, professional occupations. Many employers still distinguish among prospective employees based on the school attended and the degree earned. Early tracking is particularly troubling in those education systems where students cannot easily change tracks after their initial choice.

In the classroom

Teachers, too, have a large role to play. Many recognise that handling cultural diversity in class is difficult. Indeed, large proportions of teachers in several countries feel they need more professional development in the area of teaching in a multicultural or multilingual setting (Figure 4.18). This feeling of unpreparedness is notable in Latin American countries and in the European countries that recently saw rapid increases in the linguistic and cultural diversity in schools, such as Italy and Spain.

Children in immigrant families are key actors in the process of integration, as they broker communication between members of the host community and their own families, and provide other children with opportunities to learn about different cultures. The analysis suggests that in most countries, a large majority of students without an immigrant background believe that immigrants should have the same rights as other citizens.

Interestingly, countries differ considerably as to whether having immigrant students in class fosters positive attitudes, among students without an immigrant background, towards the rights of migrants. For example, in Bulgaria, Greece, Indonesia, Italy, Korea, Luxembourg, Mexico, the Slovak Republic and Sweden, students who have at least one immigrant student in their class are less likely than students who have no immigrant student in their class to agree that immigrants have the same rights as other citizens; but in the majority of other countries, the presence of immigrant students is associated with greater support for immigrants' rights. This suggests that social mixing will not necessarily promote social cohesion in diverse societies.

But ethnic heterogeneity is not *per se* a hindrance to learning in the classroom. Many schools recognise that minority groups have something to contribute. On average across OECD countries, only 4% of students are in schools whose principal reported that ethnic heterogeneity is a serious obstacle to learning (Figure 4.19). But there are large differences across countries in schools' preparedness to handle multilingual and multicultural student populations. Over 15% of the principals of disadvantaged schools in Belgium, France, Iceland and Qatar reported that ethnic diversity hinders learning. This difference reflects the concentration of immigrant students – those with arguably the largest learning and linguistic deficits – in disadvantaged schools. It also suggests that those schools need to start viewing ethnic differences as a learning resource, not as a liability.

What can education policy do?

The successful integration of refugees and immigrants involves a whole range of policy domains and therefore requires a whole-of-government, and indeed a whole-of-society, response. But education plays a crucial part in this. The policies and practices that countries use to integrate immigrant students into schools have a major influence on whether integration is successful or not; and countries that are unsuccessful in integrating the first generation will pay an even larger price in future generations. So what can education policy do?

Provide language instruction quickly. Combining language and content learning, from as soon as it becomes feasible, has proven to be most effective in integrating children with an immigrant background into education systems. While language assistance is important, it should be in addition to, rather than instead of, regular instruction – regardless of the age of the student or how long ago he or she arrived in the host country.

Offer high-quality early childhood education, tailored to language development. If children enter such programmes at the age of 2 or 3 they have a chance of starting school at almost the same level as non-immigrant children. Where such programmes are not available or if immigrant families are reluctant to enrol their children, targeted home visits can help families to support their child's learning at home and can also ease entry into appropriate education services.

Encourage all teachers, not just specialist teachers, to prepare themselves for diverse classrooms. All efforts to integrate immigrant children successfully depend on well-skilled and well-supported teachers, who can reflect the diversity of their student populations in their instructional approaches and who can help all students to achieve the educational goals and standards of the host country. While many classrooms are now filled with immigrants from a range of backgrounds, the teachers in these classrooms are often ill-prepared in pedagogical approaches for second-language learning or in recognising and helping children overcome the effects of trauma that many immigrant children endure.

Avoid concentrating immigrant students in the same, disadvantaged schools. It is common sense, and borne out in the evidence shown in this report, that schools that struggle to do well for domestic students will struggle even more with a large population of children who cannot speak or understand the language of instruction. Countries that distribute immigrant students across a mix of schools and classrooms achieve better outcomes for these students. A more even distribution also relieves the pressure on schools and teachers when large numbers of immigrant students arrive over a short period of time.

Re-think education policies. While ability grouping, grade repetition and tracking are harmful for all students, immigrant students are more likely to be affected by these practices. Language difficulties and cultural differences can be misinterpreted as lack of ability and potential, when this is not the case.

Reach out to immigrant parents. While teachers are critical to immigrant students' success in schools, so are their parents. Students do better when their parents understand the importance of schooling, how the school system works, and how best to support their child's progress through school.

Table of Contents

BOXES

FIGURES

TABLES

Executive Summary

The current migration crisis in Europe is unprecedented in terms of the number of people involved, but migrant flows into Europe have increased sharply throughout recent decades. In 2012, the latest cycle of the OECD Programme for International Student Assessment (PISA) for which data are available, 12% of 15-year-old students had an immigrant background, on average across OECD countries. At the same time, data from the European Social Survey reveal negative attitudes towards immigration in some countries – which can have an impact on immigrant students' sense of belonging in their new communities.

How education systems respond to immigration has an enormous impact both on whether or not immigrants are successfully integrated into their host communities and on the economic and social well-being of all members of the communities they serve, whether they have an immigrant background or not. Immigrant students perform better, and report feeling more accepted, in some countries/economies than in others – which suggests both that education policy has an impact on integration, and that countries can learn a great deal from each other about how best to achieve that goal.

Results from PISA indicate that, in most countries, first-generation immigrant students perform worse than students without an immigrant background, and students who were born in the country in which they sat the PISA test, but whose parents are foreign-born, perform somewhere between the two. What may account for these performance differences?

In many countries, immigrant students tend to be concentrated in the same schools. The concentration of immigrant students in schools does not, in itself, have to have adverse effects on student performance or on integration efforts. Indeed, PISA data show that it is not the concentration of immigrant students in a school but, rather, the concentration of socio-economic disadvantage in a school that hinders student achievement. The OECD average difference in mathematics performance between students who attend schools where more than 25% of students are immigrants compared to students who attend schools with no immigrant students is 18 score points – the equivalent of around 6 months of schooling. But after accounting for the socio-economic status of the students and schools, that difference is more than halved – to 5 score points.

Many newly arrived immigrant students cannot yet read or speak well – if at all – the predominant language of their host countries. On average, 64% of first-generation immigrant students and 41% of second-generation immigrant students speak a language at home that is different from the language in which the PISA test was conducted. Not surprisingly, students who do not speak the language of assessment perform worse on the PISA reading test than students who do – so much so that, once the language students speak at home is taken into account, the performance gap in reading between first-generation immigrant students and non-immigrant students shrinks considerably.

Even though PISA consistently shows that attendance at pre-primary school for more than one year is associated with better school outcomes among 15-year-olds, the students who could most benefit from these programmes – disadvantaged and immigrant students – are those least likely to participate. For example, 15-year-old immigrant students are 20% less likely than students with no immigrant background to have attended pre-primary education, on average.

Certain school policies, like grade repetition and tracking, also affect immigrant students' progress through school. For example, 15-year-old immigrant students are 3.4 times more likely than non-immigrant students to have repeated a grade either in primary or secondary school, on average across OECD countries;

and they are 44 percentage points more likely than non-immigrant students to be enrolled in vocational programmes – which not only limit the academic skills they may acquire, but also hinder access to high-status professional occupations later on.

And while more and more schools recognise that minority students have a lot to contribute to the classroom – on average across OECD countries, only 4% of students attend schools whose principal reported that ethnic heterogeneity is a serious obstacle to learning – many teachers feel ill-prepared to teach ethnically diverse classes. Large proportions of teachers in several countries reported, through the 2013 OECD Teaching and Learning International Survey (TALIS), that they need more professional development in the area of teaching in a multicultural or multilingual setting. The proportions are strikingly large in Latin American countries and in the European countries that recently saw rapid increases in the linguistic and cultural diversity in their schools, notably Italy and Spain.

Despite these considerable obstacles to success in school, immigrant students hold high aspirations for themselves. Among the countries and economies that participated in PISA 2006, immigrant students in 14 countries and economies were more likely than non-immigrant students to expect to be working as professionals or managers when they were 30; and in 26 countries/economies, immigrant students' career expectations were similar to those held by non-immigrant students. Expectations for higher education and careers are often self-fulfilling prophecies: students who hold ambitious – but realistic – expectations for their future are more likely to put greater effort into their learning and make better use of the education opportunities available to them.

How well immigrant students do at school is not only related to their attitudes, socio-economic status and prior education, but also to the quality and receptiveness of the host-country's education system. How can education systems help immigrant students to integrate into their new communities?

Immediate policy responses

- Provide sustained language support, within regular classrooms as soon as it becomes feasible.
- Encourage immigrant parents to enrol their young children in high-quality early childhood education.
- Build the capacity of all schools attended by immigrant students.

High-impact, medium-term responses

- Avoid concentrating students with an immigrant background in disadvantaged schools.
- Avoid ability grouping, early tracking and grade repetition.
- Provide extra support and guidance to immigrant parents.

Responses to strengthen integration

- Support innovation and experimentation, evaluate results and target funding to what works.
- Demonstrate the value of cultural diversity.
- Monitor progress.

While immigrant students often face cultural and social barriers that compound the effects of socio-economic disadvantage, PISA data show that in some countries, for example the United States, the share of disadvantaged students who perform among the top quarter of all PISA students is larger among immigrant students than among non-immigrant students. These highly motivated students, who managed to overcome the double disadvantage of poverty and an immigrant background, have the potential to make exceptional contributions to their host countries.

Chapter 1
Recent Trends in Immigration and Education

Education systems have a crucial role to play in helping immigrant students to integrate into their new communities. This chapter briefly discusses trends in migration over the past half century, including changes in the numbers and profiles of immigrant students in OECD countries over the past decade. The chapter then examines the impact of immigration on education systems.

Note regarding data from Israel

The statistical data for Israel are supplied by and are under the responsibility of the relevant Israeli authorities. The use of such data by the OECD is without prejudice to the status of the Golan Heights, East Jerusalem and Israeli settlements in the West Bank under the terms of international law.

In 2015, Europe recorded an unprecedented number of asylum seekers: as many as one million. An estimated 350 000 to 450 000 people could be granted refugee or similar status, more than in any previous European refugee crisis since World War II (OECD, 2015a). While the current migration crisis in Europe is unprecedented in terms of the number of people involved, migrant flows into Europe have increased sharply throughout recent decades, except during the most recent economic crisis (OECD, 2015b; Castles and Miller, 2003).

Migration is profoundly changing the demand for the skills societies need to promote social cohesion. It demands the capacity for adaptation among both people with no immigrant background and immigrant populations. Education systems have a crucial role to play in developing these skills, and more should be done to ensure that they are equipped with the tools to do so.

Immigration over the past 50 years

The post-World War II years saw large movements of workers crossing borders to fill jobs for which there were not enough non-immigrant workers in many European countries. At the same time, the traditional settlement countries of Australia, Canada, New Zealand and the United States resumed admitting immigrants, a practice that had been interrupted by the two World Wars and the great Depression. Workers arrived from across the globe as the settlement countries abandoned former restrictive policies, sometimes based on geographic origin.

The oil crisis of the 1970s slowed labour migration as economies adjusted to higher energy prices; but migration did not stop. Many workers remained where they had settled and brought over their families from abroad. Others fled their homelands in the wake of civil wars and political persecution. The transfer of wealth turned the Gulf States into magnets for workers moving across continents to take jobs in oil production, construction, commerce and domestic help.

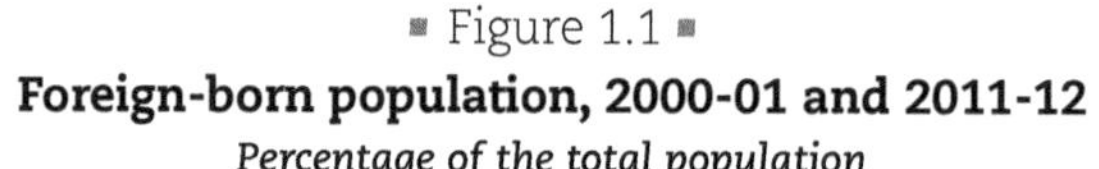

▪ Figure 1.1 ▪

Foreign-born population, 2000-01 and 2011-12

Percentage of the total population

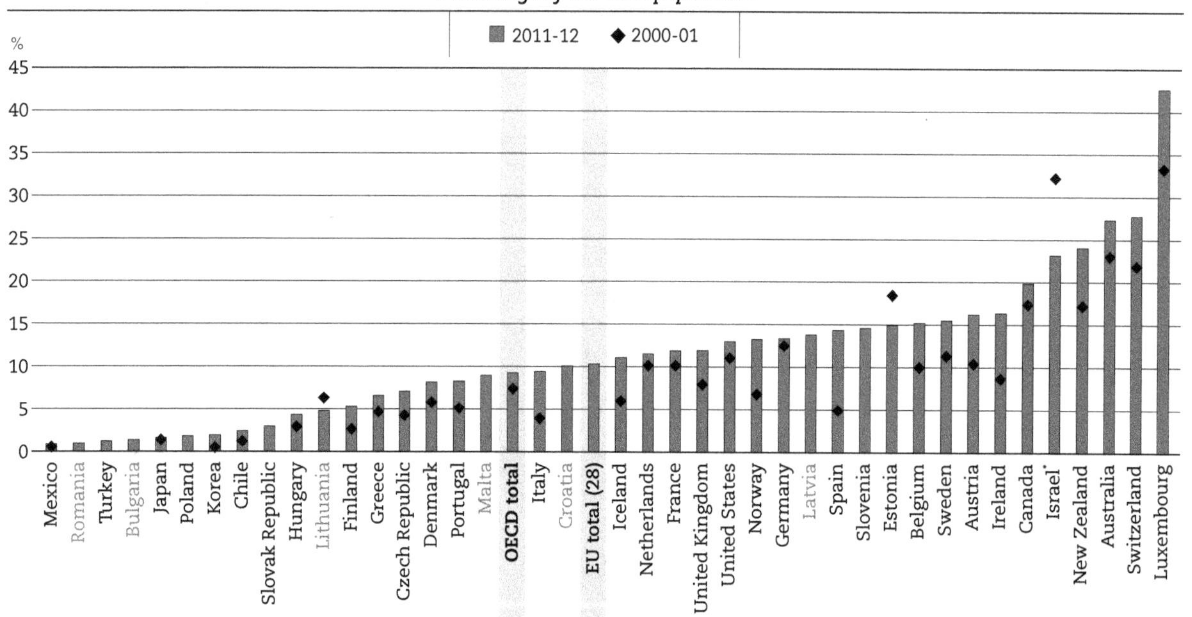

Notes: Korea and Japan determine who is an immigrant on the basis of nationality, not on the basis of country of birth.

Lithuanian data are from 2002.

* See note at the beginning of this chapter.

Source: OECD (2015), *Indicators of Immigrant Integration 2015: Settling In*, OECD Publishing, Paris. OECD Database on International Migration (2000-01 and 2010-11). Eurostat Database on International Migration and Asylum for non-OECD EU member countries (2012-13). European Union Labour Force Survey (EU-LFS) 2012-13 for Croatia and Turkey.

Underlying data for the figures in this chapter can be found at www.oecd.org/edu/school/Immigrant-Students-Chapter1-Figures.xlsx.

More than a decade later, the fall of the Iron Curtain ushered in a new era of international migration, as barriers to out-migration, if not to immigration, came down almost everywhere. In addition, economic globalisation created needs and opportunities for workers, both skilled and less skilled, in new centres of development, production and growth, such as China, India, Korea, Malaysia, Singapore and Thailand. At the same time, most former OECD emigration countries, such as Italy and Spain, became immigration countries, showing immigration rates (before the global economic crisis) that were, on average, as large as those of traditional OECD immigration countries (OECD, 2013a).

Figure 1.1 shows that the share of the population that was foreign-born has been increasing in recent years. While the average increase between 2000 and 2012 was of two percentage points across OECD countries, some countries, like Luxembourg and Spain, saw the percentage of their foreign-born population rise by more than nine percentage points in a decade.

Perhaps even more noteworthy is the fact that *immigrants have become more diverse* in most countries. For example, data from the OECD Database of Immigrants in OECD countries (DIOC) show that among the immigrant population in France, the share from the top five countries of origin declined from 57% in 2000 to less than 50% in 2010. Globally, it is migration from Asia which is on the rise (OECD and European Union 2015, p. 69). In 2010, China was the second main source of highly-educated immigrants to Canada, the third source to Australia, and the fourth source to the United States and New Zealand. In 1980, China did not appear among the main source countries of skilled immigrants to any of those countries (Brücker et al. 2013).

These trends reveal major changes that are not only quantitative, but also qualitative: the number of immigrants into many OECD countries is increasing, and so is the diversity and heterogeneity of immigrant groups. Increases in the quantity and diversity of immigrants will also require that host communities change – to develop the skills needed to adapt to new concepts of identity, culture and citizenship. Policy responses will also be tested. They will have to become increasingly tailor-made to respond to the needs of diverse immigrant populations. However, increases in diversity also open greater opportunities for host communities as the pool of talent that countries can draw upon becomes larger and opportunities for cultural exchange strengthened (Alesina and La Ferrara, 2005)

Trends in the number and profile of immigrant students

Migration is also affecting the classroom, as teachers and educators adapt their practices to cater to diverse student populations. In 2012, the latest PISA cycle for which data are available, 11% of 15-year-old students had an immigrant background, on average across OECD countries. Around 6% of all immigrants were second-generation immigrants (meaning that they were born in the country where they sat the PISA test to foreign-born parents), and 5% were first-generation immigrants (meaning that both they and their parents were born abroad) (Figure 1.2).

Box 1.1. Definition of immigrant students in PISA

PISA distinguishes between four types of student immigration status:

- **First-generation immigrant students** are the foreign-born students whose parents were also foreign born.
- **Second-generation immigrant students** are the students who were born in the country of assessment but whose parents are foreign born.
- **Students with an immigrant background** include both first- and second-generation immigrant students. In this report, they are also referred to as "immigrant students".
- **Students without an immigrant background** were born in the country of assessment or have at least one parent who was born in that country/economy. In this report, they are also referred to as "non-immigrant students".

The number of students with an immigrant background varies considerably across countries and economies. In Macao-China, Qatar and the United Arab Emirates, more than half of the student population had an immigrant background, while in as many as 19 countries and economies, immigrants accounted for less than 1% of all 15-year-old students (OECD, 2013b).

Despite the surge in migration over the past decades, the growth in the number of foreign-born students has not affected all countries equally; many countries saw only small increases in the number of foreign-born students. Figure 1.2 shows that the share of 15-year-old students who are first-generation immigrants grew by only around 0.4 percentage point, on average across OECD countries, between 2003 and 2012. However, this share grew by as much as 6 percentage points in Ireland, 5.6 percentage points in Spain and 3.8 percentage points in Italy. In some small countries, like Austria, Luxembourg and Switzerland, and in the more traditional immigration countries, like Canada and the United States, changes in the profile of student populations were the result of growing numbers of second-generation immigrants.

■ Figure 1.2 ■

Trends in the number of first- and second-generation immigrants

■ 2012 ◆ 2003

Percentage of second-generation immigrant students

%
60
50
40
30
20
10
0

Korea
Indonesia
0.1 Poland
Uruguay
0.2 Japan
Tunisia
Brazil
Slovak Republic
Mexico
Thailand
0.5 Iceland
Turkey
0.9 Hungary
0.9 Czech Republic
0.9 Spain
1.5 Finland
0.7 Ireland
1.6 Italy
Portugal
3.8 Greece
-3.9 Latvia
2.5 Norway
2.7 Denmark
2.5 OECD average 2003
Russian Federation
1.7 Belgium
Netherlands
3.0 Sweden
3.0 New Zealand
France
3.7 Germany
6.8 Austria
Australia
6.5 United States
7.4 Canada
8.5 Switzerland
12.5 Liechtenstein
-2.4 Hong Kong-China
12.9 Luxembourg
-8.2 Macao-China

Percentage of first-generation immigrant students

%
30
20
10
0

Korea
Poland
Thailand
Tunisia
Indonesia
Japan
Turkey
Slovak Republic
Uruguay
Brazil
-0.8 Latvia
-1.4 Hungary
-1.0 Mexico
1.0 Czech Republic
Finland
Netherlands
2.0 Iceland
-5.7 Germany
Denmark
-3.8 Russian Federation
Portugal
1.4 Norway
1.5 France
0.4 OECD average 2003
3.8 Italy
-3.6 Austria
Sweden
Greece
United States
-4.3 Switzerland
1.8 Belgium
5.6 Spain
6.0 Ireland
Australia
2.2 Canada
Liechtenstein
-6.2 Hong Kong-China
Macao-China
3.6 New Zealand
Luxembourg

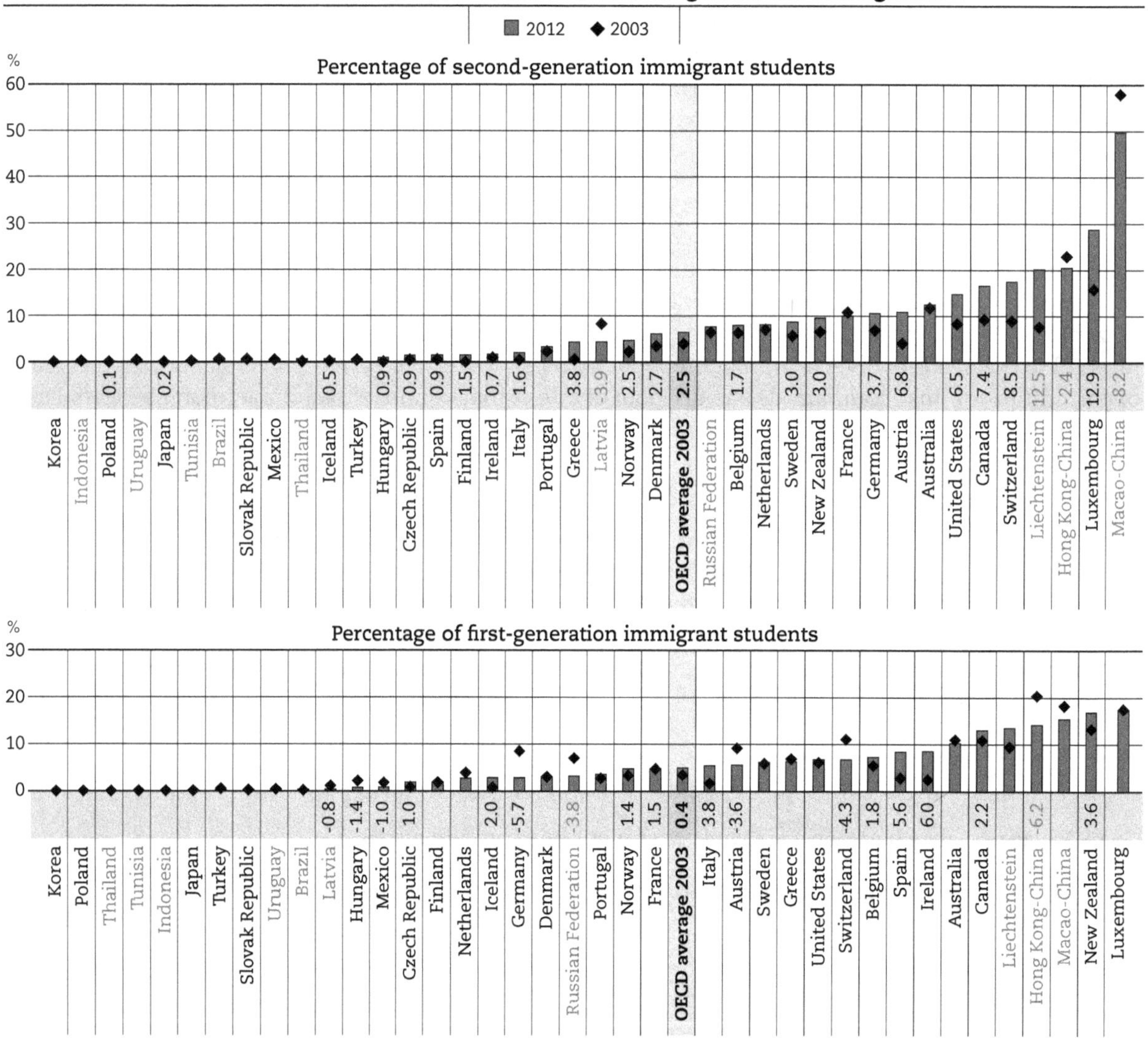

Notes: Only countries and economies with comparable data from PISA 2003 and PISA 2012 are shown.

The percentage-point difference between 2003 and 2012 in the share of students with an immigrant background is shown next to the country/economy name. Only statistically significant differences are shown.

OECD average 2003 includes only OECD countries with comparable data since PISA 2003.

For each chart, countries and economies are ranked in ascending order of the percentage of students in 2012.

Source: OECD, PISA 2012 Database.

Underlying data for the figures in this chapter can be found at www.oecd.org/edu/school/Immigrant-Students-Chapter1-Figures.xlsx.

■ Figure 1.3 ■

Relationship between the percentage of immigrant students and a school system's average performance in reading

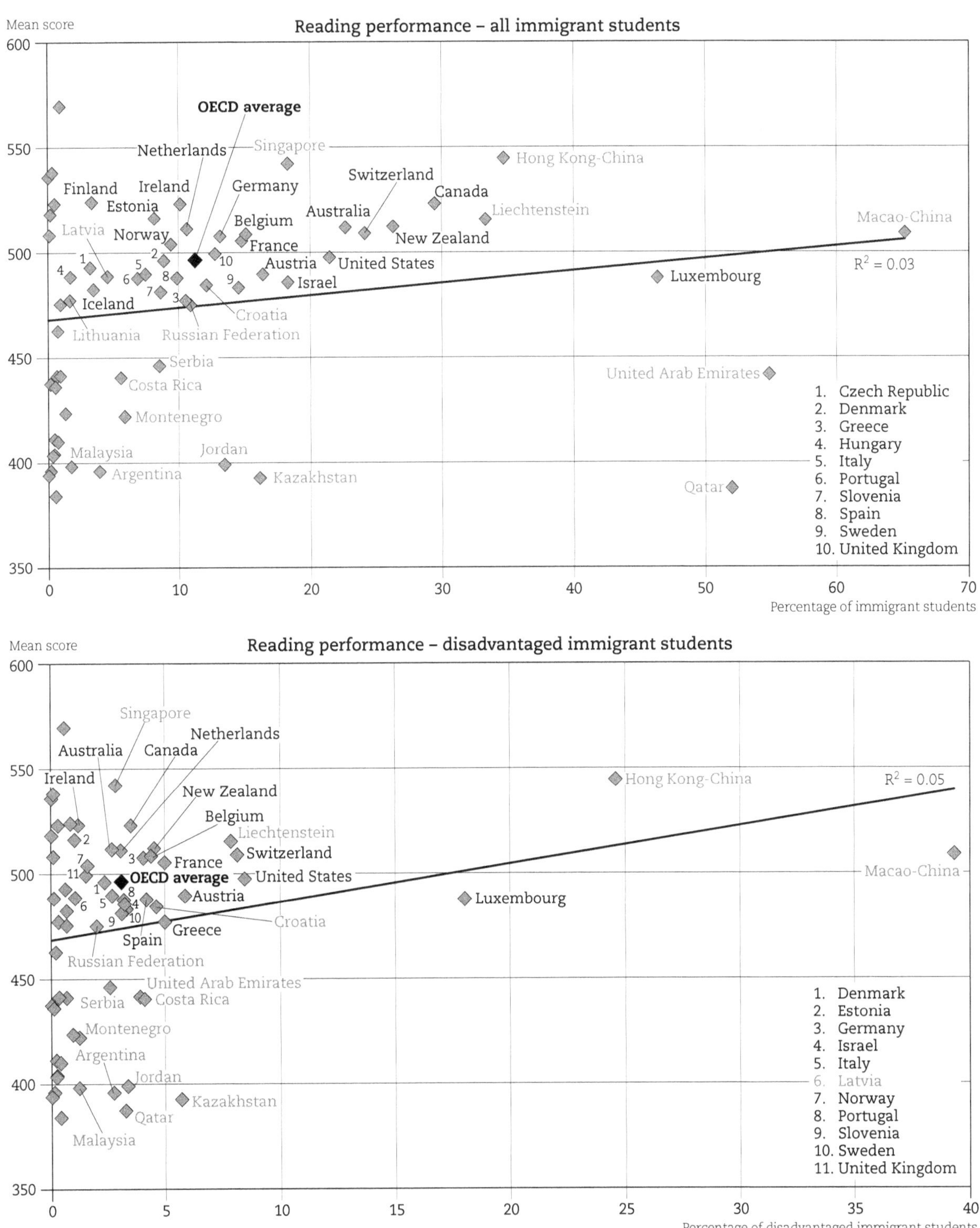

Note: Disadvantaged immigrant students are defined as those immigrant students whose PISA *index of economic, social and cultural status* is in the bottom quarter of all students in OECD countries.

Source: OECD, PISA 2012 Database.

Underlying data for the figures in this chapter can be found at www.oecd.org/edu/school/Immigrant-Students-Chapter1-Figures.xlsx.

Although geopolitical instability and environmental risks might lead to even greater migrant flows towards OECD countries in the years to come, data from PISA 2012 suggest that migration has not been associated with declining education standards in host communities. In fact, Figure 1.3 shows that there is no significant association between the share of immigrant students and the performance of a school system, as measured through the mean score on the PISA reading assessment. This relationship does not seem to be affected by the composition of the immigrant population. Figure 1.3 shows, in fact, that there is no clear association between the share of immigrant students who are socio-economically disadvantaged and a school system's performance in reading.

The way in which education systems respond to migration has an enormous impact both on whether or not immigrants are successfully integrated into their host communities and on the economic and social well-being of all members of the communities they serve, whether they have an immigrant background or not. Some education systems face more pressure than others: because they need to integrate a larger number of school-aged immigrants, because the profile of the immigrants makes them particularly vulnerable (for example, because their native language is very different from the language spoken in their host community), or because they and their parents are socio-economically disadvantaged.

While it is true that many immigrants endure economic hardship and precarious living conditions, this is often the result of displacement. At the same time, many immigrants bring to their host countries valuable skills and human capital. Figure 1.4 illustrates this point by showing the percentage of first-generation immigrant students with at least one parent who is as educated as the average parent of 15-year-old students in the country of residence. On average across OECD countries, 58% of the first-generation immigrants who took part in PISA 2012 had at least one parent who had attended school for as many years as the average parent, while in 2003, 62% of first-generation students did. This decline was due to a large influx of poorly educated immigrant families into Greece and, to a lesser extent, into Ireland and New Zealand.

▪ Figure 1.4 ▪

First-generation immigrant students with educated parents

Percentage of first-generation immigrant students with at least one parent as educated as the average parent of non-immigrant students in the host country

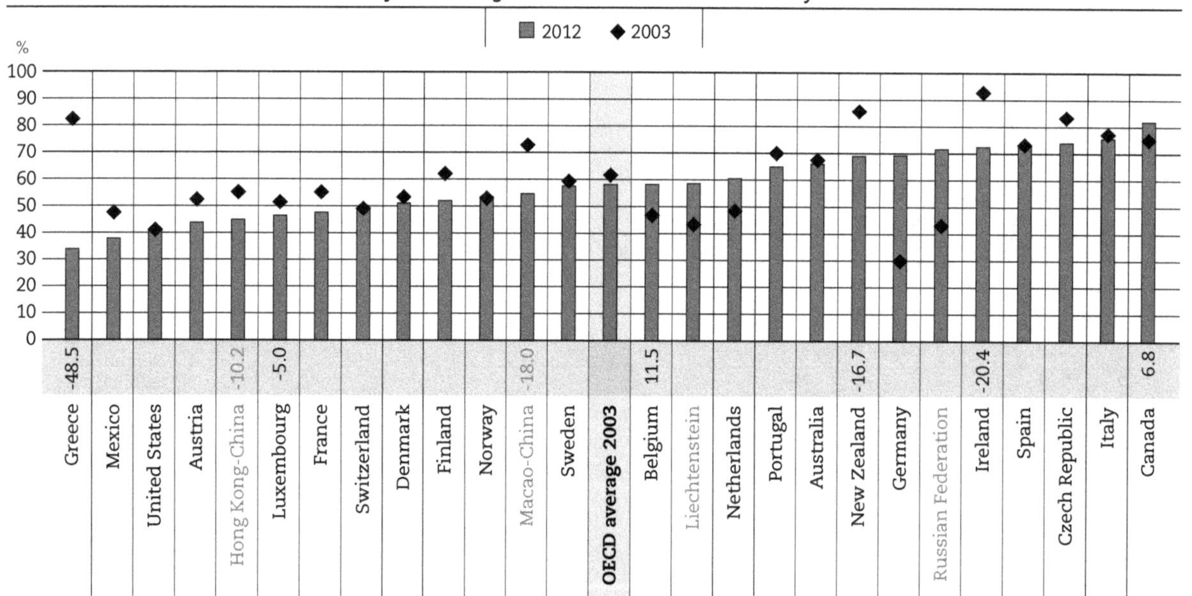

Notes: Only countries and economies with comparable data from PISA 2003 and PISA 2012 are shown.

The percentage-point difference between 2003 and 2012 is shown next to the country/economy name. Only statistically significant differences are shown.

OECD average 2003 includes only OECD countries with comparable data since PISA 2003.

For each chart, countries and economies are ranked in ascending order of the percentage of students in 2012.

Source: OECD, PISA 2012 Database.

Underlying data for the figures in this chapter can be found at www.oecd.org/edu/school/Immigrant-Students-Chapter1-Figures.xlsx.

Figure 1.4 shows that even in Greece, which received a large influx of comparatively poorly educated immigrants in recent years, in around one-third of families of new immigrants at least one parent had attended school for as long as it is customary in Greece. In the vast majority of countries with available data, more than one in two students who were not themselves born in the country in which they sat the PISA test in 2012 had at least one parent with a similar level of education as their peers who did not have an immigrant background. While this reflects selective immigration policies in countries like Australia and Canada, it also reflects improvements in schooling in many of the countries of origin of immigrants entering OECD countries. These relatively high levels of education among immigrants are also a result of the fact that high-skilled people tend to emigrate from poorer countries in greater numbers than low-skilled people (Doquier and Rapoport, 2012).

Stalled rates of participation in post-secondary education programmes in countries such as Italy and Spain are increasing the demand for a highly qualified workforce in OECD countries. Even during the height of the recent economic crisis, many employers lamented shortages of qualified workers in key sectors of the economy. Many immigrants can offer education and skills that host countries could better use and reward (Sumption, 2013).

However, many immigrants do not see their qualifications and skills recognised in the labour market of their host countries (Friedberg, 2000; OECD/European Union, 2014; OECD, 2014). Data from the 2012 Survey of Adult Skills, a product of the OECD Programme for the International Assessment of Adult Competencies (PIAAC), reveal that foreign-born adults are considerably more likely to report being overqualified than comparable native-born adults. Figure 1.5 suggests that, except for the Czech Republic, the Slovak Republic and the United States, when comparing foreign-born and native-born adults who attended school for a similar number of years, who are of the same age, gender and marital status, who work in establishments of the same size, who work the same number of hours and who have similar contracts, foreign-born adults are more likely to report that they hold higher qualifications than those needed to get the job in which they are currently working. These differences may reflect differences in the quality of the education systems in the countries of origin of the foreign-born adults surveyed in PIAAC. They may also reflect the fact that many foreign-born adults are held back by language and cultural barriers.

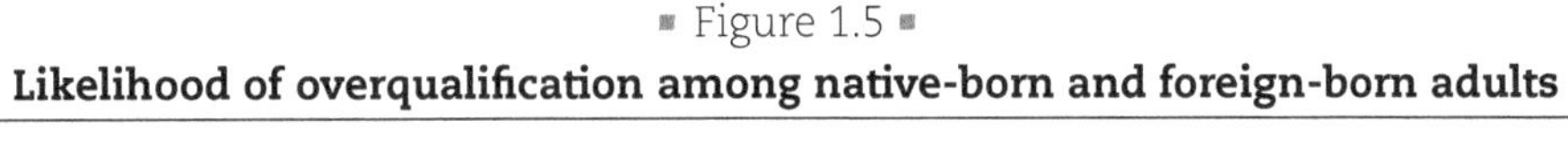

■ Figure 1.5 ■

Likelihood of overqualification among native-born and foreign-born adults

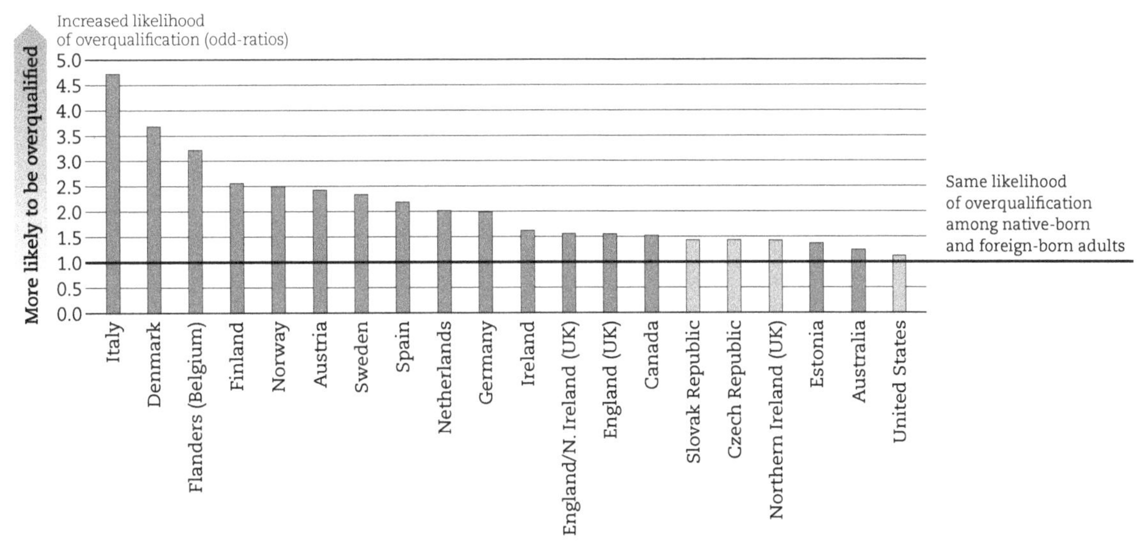

Note: Differences between foreign-born and native-born adults that are statistically significant at the 5% level are marked in a darker tone. Over-qualification is defined relative to the qualification needed to get their job, as reported by respondents to the Survey of Adult Skills. Results are adjusted for years of education, age, gender and marital status, establishment size, hours worked and contract type.

Countries and economies are sorted in descending order of the increased likelihood that foreign-born adults will report being overqualified (odd ratios).

Source: OECD, Survey of Adult Skills (PIAAC 2012).

Underlying data for the figures in this chapter can be found at www.oecd.org/edu/school/Immigrant-Students-Chapter1-Figures.xlsx.

Failure to be able to use productively the skills immigrants bring means that many immigrants see no return on the investments they made in acquiring those skills. As a result, they often must accept low wages and face spells of unemployment – both of which could have consequences for their children's education. Host communities also stand to lose, since they often support immigrants and their families financially, through social welfare programmes. Immigrants who are employed and using their skills productively could repay any initial public investment in their integration and contribute to economic growth and development by paying taxes, contributing to pension schemes, and participating in the local economy.

The variation across countries in performance differences between immigrant students and students without an immigrant background, even after accounting for socio-economic status, suggests that policy has an important role to play in reducing, if not eliminating entirely, the disadvantage that accompanies displacement. But given the diversity of immigrant student populations across countries, designing education policies to address those students' specific needs – particularly that of language instruction – is not an easy task; and education policy alone is unlikely to address all the factors related to differences in performance between immigrant and non-immigrant students.

For example, immigrant students' performance in PISA is more strongly (and negatively) associated with the concentration of socio-economic disadvantage in schools than with the concentration of immigrants or of students who speak a different language at home than the one in which they are taught at school. Reducing the concentration of disadvantage in schools may require changes in other social policy, such as housing or welfare, to encourage a more balanced social mix in schools.

The following chapter examines in detail how immigrant students fare in different education systems. The novelty of the approach taken in this report is that analyses are conducted examining both achievement and non-achievement outcomes and use several different groups for comparison: non-immigrant students who are enrolled in the same education system as immigrant students, socio-economically disadvantaged non-immigrant students, previous cohorts of immigrant students in the same education system, and immigrant students enrolled in a different education system. This approach is necessary if the analyses are to provide specific pointers for education practitioners and policy makers as they design and implement integration policies.

References

Alesina, A. and **E. La Ferrara** (2005), "Ethnic diversity and economic performance", *Journal of Economic Literature*, Vol. 43, pp. 762-800.

Brucker, H., S. Capuano and **A. Marfouk** (2013), *Education, Gender and International Migration: Insights from a Panel-Dataset 1980-2010*, mimeo, IAB, Nuremberg.

Castles, S. and **M.J. Miller** (2003), *The Age of Migration*, 3rd edition, Guilford Press, New York.

Docquier, F. and **H. Rapoport** (2012), "Globalization, brain drain and development", *Journal of Economic Literature*, Vol. 50/3, pp. 681-730.

Friedberg R.M. (2000), "You can't take it with you? Immigrant assimilation and the portability of human capital", *Journal of Labor Economics*, Vol. 18, No. 2, pp. 221-225.

OECD (2015a), "Is this humanitarian migration crisis different?" *Migration Policy Debates*, No. 7, September 2015, OECD, Paris, www.oecd.org/els/mig/Is-this-refugee-crisis-different.pdf.

OECD (2015b), *International Migration Outlook 2015*, OECD Publishing, Paris. http://dx.doi.org/10.1787/migr_outlook-2015-en.

OECD (2014), *International Migration Outlook 2014*, OECD Publishing, Paris, http://dx.doi.org/10.1787/migr_outlook-2014-en.

OECD (2013a), *International Migration Outlook 2013*, OECD Publishing, Paris, http://dx.doi.org/10.1787/migr_outlook-2013-en.

OECD (2013b), *Excellence through Equity: Giving Every Student the Chance to Succeed*, PISA, OECD Publishing, Paris, http://dx.doi.org/10.1787/9789264201132-en.

OECD/European Union (2015), *Indicators of Immigrant Integration 2015: Settling In*, OECD Publishing, Paris. http://dx.doi.org/10.1787/9789264234024-en.

OECD/European Union (2014), *Matching Economic Migration with Labour Market Needs*, OECD Publishing, Paris, http://dx.doi.org/10.1787/9789264216501-en.

Sumption, M. (2013), *Tackling Brain Waste: Strategies to Improve the Recognition of Immigrants' Foreign Qualifications*, Migration Policy Institute, accessed on 3/11/2015 www.migrationpolicy.org/research/tackling-brain-waste-strategies-improve-recognition-immigrants-foreign-qualifications.

Chapter 2
Immigrant Students' Performance and Sense of Belonging at School

In most countries, first-generation immigrant students perform worse than students without an immigrant background, and second-generation immigrant students perform somewhere between the two. This chapter examines how host-country education systems and immigrant students' socio-economic status are associated with immigrant students' performance at school. It also discusses the extent to which immigrant students feel that they belong at school, which is a good reflection of whether or not they have integrated well into their new communities.

Note regarding data from Israel

The statistical data for Israel are supplied by and are under the responsibility of the relevant Israeli authorities. The use of such data by the OECD is without prejudice to the status of the Golan Heights, East Jerusalem and Israeli settlements in the West Bank under the terms of international law.

■ Figure 2.1 ■

Immigrant students' performance in reading, mathematics and problem solving

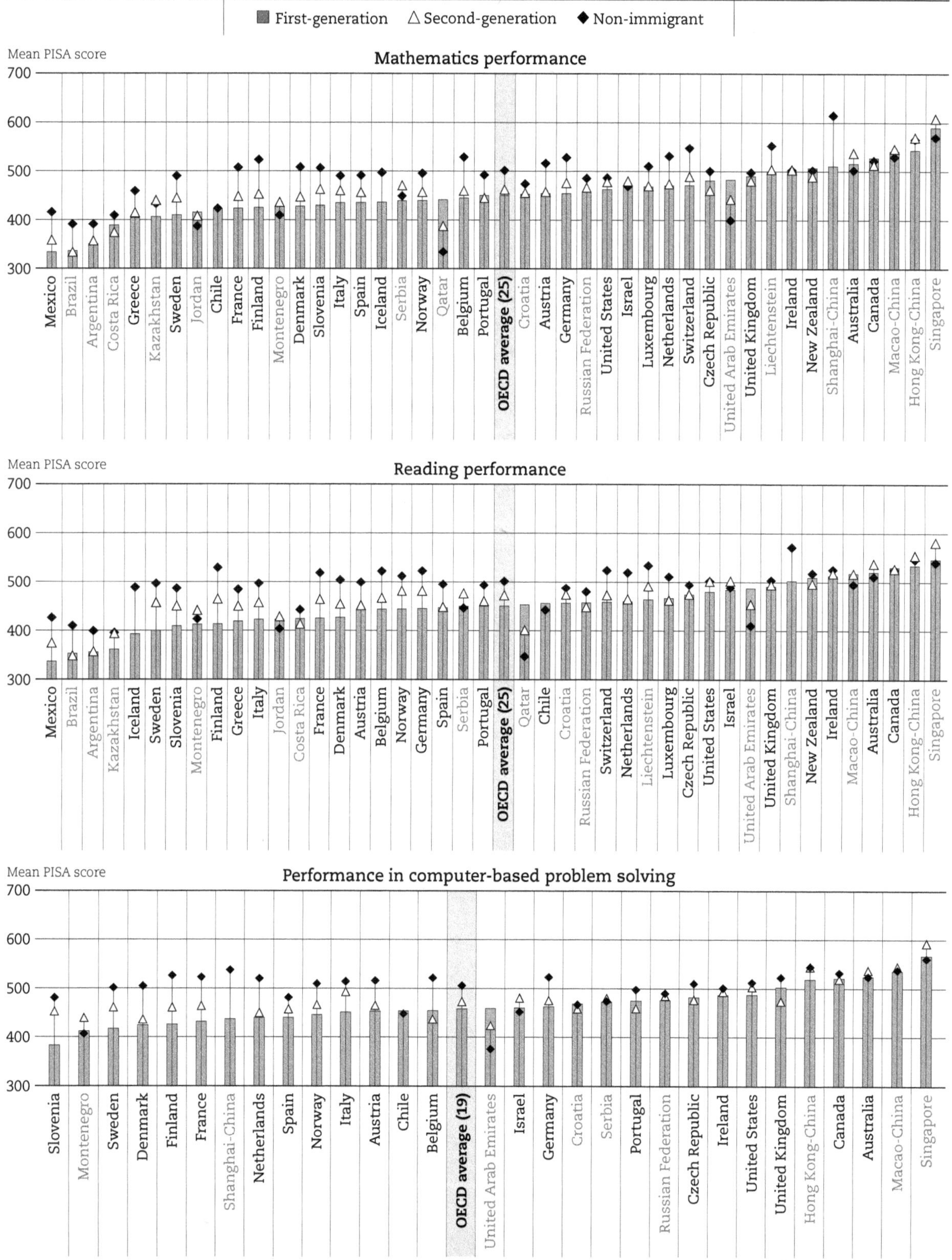

Note: OECD averages (25,19) include only countries with valid data on first- and second-generation immigrant students.
For each chart, countries and economies are ranked in ascending order of the mean score of first-generation immigrant students.
Source: OECD, PISA 2012 Database.
Underlying data for the figures in this chapter can be found at www.oecd.org/edu/school/Immigrant-Students-Chapter2-Figures.xlsx.

Figure 2.1 shows how immigrant students perform in reading, mathematics and problem solving in different education systems. Because immigrants often speak a language at home that is different from the language of the PISA assessment, it is important to consider differences in students' ability to understand and manipulate texts, solve mathematics problems, and solve problems that are formulated in simple language and that require little knowledge of mathematics.

Results indicate that, in most countries, first-generation immigrant students perform worse than students without an immigrant background, and second-generation immigrant students perform somewhere between the two. Figure 2.1 also shows that although many migrants have lower relative performance when compared to students without an immigrant background in their country, they can perform at very high levels by international standards and that the performance gap between first-generation students and students without an immigrant background tends to be wider in reading than in mathematics or problem solving. This suggests that language barriers to text comprehension may be key in explaining the gap in academic performance between these two groups of students.

■ Figure 2.2 ■

Change between 2003 and 2012 in the share of students with an immigrant background who are low performers in both mathematics and reading

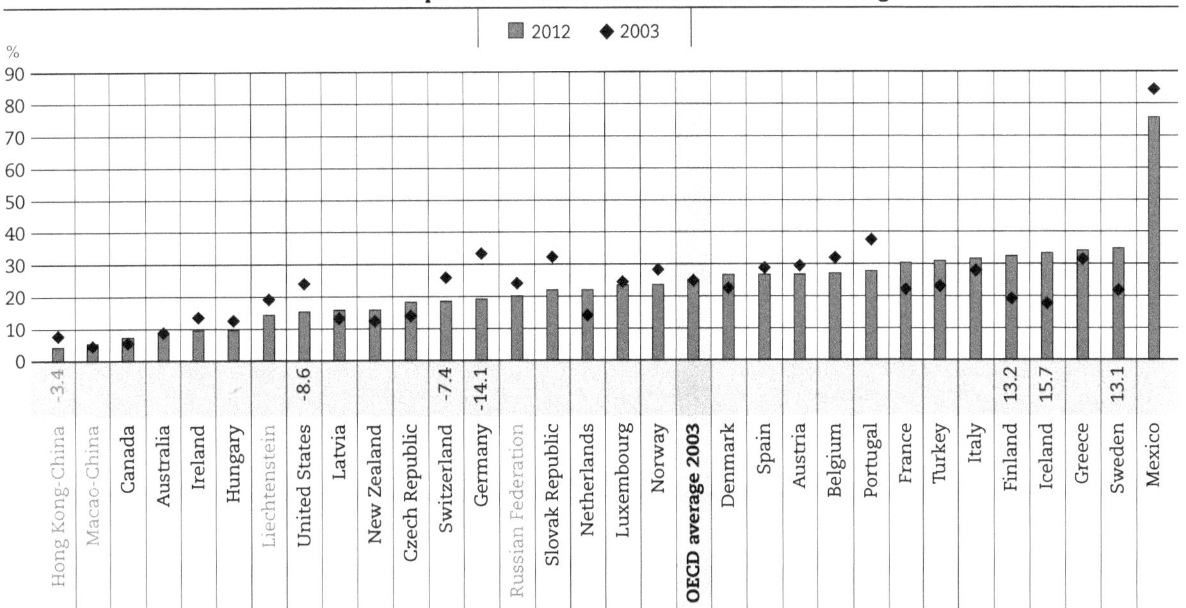

Notes: Only countries and economies with comparable data from PISA 2003 and PISA 2012 are shown.
Changes between PISA 2003 and PISA 2012 that are statistically significant are shown next to the country/economy name.
OECD average 2003 includes only OECD countries with comparable data since PISA 2003.
Countries and economies are ranked in ascending order of the percentage of students in 2012.
Source: OECD, PISA 2012 Database.
Underlying data for the figures in this chapter can be found at www.oecd.org/edu/school/Immigrant-Students-Chapter2-Figures.xlsx.

A worrying problem for immigrant students and education systems is that often students with an immigrant background not only have language barriers to overcome and difficulties in understanding the set of social and cultural rules that implicitly establish the functioning of their host community, they also lag behind their peers academically in most subjects. Figure 2.2 shows that, on average across OECD countries, as many as 25% of students with an immigrant background were low performers in mathematics and reading in 2012, meaning that they did not perform at the PISA baseline level of proficiency in either of the two main subjects examined in PISA. By comparison, 12% of students without an immigrant background were low performers in those subjects.

In some countries, the proportion of students with an immigrant background who were low achievers in mathematics and reading was particularly large and, even more worryingly, grew between 2003 and 2012.

In Finland, Iceland and Sweden, the proportion of students with an immigrant background who did not make the grade in reading and mathematics grew by more than 10 percentage points between 2003 and 2012. Germany, on the other hand, saw the largest decline – of more than 10 percentage points – in the proportion of students with an immigrant background who were low performers in those two subjects.

The role of host-country education systems

Figure 2.1 shows that immigrant students tend to perform at high levels in countries with very selective immigration policies. This fact seems to support the idea that the large differences in the performance of immigrant students can be explained by the immigrants themselves. However, while the culture and the education acquired before migrating clearly matter, the performance of immigrant students is also strongly related to the characteristics of education systems in host countries.

Figure 2.3 illustrates this point by pooling data from PISA 2003, 2006, 2009 and 2012. The figure shows, for a selected group of countries with available information, how immigrant students from the same origin and similar socio-economic status perform across different destination countries. On average, students from Arabic-speaking countries who settled in the Netherlands score 100 points higher in mathematics than those who settled in Qatar, after accounting for socio-economic differences. Albanian students in Greece score 50 points higher in mathematics than Albanian students with similar socio-economic status who settled in Montenegro – a difference that is very close to the average performance difference between Greece and Montenegro. Students born in mainland China score above the OECD average across several destination countries, but they tend to perform better in Hong Kong-China than in Macao-China.

■ Figure 2.3 ■

Immigrant students' performance in mathematics, by country of origin and destination

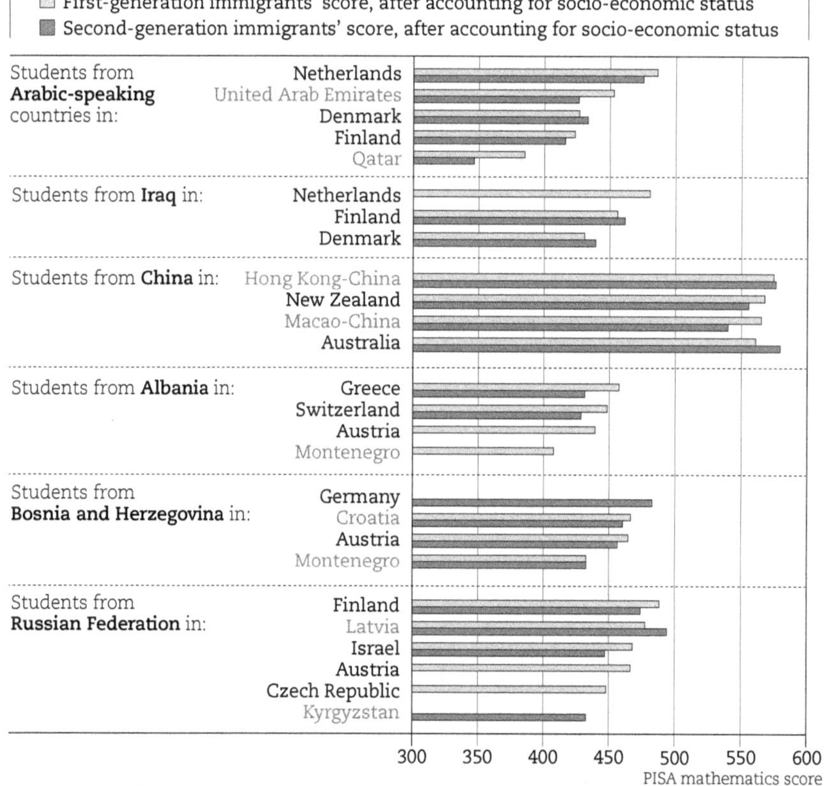

Notes: The estimates are obtained by pooling data from the PISA 2003, PISA 2006, PISA 2009 and PISA 2012 databases.

The average performance by immigrant group and destination country accounts for differences in socio-economic status. It corresponds to the predicted performance of the group if all the immigrant students who migrated from that country of origin and all the non-immigrant students across all the destination countries shared the same socio-economic status of the average student.

Only destination countries with data on at least 20 immigrant students are shown.

Source: OECD, PISA 2003, 2006, 2009, 2012 Databases.

Underlying data for the figures in this chapter can be found at www.oecd.org/edu/school/Immigrant-Students-Chapter2-Figures.xlsx.

■ Figure 2.4 ■

Change between 2003 and 2012 in mathematics performance, by difference in immigrant background

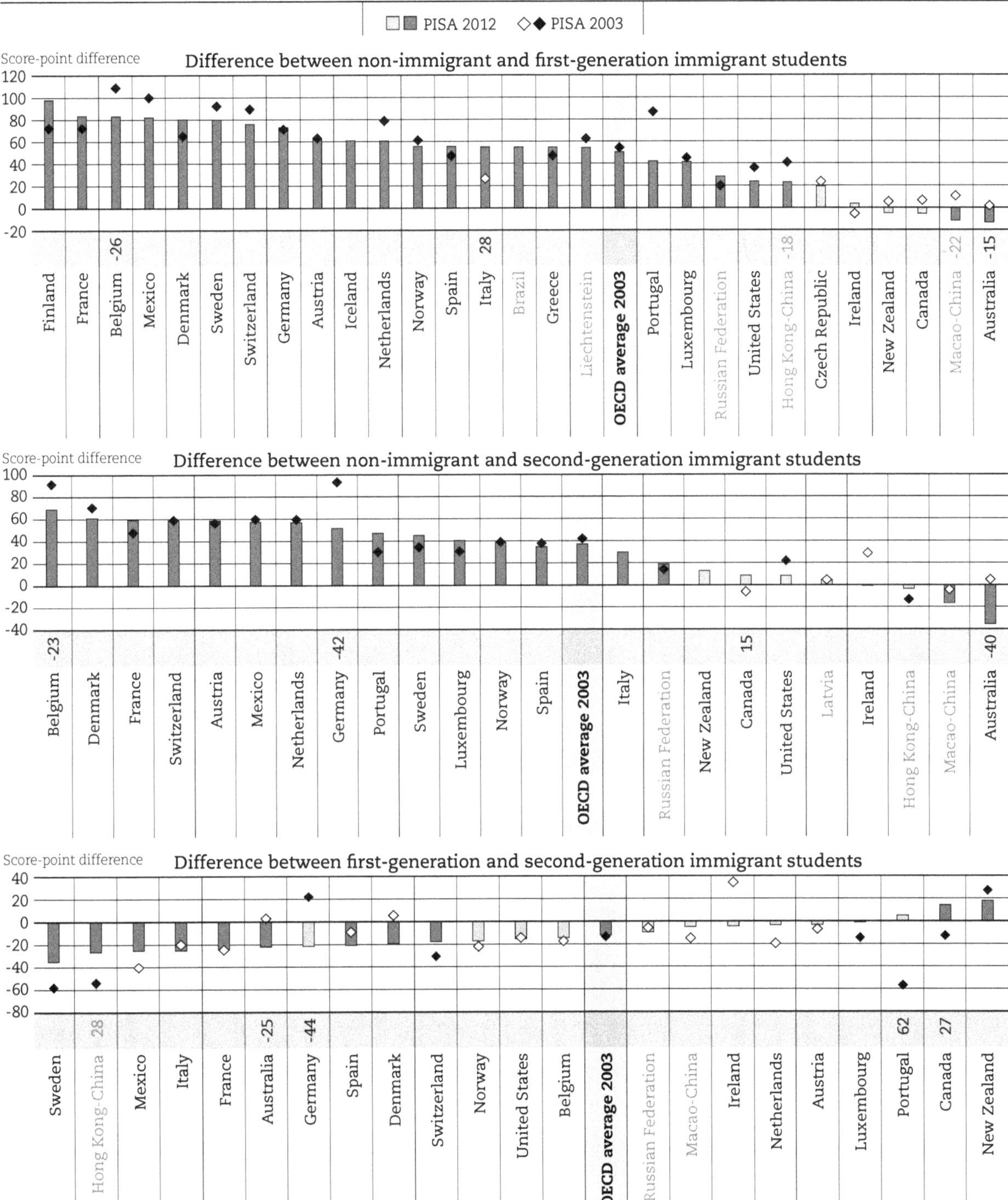

Notes: Only countries and economies with comparable data from PISA 2003 and PISA 2012 are shown.

Statistically significant differences are marked in a darker tone.

Changes between PISA 2003 and PISA 2012 in mathematics performance that are statistically significant are shown next to the country/economy name.

OECD 2003 average includes only OECD countries with comparable data since PISA 2003.

For the first and the second charts, countries and economies are ranked in descending order of the score-point difference in mathematics in 2012; for the third chart, countries and economies are ranked in ascending order.

Source: OECD, PISA 2012 Database.

Underlying data for the figures in this chapter can be found at www.oecd.org/edu/school/Immigrant-Students-Chapter2-Figures.xlsx.

■ Figure 2.5 ■

Change between 2003 and 2012 in mathematics performance, by immigrant background

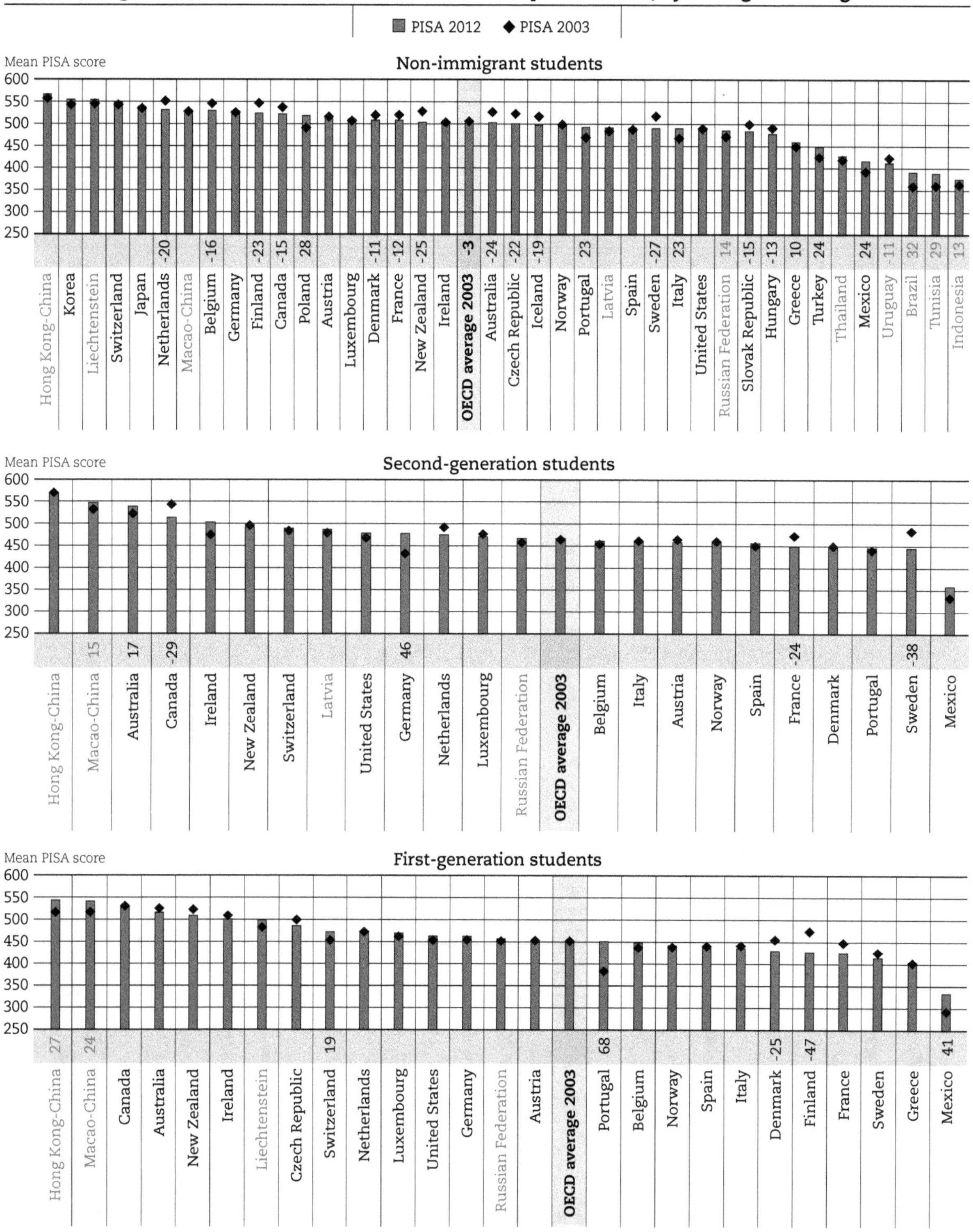

PISA 2012 ◆ PISA 2003

Mean PISA score

Non-immigrant students

600
550
500
450
400
350
300
250

Hong Kong-China
Korea
Liechtenstein
Switzerland
Japan
Netherlands -20
Macao-China
Belgium -16
Germany
Finland -23
Canada -15
Poland 28
Austria
Luxembourg
Denmark -11
France -12
New Zealand -25
Ireland
OECD average 2003 -3
Australia -24
Czech Republic -22
Iceland -19
Norway
Portugal 23
Latvia
Spain
Sweden -27
Italy 23
United States
Russian Federation 14
Slovak Republic -15
Hungary -13
Greece 10
Turkey 24
Thailand
Mexico 24
Uruguay -11
Brazil 32
Tunisia 29
Indonesia 13

Mean PISA score

Second-generation students

600
550
500
450
400
350
300
250

Hong Kong-China
Macao-China 15
Australia 17
Canada -29
Ireland
New Zealand
Switzerland
Latvia
United States
Germany 46
Netherlands
Luxembourg
Russian Federation
OECD average 2003
Belgium
Italy
Austria
Norway
Spain
France -24
Denmark
Portugal
Sweden -38
Mexico

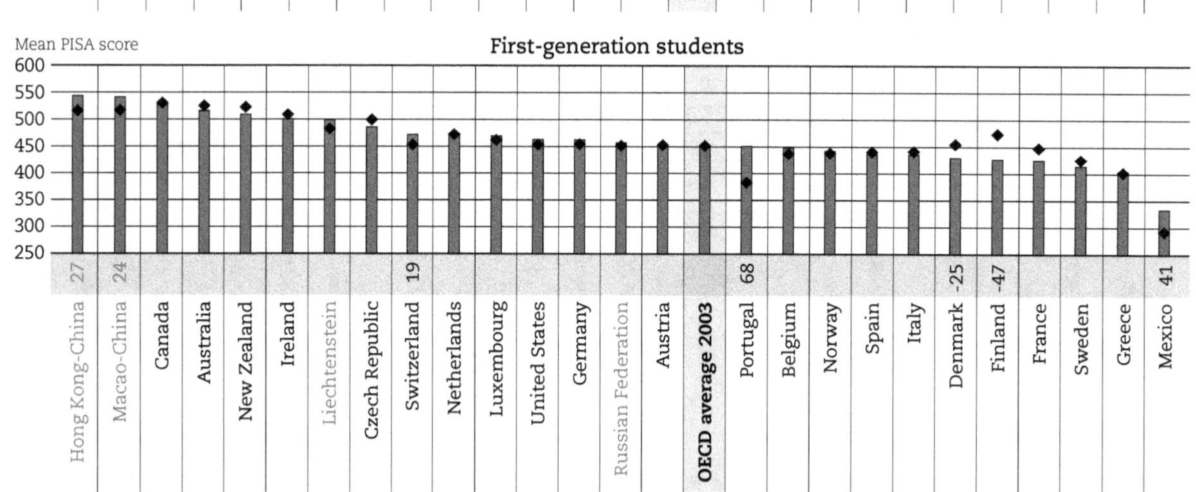

Notes: Only countries and economies with comparable data from PISA 2003 and PISA 2012 are shown.

Changes between PISA 2003 and PISA 2012 in mathematics performance that are statistically significant are shown next to the country/economy name.

OECD 2003 average includes only OECD countries with comparable data since PISA 2003.

For each chart, countries and economies are ranked in descending order of the mean score in mathematics in 2012.

Source: OECD, PISA 2012 Database.

Underlying data for the figures in this chapter can be found at www.oecd.org/edu/school/Immigrant-Students-Chapter2-Figures.xlsx.

Of course, it is not only socio-economic status that contributes to differences in performance of immigrant students from the same country of origin who settle in different destination countries; other factors also play a role, including students' own motivation or the level of support they receive from their parents. But these findings suggest that education systems play an important role in integrating the children of immigrants. Indeed, differences in the performance of immigrant students across OECD countries are only partly due to the socio-economic and cultural profile of the immigrant students in those countries; they are also related to the capacity of schools in host communities to nurture the talents of students with different intellectual and cultural backgrounds.

Changes in the performance of immigrant students over time also suggest that education policies can complement social policies in fostering integration (Figure 2.4 and Figure 2.5). The performance difference in mathematics between students with and without an immigrant background decreased, on average, by around 10 score points between 2003 and 2012 (OECD, 2013). However, the OECD average masks large differences across countries. For example, in less than one decade Germany managed to improve the mathematics performance of second-generation immigrant students by 46 score points – the equivalent of more than one year of formal schooling (Figure 2.5). In Portugal, first-generation immigrant students performed much better in 2012 than in 2003, and that improvement was greater than the improvement observed among students without an immigrant background (Figure 2.5). In Italy, the performance gap in mathematics between first-generation immigrant students and students without an immigrant background widened by 28 score points – from a 26-point difference, which was not statistically significant, in 2003 to a difference of 55 score points in 2012 (Figure 2.4). This change reflected an improvement in mathematics performance among students without an immigrant background between 2003 and 2012, but no concurrent improvement in performance among first- and second-generation immigrant students. In Canada, France and Sweden, the performance of both second-generation students and students without an immigrant background deteriorated between 2003 and 2012, but the decline among second-generation immigrant students was particularly steep (Figure 2.5).

Socio-economic status and immigrant students' performance

When examining trends in performance differences between immigrant students and students without an immigrant background, it is important to consider them in the context of changes in the socio-economic profile of students. This allows for a determination of whether changes are due to differences in the profile of immigrant students or differences in how education systems cater to the particular needs of immigrant students.

Changes in the performance differential between immigrant students and students without an immigrant background partly reflect the improved socio-economic background of immigrant students. Education outcomes have improved in many countries of origin, and migration policies have become increasingly skill-selective. Global progress in improving adult literacy rates, one of the Education for All goals, has been mostly the result of increasing educational attainment among younger adults rather than improvement within the cohorts of adults who are past school age (UNESCO, 2015).

These positive trends in educational attainment among immigrants entering OECD countries are reflected in the educational background of the parents of immigrant students who sat the PISA test in 2003 and 2012. Figure 2.6 shows that the percentage of students whose mother had not earned an upper secondary degree decreased by 6 percentage points during the period, on average. However, changes in the composition of immigrant populations have not been uniform across all PISA-participating countries and economies. For example, in Germany in 2003, 65% of immigrant students were raised by a mother who had not attained upper secondary education; by 2012, this percentage had fallen to 44%. Among the countries using points tests to screen entry into their territories in favour of better-qualified migrants, Australia and New Zealand further reduced their traditionally small share of immigrant students from low-educated families – but so did Sweden, which has very different immigration policies.

▪ Figure 2.6 ▪

Trends between 2003 and 2012 in the percentage of students with a low-educated mother

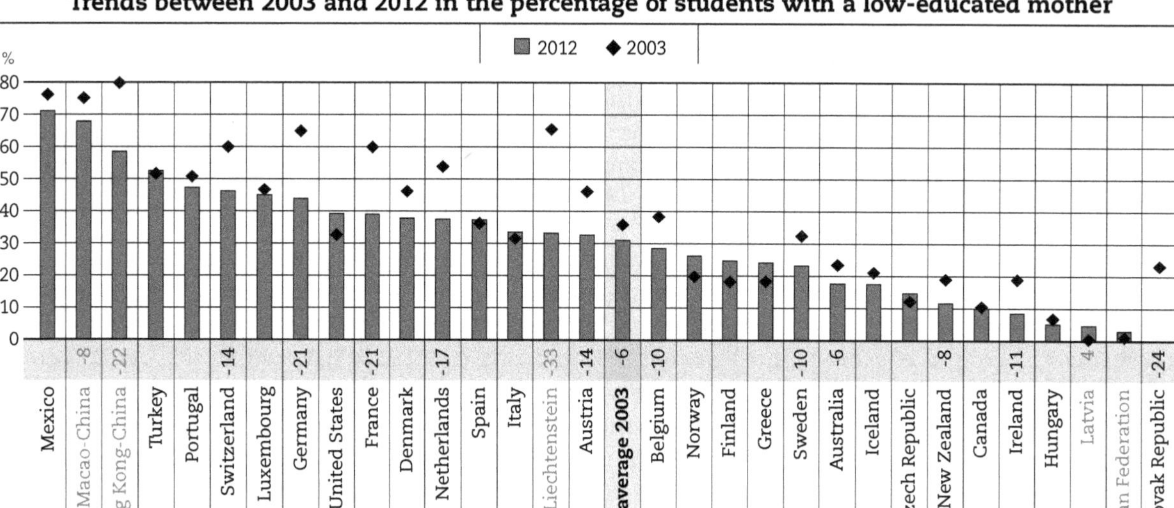

Notes: Only countries and economies with comparable data from PISA 2003 and PISA 2012 are shown.

Low-educated mothers' highest level of education is lower secondary (ISCED 2) or less.

Only statistically significant percentage-point differences between PISA 2003 and PISA 2012 in the share of students with an immigrant background and in the percentage of students with an immigrant background who have a low-educated mother are shown above the country/economy name.

OECD average 2003 includes only countries with comparable data since PISA 2003.

Countries and economies are ranked in descending order of the percentage of students with an immigrant background in 2012.

Source: OECD, PISA 2012 Database.

Underlying data for the figures in this chapter can be found at www.oecd.org/edu/school/Immigrant-Students-Chapter2-Figures.xlsx.

Sense of belonging at school

When families move to a new country, it is often with the parents' hope of offering their children a better living standard and a brighter future. However, children of immigrants have to overcome many barriers in order to succeed at school. For some, the lack of familiarity with the language of instruction and precarious living conditions can turn the first years spent in their new country into a particularly stressful experience.

Figure 2.7 suggests that good integration policies can reduce some of the long-term effects of this stress. In fact, results from PISA 2012 indicate that, in many countries, first- and second-generation immigrant students express similar levels of happiness as students who do not have an immigrant background. In several non-European countries, first-generation immigrant students even express a higher level of happiness at school than other students. This is the case in Australia, Canada, New Zealand, Qatar, the United Arab Emirates and the United States. This may occur because schools are environments where immigrant students are given opportunities – and dedicated support – for socialisation and integration in a new community and because they see schools as bearing the fruits of the sacrifices they and their families made. But in other countries, such as Brazil, Israel, Italy, Montenegro, Serbia, Spain and Sweden, first-generation immigrant students express a considerably lower level of happiness at school than their 15-year-old peers.

In 2003 and 2012, PISA also monitored students' sense of belonging at school by asking students whether they strongly agreed, agreed, disagreed or strongly disagreed that they feel like they belong at school. Schools are a crucial social environment for 15-year-olds. Therefore, students' subjective evaluations on the level of their connection with and within their school, and whether their need to feel a part of the school community is met, can be seen as important indicators of a school's ability to foster a sense of well-being that is not related to academic achievement (Maslow, 1954; Deci and Ryan, 1991; Vallerand, 1997; Baumeister and Leary, 1995).

■ Figure 2.7 ■

Happiness at school, by immigrant background

Percentage of students who reported feeling happy at school

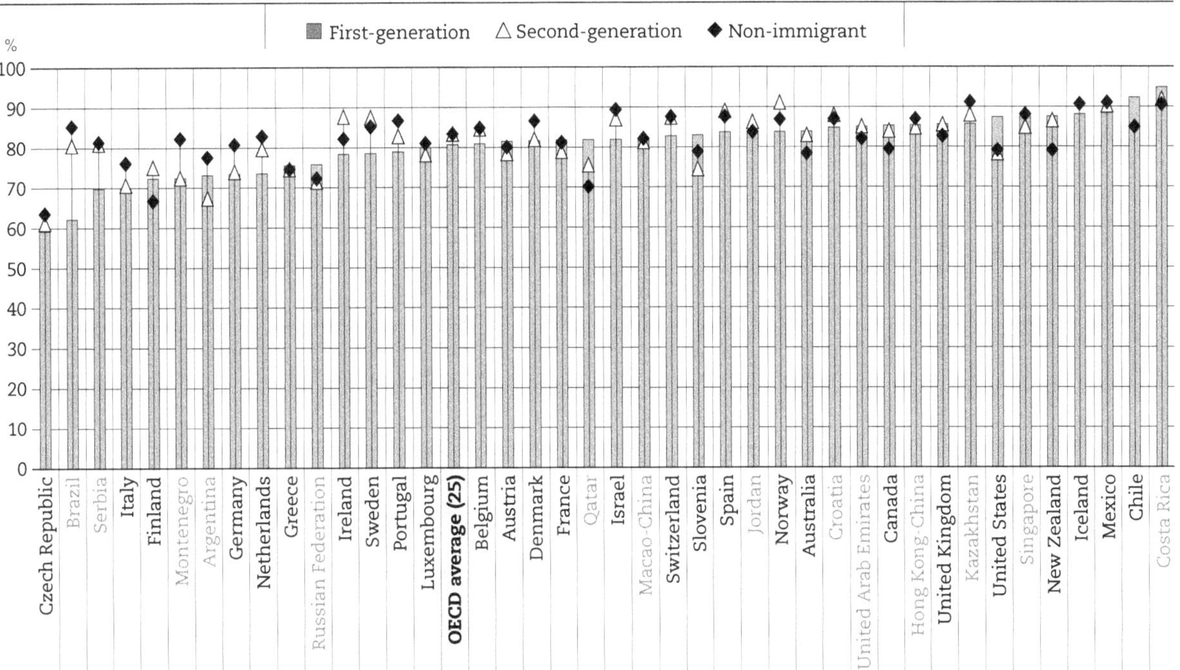

Note: OECD average (25) includes only countries with valid data on first-generation immigrants

Countries and economies are ranked in ascending order of the percentage of first-generation immigrant students who agree or strongly agree with the statement that they feel happy at school.

Source: OECD, PISA 2012 Database.

Underlying data for the figures in this chapter can be found at www.oecd.org/edu/school/Immigrant-Students-Chapter2-Figures.xlsx.

Students' sense of belonging is not only important in itself – because promoting positive affective states among children is a worthwhile goal – but also because it is likely to be associated with lower rates of school dropout and to promote healthy social and psychological development among children and adolescents. Countries vary widely not only in the overall percentage of students who agree or strongly agree that they feel like they belong at school, but also in the extent to which first- and second-generation immigrant students are more or less likely than students without an immigrant background to feel that they belong at school.

In Belgium, Ireland, Luxembourg and Portugal, first-generation immigrant students expressed the most alienation from education systems as compared to students without an immigrant background. Integration unfolds over time in Luxembourg, Norway and Spain, where second-generation immigrant students expressed a stronger sense of belonging at school than first-generation immigrant students. In Australia, Canada, New Zealand and Qatar, the percentages of both first- and second-generation immigrant students who reported that that feel they belong at school were higher than the percentage of non-immigrant students who so reported. All four of these countries adopt highly selective immigration policies (Figure 2.8).

Figure 2.9 shows that the gap in sense of belonging between first-generation immigrant students and students who do not have an immigrant background did not change between 2003 and 2012, on average across OECD countries. However, this gap widened in France and Switzerland during the same period, while in Canada and New Zealand students without an immigrant background expressed less of a sense of belonging in 2012 than they did in 2003, with no comparable decline among first-generation immigrant students. In Australia, there was a decline among both groups, but this was more pronounced among students without an immigrant background, resulting in lower overall levels of sense of belonging in 2012 and a smaller gap between first-generation immigrant students and students without an immigrant background.

■ Figure 2.8 ■

Sense of belonging at school, by immigrant background

Percentage of students who reported that they feel like they belong at school

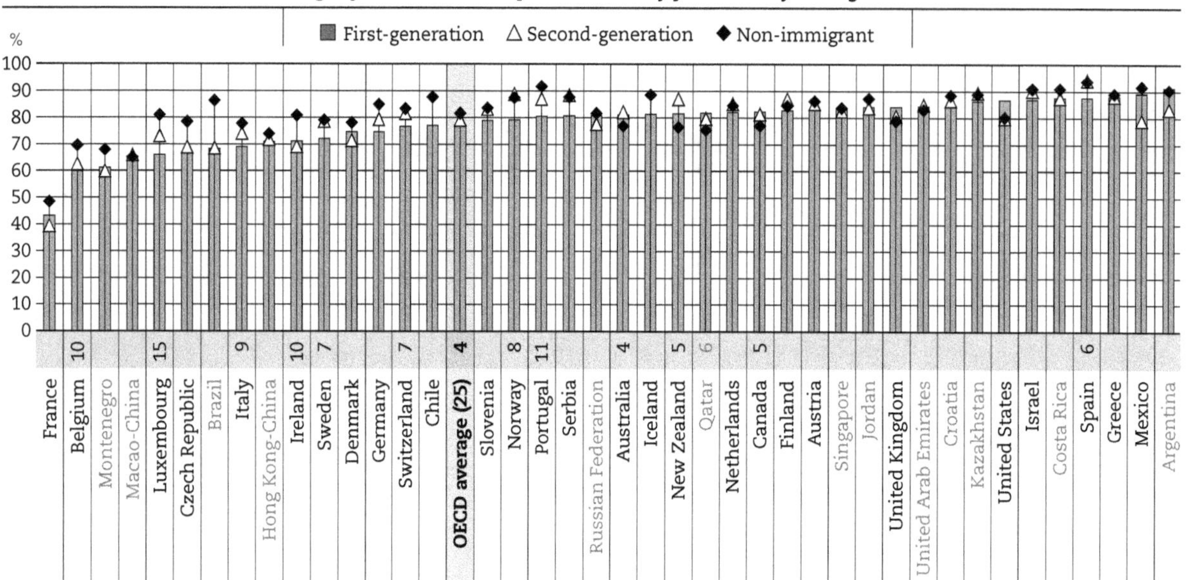

Notes: Statistically significant percentage-point differences between first-generation immigrant students and non-immigrant students who reported that they feel like they belong at school are shown next to the country/economy name.

OECD average (25) includes only countries with valid data on first- and second-generation immigrants.

Countries and economies are ranked in ascending order of the percentage of first-generation immigrant students who reported that they feel like they belong at school.

Source: OECD, PISA 2012 Database.

Underlying data for the figures in this chapter can be found at www.oecd.org/edu/school/Immigrant-Students-Chapter2-Figures.xlsx.

■ Figure 2.9 ■

Trends between 2003 and 2012 in students' sense of belonging at school

Percentage-point difference (PISA 2012 minus PISA 2003)

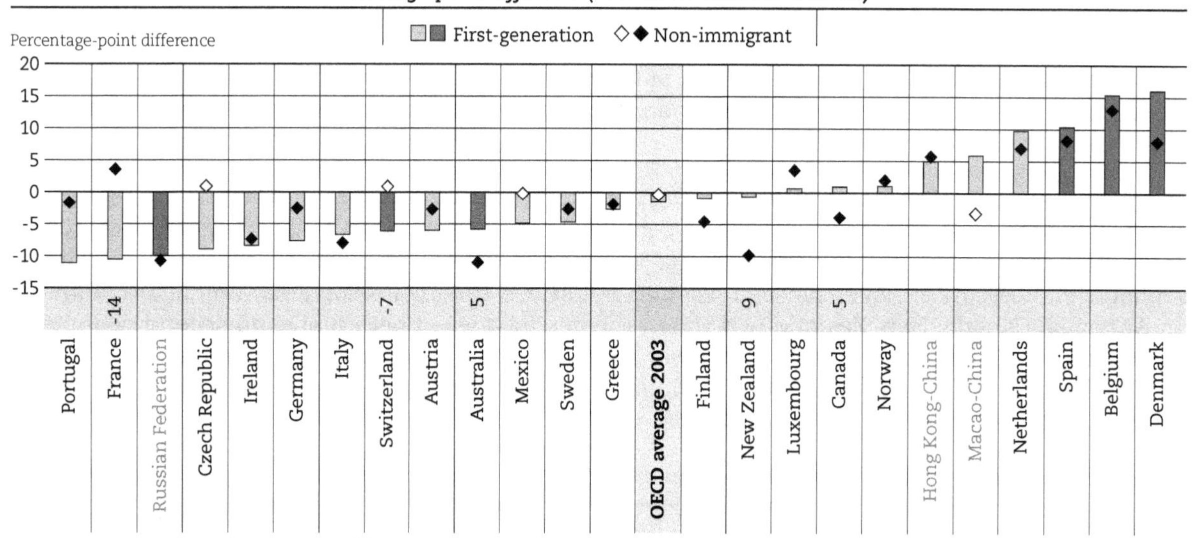

Notes: Only countries and economies with comparable data from PISA 2003 and PISA 2012 are shown.

Statistically significant changes are marked in a darker tone.

Changes between PISA 2003 and PISA 2012 in the difference in sense of belonging at school between first-generation immigrant and non-immigrant students that are statistically significant are shown next to the country/economy name.

OECD average 2003 includes only OECD countries with comparable data since PISA 2003.

Countries and economies are ranked in ascending order of the percentage of first-generation immigrant students.

Source: OECD, PISA 2012 Database.

Underlying data for the figures in this chapter can be found at www.oecd.org/edu/school/Immigrant-Students-Chapter2-Figures.xlsx.

Figure 2.10 offers a more fine-grained comparison by showing the percentage of immigrant students who reported that they feel like they belong at school by country of origin and country of destination. Results illustrate that almost 90% of students from Iraq who settled in Finland reported feeling like they belong at school, but only 69% of students from Iraq who settled in Denmark reported the same. Similarly, only 64% of students who migrated to Denmark from Turkey reported feeling like they belong at school while 93% of those who migrated to Finland so reported. And while 73% of students who migrated from Arabic-speaking countries to Denmark reported that they feel like they belong at school, 90% of those who migrated to Finland so reported. These results suggest that the psychological well-being of immigrant students is affected not only by cultural differences between the heritage and host country's culture, but also by how schools and communities help them to deal with daily problems of living, learning and communicating.

▪ Figure 2.10 ▪

Immigrant students' sense of belonging at school, by country of origin and destination

Percentage of students with an immigrant background who reported that they feel like they belong at school

Notes: The estimates are obtained by pooling data from the PISA 2003 and PISA 2012 databases.

The coverage of destination countries is limited by the fact that only some countries collect detailed information on immigrants' country of birth. Only destination countries with data on at least 20 immigrant students of the same origin are shown.

Source: OECD, PISA 2003, 2006, 2009, 2012 Databases.

Underlying data for the figures in this chapter can be found at www.oecd.org/edu/school/Immigrant-Students-Chapter2-Figures.xlsx.

References

Baumeister, R.F. and **M.R. Leary** (1995), "The need to belong: Desire for interpersonal attachments as a fundamental human motivation", *Psychological Bulletin*, Vol. 117, pp. 497-529.

Deci, E.L. and **R.M. Ryan** (1991), "A motivational approach to self: Integration in personality", *Nebraska Symposium on Motivation: Perspectives on Motivation*, Vol. 38, pp. 237-288.

Maslow, A. (1954), *Motivation and Personality*, Harper and Row, New York.

OECD (2013), *Excellence through Equity: Giving Every Student the Chance to Succeed*, PISA, OECD Publishing, Paris, http://dx.doi.org/10.1787/9789264201132-en.

UNESCO (2015), *Education for All Global Monitoring Report 2015: Achievement and Challenges*, UNESCO, Paris.

Vallerand, R.J. (1997), "Toward a hierarchical model of intrinsic and extrinsic motivation", in M.P. Zanna (ed.), *Advances in Experimental Social Psychology*, Academic Press, New York.

Chapter 3
Attitudes Towards Immigrants

Immigrant students' well-being and development is shaped by their own and their family's interactions with the different groups in their host communities. Despite the important role immigrants play in the labour market and culture of host countries, negative attitudes towards immigration are widespread in many countries. This chapter draws on data from the European Social Survey and the International Civic and Citizenship Education Study to examine host communities' attitudes towards immigrants entering their countries, and how those attitudes have evolved over time. Results from the OECD Teaching and Learning International Survey (TALIS) are also examined to determine whether teachers feel well-equipped to teach classes of diverse students.

Note regarding data from Israel

The statistical data for Israel are supplied by and are under the responsibility of the relevant Israeli authorities. The use of such data by the OECD is without prejudice to the status of the Golan Heights, East Jerusalem and Israeli settlements in the West Bank under the terms of international law.

For most immigrant children and adolescents, schools represent a, if not the, major entry point into their new society (Gibson, 1991). Schools introduce immigrant students to the norms, values and expectations of their host societies (Vedder and Horenczyk, 2006) and are the main arena where different groups of young people in the community can meet, establish friendships and acknowledge differences. Schools can thus play a vital role in developing harmonious intercultural relations.

However, educational institutions often reproduce the same dynamics that are prevalent in societies at large. In communities where foreign-born people are viewed and treated as "second class" citizens, the children of immigrants receive no additional assistance and schools become a source of stress and frustration.

Positive intergroup relations help immigrant students to adjust to their new surroundings. All adolescents who do not enjoy positive, supportive relationships with their parents, teachers and peers are, in fact, at risk of psychological distress and underperformance at school (Wentzel, 1998). Students' perceptions of support and caring from teachers and peers are related to motivation, perceived competence and investment of effort – all factors that clearly contribute to academic performance.

■ Figure 3.1 ■

Relationship between sense of belonging at school and reading performance

Difference between non-immigrant and first-generation immigrant students after accounting for socio-economic status

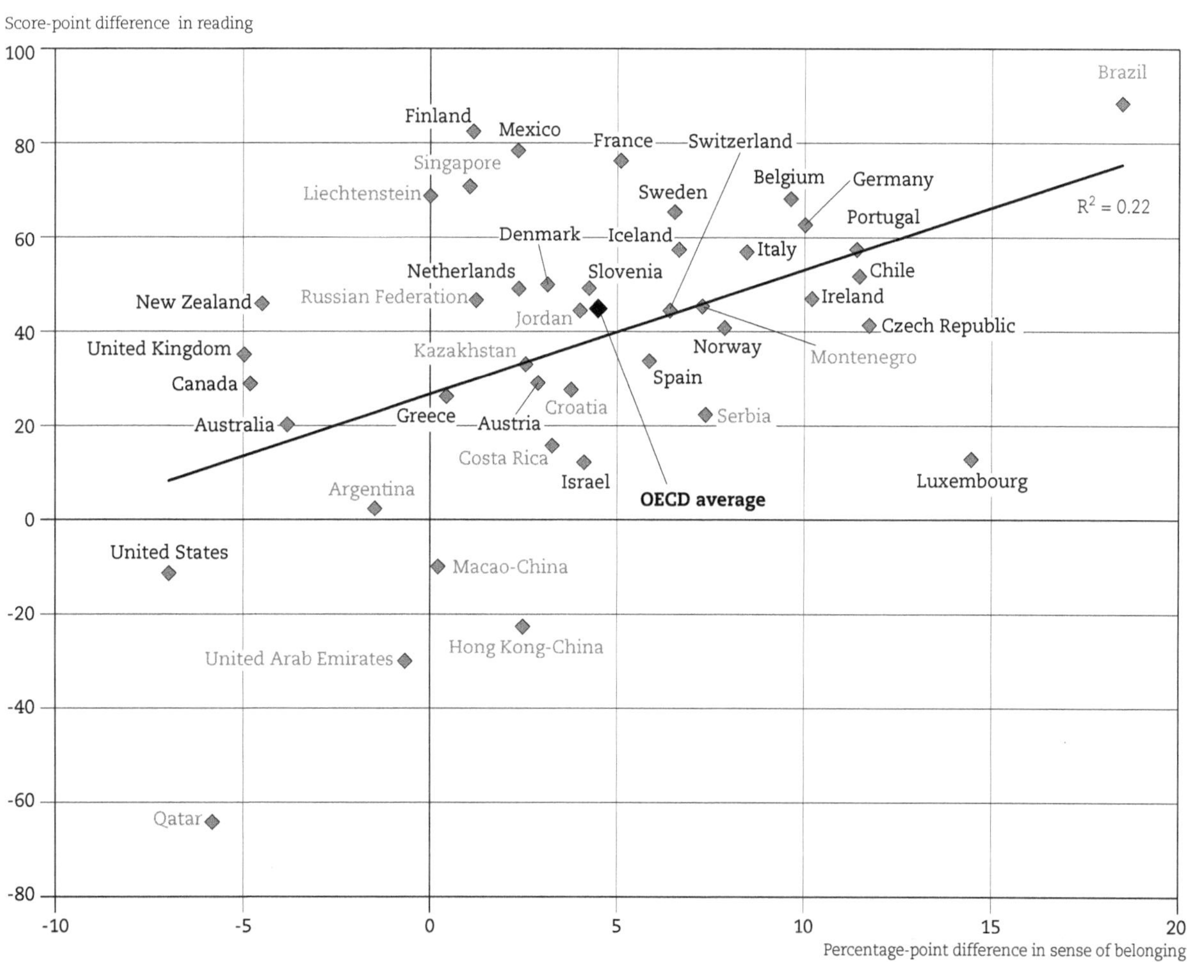

Note: Sense of belonging is defined as the percentage of students who reported that they feel like they belong at school.
Source: OECD, PISA 2012 Database.
Underlying data for the figures in this chapter can be found at www.oecd.org/edu/school/Immigrant-Students-Chapter3-Figures.xlsx.

Figure 3.1 shows that the performance gap between immigrant and non-immigrant students is smaller in countries where the difference in the sense of belonging between the two groups is also smaller. While it is not easy to disentangle the direction of the causal relationship between sense of belonging at school and academic performance, it seems clear that those systems that are better able to promote a sense of belonging among immigrant students are in a better position to capitalise on these students' academic potential and promote their academic skills.

Beyond academic achievement, students' well-being and development is shaped by their own and their family's interactions with the different groups in their host communities. It is thus important to consider immigrant students' adjustment at school from the perspective of their psychological adaptation. Psychological adaptation refers to "a set of psychological outcomes, including a sense of personal and cultural identity, good mental health, and the achievement of personal satisfaction in the new cultural context" (Berry, 1997).

Perceptions of discrimination are a psychological reality for many immigrants and the most serious threat to their psychological adaptation. More than 20% of the native-born children of immigrants in Europe consider themselves to be members of a group that is or has been discriminated against on the grounds of ethnicity, nationality or race (OECD, 2015). Perceptions of discrimination in Europe are more common among the native-born children of immigrants than among their peers who have actually immigrated. Discrimination contributes to young immigrants' self-perception as outsiders, which exacerbates their difficulty in finding the inner resilience to overcome social barriers and deal effectively with daily problems.

Attitudes towards immigrants in destination countries

Discriminatory attitudes are often viewed as typical of those who have little exposure to "others". But the increases in migration flows mean that most people have had some direct contact with those who speak different languages, eat different foods, hold different religious beliefs and follow different traditions. Many appreciate the economic and social contributions migrants make to their communities. For example, given falling fertility rates and lack of qualified workers in key sectors of the economy, many OECD countries stand to benefit from immigration.

Yet despite the important role immigrants play in the labour market of host countries, the value of immigration is often not properly understood by resident populations, and negative attitudes towards immigration are widespread in many countries (Davidov et al., 2008). The surge of international migration over the past few decades has created tensions in many OECD countries and has led to the adoption of more restrictive immigration policies favouring a more selective intake of skilled migrants (OECD, 2015).

Using data from the European Social Survey, Figure 3.2 details public attitudes towards immigration in European countries – including some of the countries that are facing the largest inflows of migrants as a result of current geopolitical instabilities. Migration flows are placing great demands on many European political leaders and welfare systems. Some citizens, already worried about the state of the economy and the impact of the reforms in social welfare systems introduced in the aftermath of the economic crisis, regard both migrants and political institutions with distrust.

In 2012, residents in European countries were asked to report whether they believe that their country is made a worse or better place to live by immigrants coming from other countries. Respondents were asked to use a scale ranging from 0 (worse place to live) to 10 (better place to live). On average across the countries shown in Figure 3.2, residents assigned a value of 5 on the scale, while individuals living in Iceland and Sweden reported mean values close to 6.5. By contrast, residents in the Czech Republic, France, Hungary, Italy, Portugal, the Russian Federation and the Slovak Republic reported mean values of below 4.5, signalling a greater prevalence of negative attitudes towards immigrants.

■ Figure 3.2 ■

Attitudes towards immigration in European countries

Individual reports on whether immigrants make the country a better or worse place to live

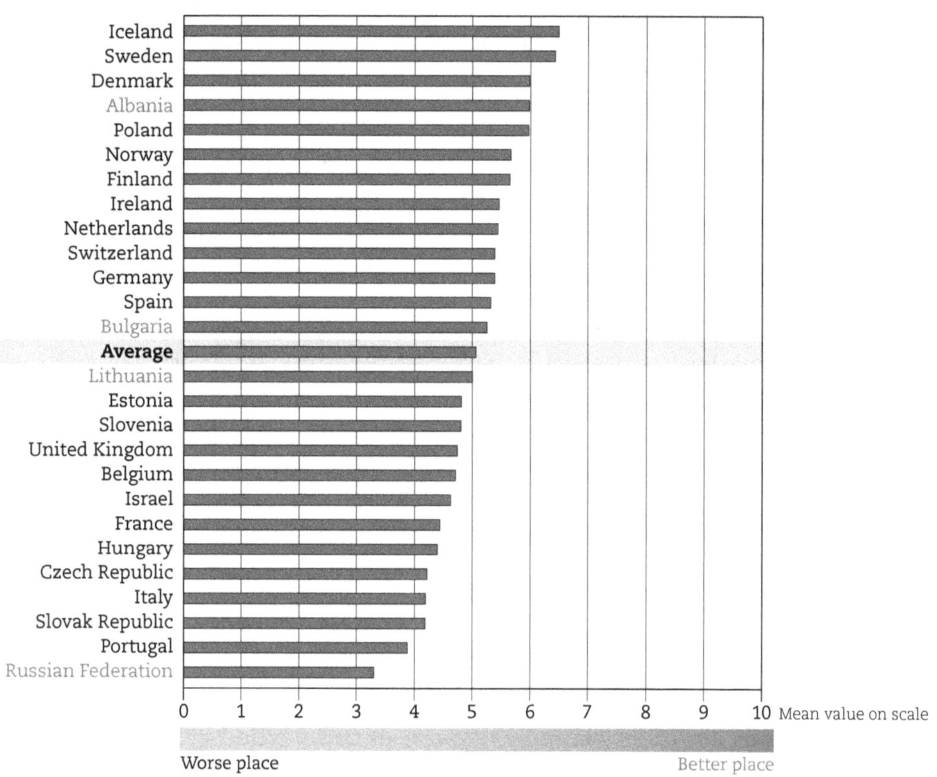

Notes: Respondents were aged between 16 and 65.

Respondents were asked to report whether they believe that their country is made a better or worse place to live by immigrants coming from other countries, using a scale ranging from 0 (worse place to live) to 10 (better place to live).

Countries are ranked in descending order of the mean value on the scale.

Source: European Social Survey 2012, Round 6.

Underlying data for the figures in this chapter can be found at www.oecd.org/edu/school/Immigrant-Students-Chapter3-Figures.xlsx.

Trends in attitudes towards immigrants

The European Social Survey has been monitoring attitudes towards immigration in Europe since 2000. It is therefore possible to monitor trends between 2000 and 2012 to understand whether perceptions towards immigration have changed over the period. Between 2000 and 2012, the economic climate changed dramatically in many European countries, and so did migration flows. Individuals participating in the survey were asked to report the extent to which they thought that their country should allow people from poorer countries outside of Europe to come and live in their country, using a scale ranging from 1 (allow many) to 4 (allow few). Figure 3.3 shows that, on average in 2012, residents in the Czech Republic, Hungary and Israel tended to indicate that they preferred their country to allow few people from poorer countries outside Europe to settle in their country, while residents in Germany, Norway, Poland and Sweden expressed stronger support for allowing many migrants to settle in their countries.

Figure 3.3 also reveals that, on average, attitudes towards immigration changed little between 2000 and 2012. If anything, there was a small increase in support for allowing more immigrants from poorer countries outside of Europe to settle in respondents' countries. However, attitudes seem to have grown more polarised over time. Support for immigrants appears to have grown stronger in Germany, Norway, Poland and Sweden, where, in 2000, residents had already expressed comparatively positive attitudes towards allowing many immigrants to settle, while support diminished in those countries whose citizens had comparatively negative attitudes towards allowing migrants to settle, such as the Czech Republic and Israel.

■ Figure 3.3 ■

Trends between 2000 and 2012 in attitudes towards immigrants from poorer countries outside of Europe

Based on responses to question of whether to allow many or few immigrants from poorer countries outside of Europe

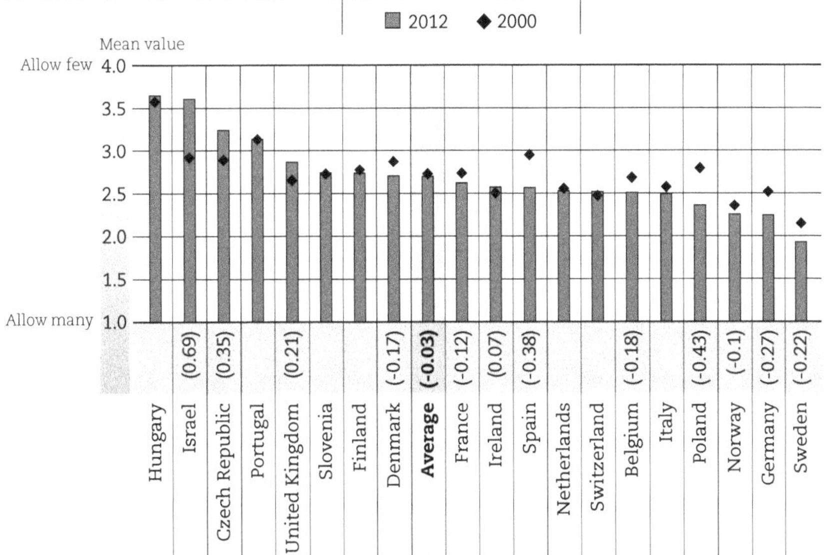

Note: The difference between 2000 and 2012 in the mean values of the scale is marked next to the country name in parentheses when this was statistically significant at the 5% level.

Countries are ranked in descending order of the mean value in 2012.

Source: European Social Survey 2000, Round 1; European Social Survey 2012, Round 6.

Underlying data for the figures in this chapter can be found at www.oecd.org/edu/school/Immigrant-Students-Chapter3-Figures.xlsx.

Data from the European Social Survey also reveal negative attitudes towards immigration in some countries, but a close look shows that these are only partly fueled by perceived economic threats; in many cases, they are shaped by perceived cultural threats. Figure 3.4 shows trends between 2000 and 2012 in responses to a question on whether individuals believe that their country should allow people of the same race or ethnic group as the majority of citizens in the country to settle. It also shows trends in responses to a related question: whether individuals believe that their country should allow people of a different race or ethnic group to settle in the country. The scale ranged from 1 (allow many) to 4 (allow few).

Figure 3.4 clearly shows that individuals tend to hold the door open to individuals who share their race or ethnic group but are more reluctant to do so for large influxes of individuals who are different from themselves. Diversity imposes extra demands on individuals (Putnam, 2007, Sturgis et. al 2014). Even in countries where increases in favourable attitudes towards immigration are observed, such as Germany, Norway and Sweden, residents are more likely to express support for allowing more people who are similar to themselves than for allowing migrants who differ considerably in their racial and ethnic profile. Figure 3.4 also reveals that the strong negative attitudes towards immigration expressed in Hungary and Israel are directed, primarily, towards migrants from different ethnic and racial groups than resident populations.

Country-level differences in attitudes towards immigration and perceptions of the value of immigrants' contributions towards society could be due to a number of factors, including underlying differences in the composition of resident populations, differences in countries' institutional arrangements and differences in people's perceptions of their environment.

In 2012, participants in the European Social Survey were asked to indicate how satisfied they felt with the present state of the economy in their country, using a scale ranging from 0 (extremely dissatisfied) to 10 (extremely satisfied). They were also asked how they felt about the education provided in their country – a powerful mechanism for socialisation, in addition to a means to acquire the cognitive and non-cognitive skills that help to create cohesive societies. In addition, participants were asked to report if it is generally bad or good for their country's economy to allow migrants to settle in the country, and whether they feel that the cultural life of their country is diluted or enriched by people from other countries who settle among them.

■ Figure 3.4 ■

Trends between 2000 and 2012 in attitudes towards immigrants according to racial or ethnic similarity

Based on responses to question of whether to allow many or few immigrants of different or same race or ethnic group from majority

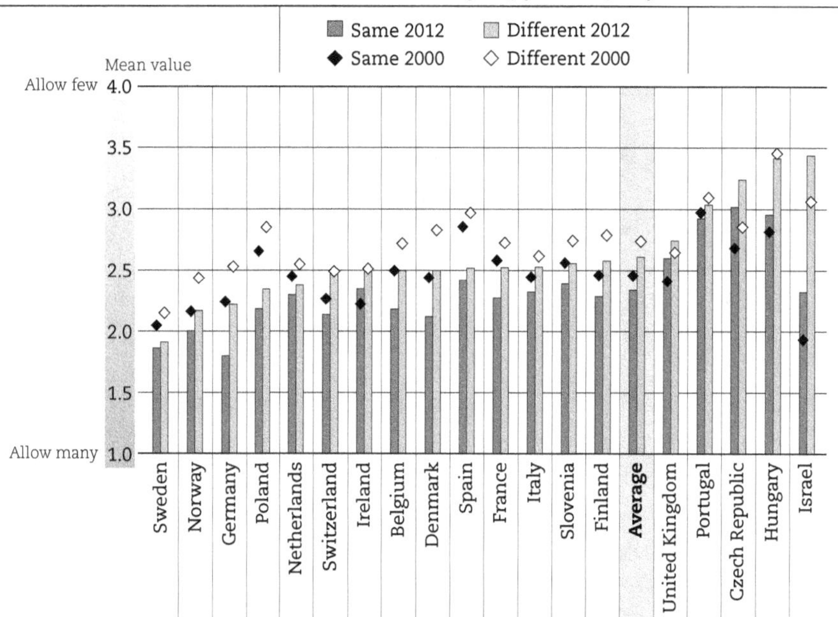

Countries are ranked in ascending order of the mean value of the scale of allowing immigrants of the same ethnic/race group in 2012.

Source: European Social Survey 2000, Round 1; European Social Survey 2012 Round 6.

Underlying data for the figures in this chapter can be found at www.oecd.org/edu/school/Immigrant-Students-Chapter3-Figures.xlsx.

Figure 3.5 indicates that in countries with widespread dissatisfaction about the state of the economy, individuals are more likely to say that immigrants can be an economic problem. Figure 3.6 shows that in countries where residents express concern about the state of the education system, immigrants are regarded as a potential threat to the cultural life of the country.

Education is strongly associated with people's attitudes towards immigrants: the better educated individuals are, the less likely they are to hold discriminatory and negative attitudes towards immigrants (Hooghe et al., 2008; Quillian, 1995; Scheepers, Gijsberts and Coenders, 2002; Kunovich, 2004; Semyonov, Rainmann and Tom-Tov, 2004; OECD, 2010a, 2010b; Borgonovi, 2012). In part, this may be because education promotes a deeper understanding of the value of diversity, fostering openness and an ability to communicate and manage relationships, in addition to providing information about the challenges faced by immigrants. However, because educational attainment is often closely related to social class, low-educated individuals may find themselves at the sharp end of the immigration issue, "competing" with immigrants for weak or weakening welfare support and limited labour market opportunities.

Although educational attainment has risen dramatically over the past decades, evidence suggests that social capital and social cohesion have been declining (Inglehart, 1999; Putnam, 2000; Pharr and Putnam 2000). Changes in how social relationships are conducted, in how members of a community interact and in institutional arrangements may make it difficult for individuals and communities, regardless of their level of education, to tolerate and accept immigrants. It is also possible that education systems, while equipping individuals with subject-specific skills, may not be doing enough to promote the types of skills needed to facilitate the acceptance and integration of immigrants into their countries. The assessment of Global Competence in the 2018 round of PISA will help education systems to assess the extent to which they manage to promote intercultural communication and understanding (Box 3.1).

■ Figure 3.5 ■

Attitudes towards immigrants based on perceptions of the state of the economy

System-level relationship

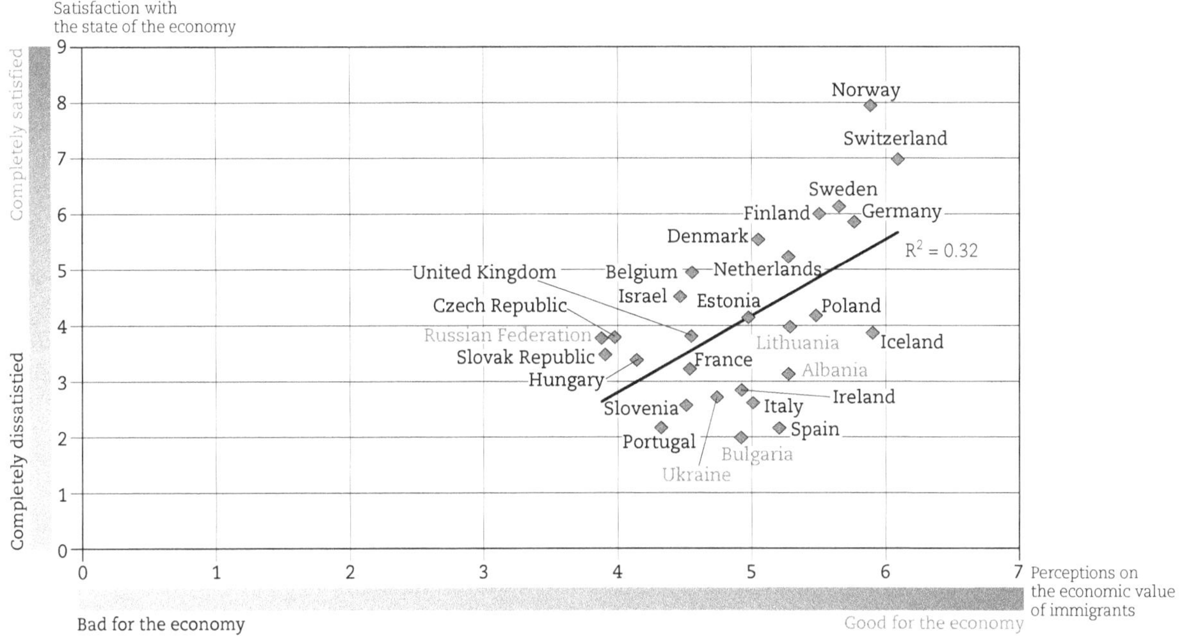

Source: European Social Survey 2012, Round 6.
Underlying data for the figures in this chapter can be found at www.oecd.org/edu/school/Immigrant-Students-Chapter3-Figures.xlsx.

■ Figure 3.6 ■

Attitudes towards immigrants based on perceptions of the state of the education system

System-level relationship

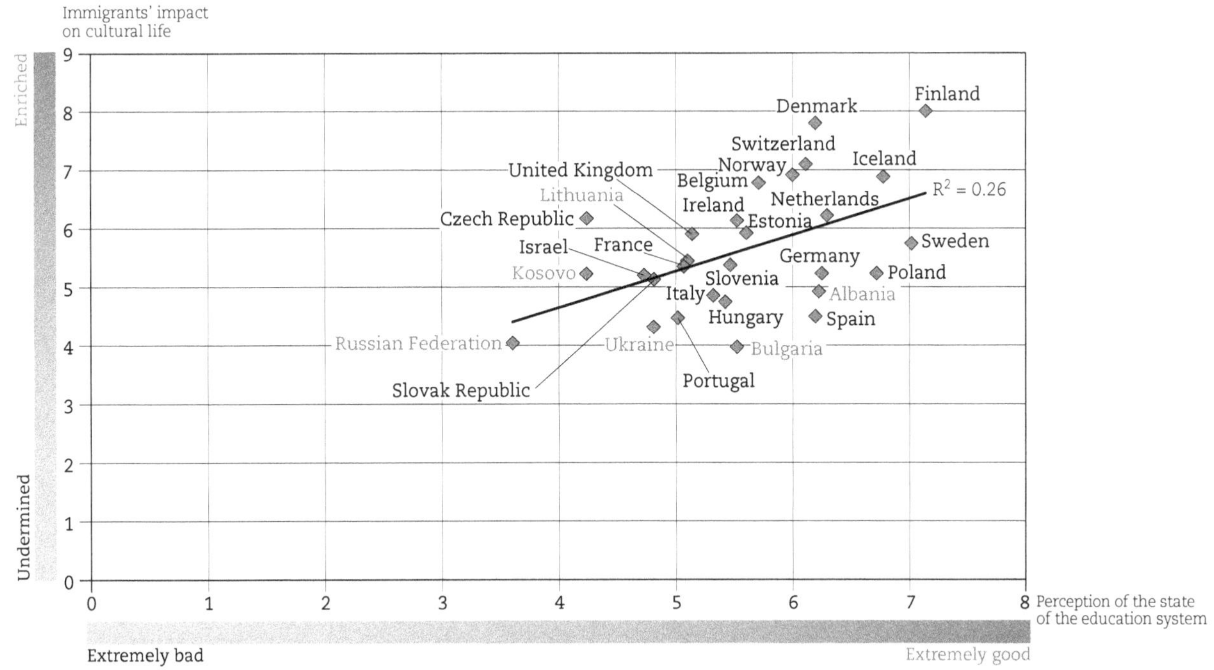

Source: European Social Survey 2012, Round 6.
Underlying data for the figures in this chapter can be found at www.oecd.org/edu/school/Immigrant-Students-Chapter3-Figures.xlsx.

Box 3.1. **The Assessment of Global Competence in PISA**

PISA-participating countries are collaborating to develop an assessment of global competence to be conducted in 2018. Global competence is defined as "the capability and disposition to act and interact appropriately and effectively, both individually and collaboratively, when participating in an interconnected, interdependent and diverse world". The assessment is built around four key dimensions:

- Communication and relationship management, which refers to the willingness and capacity to adapt one's communication and behaviour in order to interact appropriately and effectively with others holding diverse perspectives and in different contexts.
- Knowledge of and interest in global developments, challenges and trends, which refers to a learner's interest in and knowledge of cultures, major issues, events and phenomena in the world, as well as the learner's ability to understand their global significance and their implications for adapting appropriately and effectively to learning, working and living situations with others who hold diverse perspectives and in different contexts.
- Openness and flexibility, which refers to being receptive to and understanding of new ideas, people and situations, as well as to differing perspectives and practices. It also refers to the ability to seek out and understand new and differing perspectives and experiences, and to appropriately and effectively adapt one's thinking, behaviours and actions to learning, working and living situations that involve others holding diverse perspectives and in different contexts.
- Emotional strength and resilience, which refers to the ability, by developing coping mechanisms and resilience, to deal appropriately with the ambiguity, changes and challenges that these different perspectives and experiences can present.

▪ Figure 3.7 ▪

Percentage of non-immigrant students who believe that immigrants should have the same rights as other citizens, by presence of immigrants in class

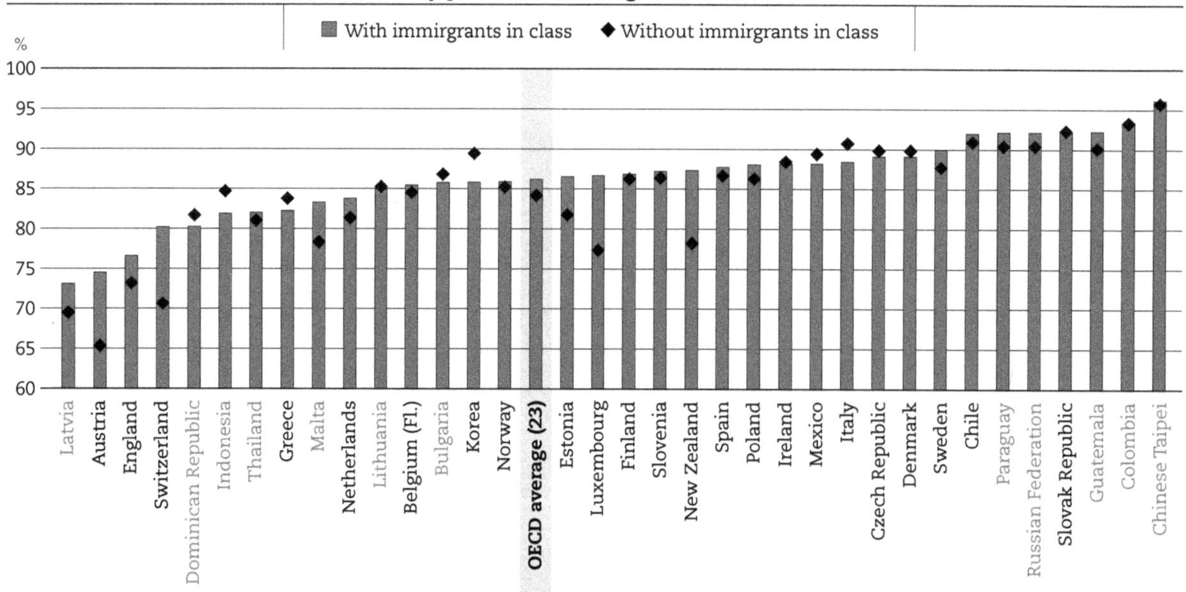

Countries and economies are ranked in ascending order of the percentage of non-immigrant students who believe that immigrants should have the same rights, and are in class with immigrant students.

Source: International Civic and Citizenship Education Study 2009.

Underlying data for the figures in this chapter can be found at www.oecd.org/edu/school/Immigrant-Students-Chapter3-Figures.xlsx.

Figure 3.7 shows that, in most countries, a large majority of students without an immigrant background believe that immigrants should have the same rights as other citizens. Interestingly, countries differ considerably as to whether having immigrant students in class fosters positive attitudes, among students without an immigrant background, towards the rights of immigrants. For example, in Austria, Estonia, New Zealand and Switzerland, students who have at least one immigrant student in their class are less likely than students who have no immigrant student in their class to agree that immigrants have the same rights as other citizens; but in the majority of other countries, the presence of immigrant students does not negatively influence, or is positively associated with, support for immigrants' rights (Figure 3.7)

This suggests that social mixing will not necessarily promote social cohesion in diverse societies. The success of integration policies rests, to a significant degree, on how well education systems promote global competence among future generations of students. Just as some education systems have been able to respond creatively to immigrant students' needs and have managed to tap these students' potential, they have also been able to foster students' capacity to act and interact appropriately and effectively with individuals who are different from themselves.

Providing opportunities to discuss and reflect on cultural differences not only helps to develop more positive societal attitudes towards cultural diversity, but can also support the well-being and family relationships of young immigrants. A clear cultural identity plays a critical role in the development of immigrant adolescents' sense of mastery and self-esteem (Berry et. al, 2006). Figure 3.8 shows that immigrant children who have opportunities to participate in celebrations of both the host country and their own heritage culture tend to report a higher level of happiness at school.

Children of immigrant families are key actors in the process of integration, as they broker communication between members of the host community and their own families and provide other children with opportunities to learn about different cultures. Teachers who understand the complexity of cultural adaptation can help immigrant children to develop good relationships with their peers while preserving positive attitudes towards the traditional values of their family.

■ Figure 3.8 ■

Participation in host- or heritage-culture celebrations and happiness at school

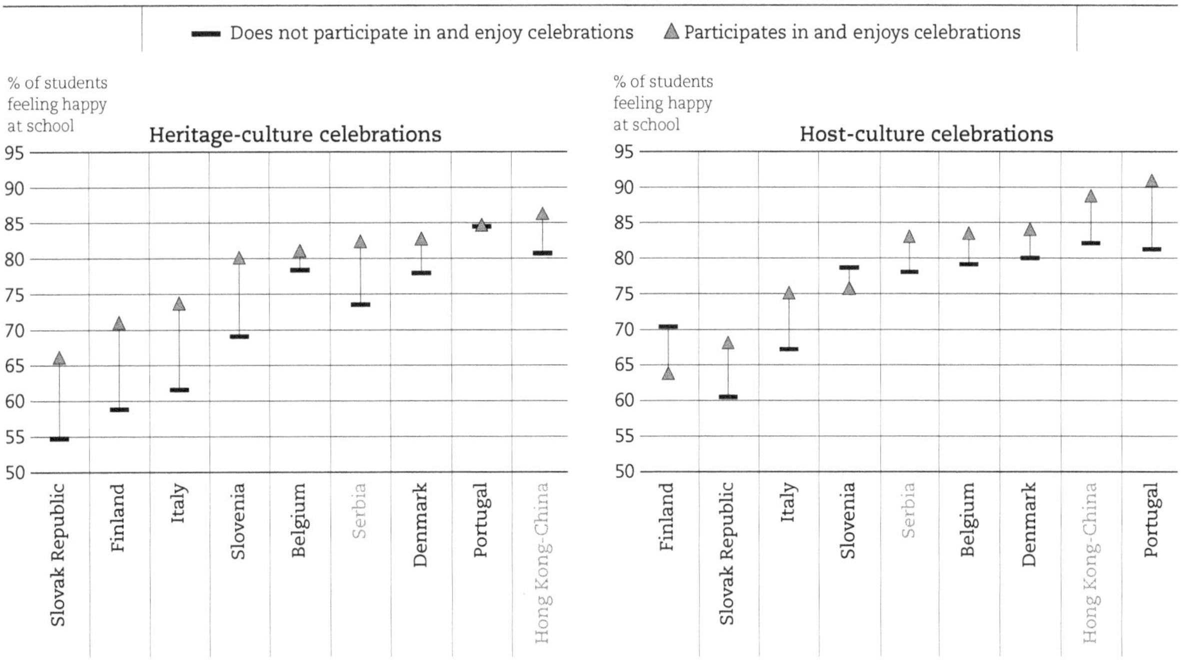

Countries and economies are ranked in ascending order of the percentage of students who reported that they feel happy at school and who participate in and enjoy these celebrations.

Source: OECD, PISA 2012 Database.

Underlying data for the figures in this chapter can be found at www.oecd.org/edu/school/Immigrant-Students-Chapter3-Figures.xlsx.

SPOTLIGHT ON REFUGEES AND EDUCATION

According to the United Nations High Commissioner for Refugees (UNHCR), there were 19.5 million refugees worldwide in 2014; 5.1 million of them were Palestinians. In 2015, Syrian nationals made the most requests for resettlement. The following list, in descending order, shows the countries of origin of refugees who made resettlement requests in 2015. The countries of first asylum from which they made those requests appear, in alphabetical order, in parentheses.

1. Syrian Arab Republic (Egypt, Iraq, Lebanon, Sudan, Syrian Arab Republic, Turkey, elsewhere)
2. Democratic Republic of the Congo (Burundi, Rwanda, Tanzania, Uganda)
3. Myanmar (Bangladesh, Malaysia, Thailand, elsewhere)
4. Iraq (Egypt, Jordan, Lebanon, Syrian Arab Republic, elsewhere)
5. Somalia (Djibouti, Ethiopia, Kenya, Rwanda, elsewhere)
6. Bhutan (Nepal, elsewhere)
7. Afghanistan (Pakistan, Islamic Republic of Iran, elsewhere)
8. Eritrea (Ethiopia, Sudan, elsewhere)
9. Sudan (Chad, Egypt, elsewhere)
10. Islamic Republic of Iran (Turkey, elsewhere)
11. Colombia (Ecuador, Venezuela, Panama)
12. Ethiopia (Egypt, Somalia, South Sudan, Sudan, elsewhere)

As this list clearly shows, developing countries hosted over 86% of the world's refugees in 2014. Some 42% of refugees resided in countries where the per capita GDP was below USD 5 000.

■ Figure 3.a ■

Major hosting and origin countries of refugees

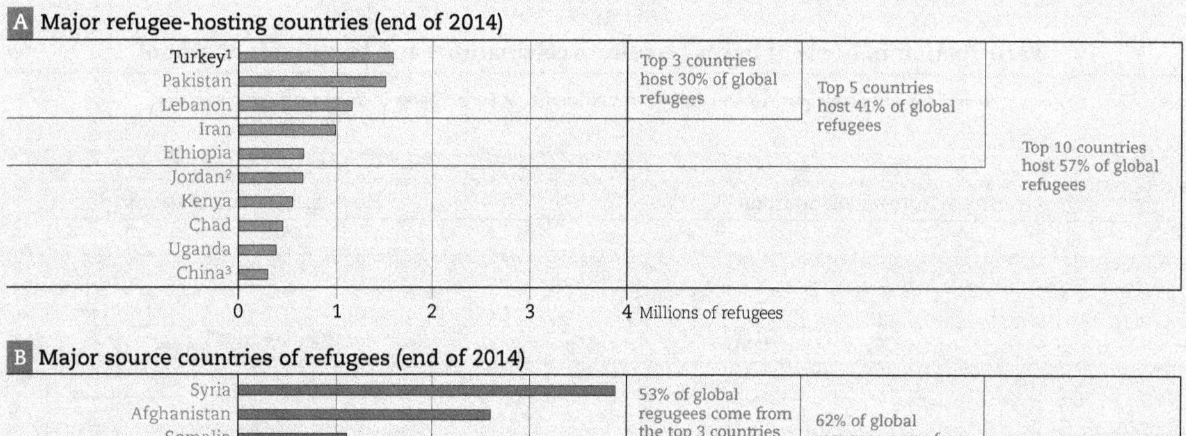

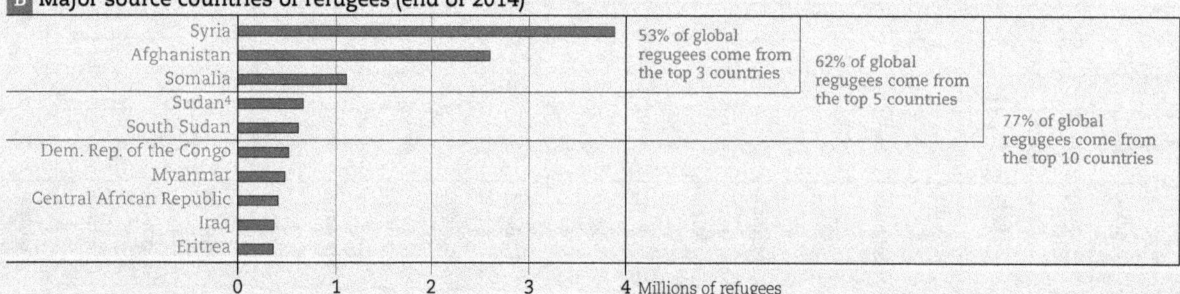

1 Refugee figure for Syrians is a government estimate.
2 Includes 29 300 Iraqi refugees registered with UNHCR in Jordan.
3 The 300 000 Vietnamese refugees are well integrated and in practice receive protection from the Government of China.
4. Figures for refugees might include citizens of South Sudan.
Source: UNHCR, Global Trends 2014.
Underlying data for the figures in this chapter can be found at www.oecd.org/edu/school/Immigrant-Students-Chapter3-Figures.xlsx.

When considering the issue of education for refugees who have been or will be resettled, it is important to keep several other facts in mind. For example, in 2014:

- Education received 2% of humanitarian funding. There has recently been a pledge from the European parliament to increase that funding to 4% by 2019. Internally displaced people also benefit from the 2% allocation. In 2014, there were 38 million internally displaced people.
- Some 51% of refugees were under 18 years old.[1]
- Some 50% of refugee children completed primary school.
- Some 35% of girls completed primary school.
- Some 25% of refugee adolescents attended secondary school.
- Only 1% of refugee youth attended post-secondary programming.[2]

In addition:

- The average number of years that a refugee is displaced is 17.
- Refugee support is traditionally funded through humanitarian mechanisms. That is changing to include development mechanisms, but it will be a gradual change, and will especially benefit stable countries that can absorb development programmes.
- Humanitarian funding for most crises usually peaks in the second year of operation and decreases steadily thereafter.
- Refugees receive the greatest amount of material and social assistance during peak funding cycles. After the cycle has peaked, criteria are applied to ensure that the most vulnerable receive the most assistance.
- Some 8% of the refugee population is considered eligible for resettlement each year. Generally, less than 1% of refugees are resettled annually. Still, almost 900 000 refugees have been resettled since 2004. There is a high likelihood that most have interacted in some way with education systems in their new countries as students or parents.
- Traditionally, the United States, Canada and Australia, in that order, have been the largest resettlement countries. Many OECD countries in Europe have policies that have allowed asylum seekers to access public services, including education.

Refugees: People who have fled armed conflict or persecution. The situation in their country of origin is so difficult that they cross an international border to access their right to international protection in the absence of protection from a country or origin government.

Asylum system: The government institution in the country of asylum that grants refugee status.

Asylum seekers: People who have requested international protection and refugee status, but whose legal status has not yet been determined by the government in the country of asylum.

First country of asylum: The first country in which refugees settle, and in which they are registered as refugees.

Migrants: People who choose to move to reunite with family, to find improved work or education opportunities, or for other reasons not related to a lack of government protection in their country of origin. Migrants can return home safely if they so choose; refugees cannot.

Resettlement:[3] The process by which the most acutely vulnerable refugees are assisted by UNHCR to gain permanent residency or citizenship in a resettlement country.

What is the education experience like for refugees in first countries of asylum?

There is nothing about being a refugee that is easy, and that includes attending school. A refugee who completes primary school, who is able to attend secondary school and possibly post-secondary or even tertiary education has tremendous resilience and supportive parents who likely completed at least some of their own formal education. Even in those contexts where access to public education is possible, there are many obstacles to participation, and most of them are related to poverty. Other barriers are related to the relative strength of the education system in the country of first asylum, and its ability to address the particular learning needs of refugee students. The following variables interact in different combinations across countries of asylum, and often within those countries. Some of the most influential variables are:

Asylum-country policy on access to public education for refugees

If access to public education is allowed or has been established, refugee children, adolescents and youth stand a better chance of attending and completing full-cycle formal education programmes. If such access cannot be established, parallel education systems based on the home country or other curricula tend to be established. The parallel systems are generally accountable primarily to themselves. They rarely continue beyond the primary level, and they lack relevant teaching and learning materials, trained teachers, and/or certification procedures. The fees or associated costs of support and materials are generally not affordable for most families and increase over time. Without sustainable, affordable access to quality education, participation and cycle completion among refugee populations suffers. UNHCR has a new policy that it hopes will encourage and support mainstreaming refugees into national systems, but it will take time, advocacy and development investment to implement fully.

Geography

In parts of the world where war has been endemic, there is a pattern of significant, sudden displacement of large populations due to conflict or food insecurity. This is true for at least three-quarters of the current refugee population. These populations seek first asylum in more stable, but not always more economically strong or secure, neighbouring countries. Generally, most of the economic and political activity in such countries is concentrated in large urban areas. More than 50% of refugees currently live in urban areas. They have better opportunities, but it is also more difficult to identify them for support if they do not request such support. If refugees settle or are settled in rural areas or encampments, access to government services may remain more of an international right than a reality. Refugee students in rural areas can usually access primary education in some form, but secondary education is difficult to find; for urban students, it is difficult to afford.

Delay

If the refugee influx population is significant, expanding or establishing formal education services can take time; the greater the delay, the greater the difficulties in getting children and adolescents into or back to school. Emergency education programmes frequently fill the gap and are sometimes the first and only exposure to academic learning for refugee populations from conflict and food-insecure regions if links to national public systems are not negotiated, guided and supported during and immediately after the emergency phase.

Education history

Many refugee children and youth from conflict or food-insecure regions have had little or limited access to education in their countries of origin. Many of their parents will have had equally limited experience in formal education. If the benefits of education are not clearly accessible to children and youth, and not apparent to families who have infrequent or no history of formal education, attendance and completion rates in displacement suffer. This is especially true when disadvantaged families must measure the costs associated with school (transport, materials, clothes) against competing essential needs.

Asylum-country policy on the right to work

In 2014, most countries of first asylum had laws that do not allow foreign nationals to work. This does not always mean that refugees don't work, but it means that they mostly have access to menial labour and substandard wages. This often means that children must work also, or stay at home with young children so that parents can work. If there are no flexible education opportunities that respond to the reality on the ground, then children in these contexts struggle to stay in school. Some refugee operations have successfully launched small-scale innovations that target working children and adolescents, or girls and young women with or without children. Bringing such programmes up to scale in the difficult operating environments where refugees live is an ongoing challenge.

Poverty and conservatism

It is common, if not a given, that refugees experience poverty. Some nomads and pastoralists may be able to continue their livelihood activities in the country of first asylum, as can entrepreneurs and others. Much depends on the practical and legal variables in the country of asylum. Some refugees depend on support from diaspora families.

Conservative cultural tendencies in refugee communities can emerge during displacement, when opportunities to earn a living change or diminish. With some exceptions, this usually translates into reduced participation of girls in education – especially once the traditionally accepted age for marriage in a given community is attained, and especially if there is a lack of female teaching staff. Sometimes marriageable age is attained before the end of primary school or basic education.

Education also becomes less of a priority for families when the economic or home-support contibutions of children and adolescents are considered essential. For families without much history of education, the benefits of school are understood to be economic. If they see little or no immediate economic benefit to participation in education, and if education also requires expenditure, it is unlikely that education will be a top priority for those families. In these contexts, UNHCR works with community and religious leaders to influence greater community buy-in for longer-term commitment to education for all children and adolescents. In general, the greater the quality of education offered in displacement, the easier it is to work with communities to change perspectives and approaches. But attaining quality education in those contexts where refugees and countries of asylum already struggle to provide it is long, slow work and requires development funding.

Teachers

The three contexts in which refugees most often find themselves also pose the greatest challenge for teachers: countries of origin in conflict, significant sudden influx, and countries of first asylum in development. In the 86% of the developing world that welcomes refugees, all have some qualified teachers, but few have enough qualified teachers for their own populations. If they do have adequate numbers of qualified teachers, they frequently do not have the budgets to employ numbers sufficient to meet the needs of the influx as well as the local community. If the influx is in a rural area, governments that agree to deploy teachers find it difficult to find enough or any of them willing to leave urban areas, or female teachers willing to leave or relocate their families. This means that, in many contexts, refugees and local community teachers with the highest levels of education – usually completion of primary or secondary school, but sometimes not even that – are engaged. Among community teachers, those with the least amount of education are generally placed in the lowest primary grades because there is a perception that the content is easier to teach and learn. Unfortunately, these are also the grades where the issues of overcrowding and pupils with a wide range of ages are most common.These teachers thus need to be able both to manage complex classroom conditions and help children reach the stage where they can read fluently and understand basic mathematics.

Difficult teaching conditions, poor incentives and lack of training lead to high teacher turnover. A number of innovations are being explored to address this critical issue of teacher quality in refugee contexts, including post-secondary opportunities for teacher training within refugee communities. The Global Partnership for Education now allows 20% of its funding to be used in emergencies for expenditures on line items such as supplemental teaching staff.

Language

The language issue in refugee contexts is comparable to that in immigration contexts, in general, but with two important differences. The first is that the language of instruction in many refugee contexts is not the native language of teachers or students. If the teachers are qualified this is not a significant issue; if they are not, it can seriously hinder learning. The second is the lack of learning materials in the language of instruction outside the classroom. UNHCR has explored several sustainable innovation pilots focusing on this issue, one of which it hopes to bring to scale in 2016.

Availability of accelerated education programmes

Most refugee children and youth who had attended school in their countries of origin will experience some kind of gap in education because of displacement. Many who have had limited education will welcome the opportunity to attend school. The chances that refugee students will remain in school are increased dramatically when they have access to catch-up, bridging or accelerated education programmes.

For students without an established background in education, accelerated education can ensure age-appropriate approaches to literacy and numeracy, encourage continuation with peers, and reduce both the incidence of overcrowded early grades and the cognitive and physical risks that can threaten younger students. For students whose educations were disrupted, catch-up and bridging classes are reassuring because they establish a sense of normalcy and routine, reduce the worry of loss, and lead back into regular programming. In each context, UNHCR tries to anticipate the need for such programming, and to introduce it. Whether that is possible depends on a number of the variables already discussed, as well as on consent from the country of first asylum and existing, certifiable accelerated curricula.

Access to affordable pre- and post-primary education

The benefits of pre-primary education are well known in development contexts. Given qualified teaching staff, sustainable, affordable programming, and community buy-in, the importance for refugees is comparable. Equally important are secondary, professional and tertiary education. All contribute to the development of self-reliance, human capital and solutions in refugee communities. Access to secondary schooling is an essential step towards ensuring that young refugees have the foundation for increased earning power and the skills to rebuild their communities. Secondary schools provide a safe space for personal development and positive social networks for adolescents whose transition to adulthood has been disrupted by instability and violence. Girls who attend secondary school are less subject to early marriage, pregnancy and sexual exploitation. In addition, in refugee contexts, seeing that the opportunities for education continue beyond primary school has a positive effect on primary school completion. Despite progress in enrolment and retention of refugee children in primary education in recent years, access to secondary education and post-secondary education for refugee adolescents and youth remains elusive.

Notes

1. *UNHCR Facts and Figures*, www.unhcr.org.uk/about-us/key-facts-and-figures.html, retrieved 2 December 2015.

2. UNHCR Education Unit, December 2015.

3. For more details, see *UNHCR Resettlement Factsheet 2014*, www.unhcr.org/524c31a09.html.

References

Berry, J.W. (1997), "Immigration, acculturation and adaptation", *Applied Psychology*, Vol. 46, pp. 5-68.

Berry, J.W., J.S. Phinney, D.L. Sam and **P. Vedder** (2006), "Immigrant Youth: Acculturation, Identity and Adaptation", *Applied Psychology: An International Review*, Vol. 55/3, pp. 303-332.

Borgonovi, F. (2012), "The relationship between education and levels of trust and tolerance in Europe", *The British Journal of Sociology*, Vol. 63, pp. 146-167.

Davidov, E., B. Meuleman, J. Billiet and **P. Schmidt** (2008), "Values and support for immigration: A cross-country comparison", *European Sociological Review*, Vol. 24/5, pp. 583-599.

Gibson, M. A. (1991), "Minorities and schooling: Some implications", in M.A. Gibson and J.U. Ogbu (eds.), *Minority Status and Schooling: A Comparative Study of Immigrant and Voluntary Minorities*, Garland, New York, pp. 357-381.

Hooghe, M., T. Reeskens, D. Stolle and **A. Trappers** (2008), "Ethnic diversity and generalised trust in Europe: A crossnational multilevel study", *Comparative Political Studies*, Vol. 42, pp. 198-223.

Inglehart, R. (1999), "Postmodernization, authority and democracy" in P. Norris (ed.), *Critical Citizens: Global Support for Democratic Government*, Oxford University Press, Oxford.

Kunovich, R.M. (2004), "Social structural position and prejudice: An exploration of cross-national differences in regression slopes", *Social Science Research*, Vol. 33, pp. 20-44.

OECD (2015), "Is this humanitarian migration crisis different?" *Migration Policy Debates*, No. 7, September 2015, OECD, Paris, www.oecd.org/els/mig/Is-this-refugee-crisis-different.pdf.

OECD (2010a), *International Migration Outlook 2010*, OECD Publishing, Paris, http://dx.doi.org/10.1787/migr_outlook-2010-en.

OECD (2010b), *Improving Health and Social Cohesion through Education*, Educational Research and Innovation, OECD Publishing, Paris, http://dx.doi.org/10.1787/9789264086319-en.

Pharr, S.J. and **R. Putnam** (eds) (2000), *Disaffected Democracies: What's Troubling the Trilateral Countries?*, Princeton University Press, Princeton.

Putnam, R.D. (2007), "E pluribus unum: Diversity and community in the twenty-first century: The 2006 Johan Skytte Prize lecture", *Scandinavian Political Studies*, Vol. 30/2, pp. 137-174.

Putnam, R.D. (2000), *Bowling Alone: The Collapse and Renewal of American Community*, Simon and Schuster, New York.

Quillian, L. (1995), "Prejudice as a response to perceived group threat: Population composition and anti-immigrant and racial prejudice in Europe", *American Sociological Review*, Vol. 60, pp. 586-611.

Scheepers, P., M. Gijsberts and **M. Coenders** (2002), "Ethnic exclusionism in European countries: Public opposition to civil rights for legal migrants as a response to perceived ethnic threat", *European Sociological Review*, Vol. 18, pp. 17-34.

Semyonov, M., R. Raijman and **A. Tom-Tov** (2004), "Population size, perceived threat, and exclusion: A mutiple-indicators analysis of attitudes toward foreigners in Germany", *Social Science Research*, Vol. 33, pp. 681-701.

Sturgis, P., I. Brunton-Smith, J. Kuha and **J. Jackson** (2014), "Ethnic diversity, segregation and the social cohesion of neighbourhoods in London," *Ethnic and Racial Studies*, Vol. 37/8, pp. 1286-1309.

Vedder, P. and **G. Horenczyk** (2006), "Acculturation and the school", in D.L. Sam and J.W Berry (eds.), *The Cambridge Handbook of Acculturation Psychology*. Cambridge University Press, Cambridge, UK, pp. 419-438.

Wentzel K.R. (1998), "Social relationships and motivation in middle school: The role of parents, teachers, and peers", *Journal of Educational Psychology*, Vol. 90, pp. 202-209.

Chapter 4

Factors Linked to Low Performance among Immigrant Students

Students with an immigrant background, particularly first-generation immigrants, tend to perform poorly at school. This chapter focuses on certain factors, including the concentration of disadvantage in the schools in which many immigrant students are enrolled, language barriers, and low participation in early childhood education, that are associated with low performance among these students.

Note regarding data from Israel

The statistical data for Israel are supplied by and are under the responsibility of the relevant Israeli authorities. The use of such data by the OECD is without prejudice to the status of the Golan Heights, East Jerusalem and Israeli settlements in the West Bank under the terms of international law.

Why do students with an immigrant background tend to do worse in school than students without an immigrant background? Results from PISA show that various factors, individually or in concert, are associated with poorer performance among this group of students.

Concentration of disadvantage

Low performance among immigrant students can be partly linked to the fact that these students tend to be concentrated in disadvantaged schools and, in turn, that a high concentration of socio-economic disadvantage tends to be associated with a larger unexplained gap in test scores between immigrant and non-immigrant students (Schnepf, 2004; Scheeweis, 2006).

When they move to a new country, many immigrants tend to settle in neighbourhoods with other immigrants, often from the same country of origin and of the same socio-economic status. They do this partly as a way to build a network of people who share their culture or their experience as immigrants and who also may be able to help newly arrived immigrants make their way through administrative procedures and perhaps even find work. They may also move to these areas because of socio-economic deprivation, which limits the range of areas where they can relocate.

Similarly, immigrant students tend to be concentrated in the same schools, sometimes because they live in the same neighbourhoods, but sometimes because school systems group them together, whether or not they are neighbours. The concentration of immigrant students in schools does not, in itself, have to have adverse effects on student performance or on integration efforts, as long as ethnic agglomerations do not become permanent enclaves whose residents have little possibility of outward – and upward – mobility.

Figure 4.1 shows that many students with an immigrant background attend schools where the proportion of other immigrant students is large; in other words, in many countries immigrant students tend to be concentrated in the same schools. Across OECD countries, the concentration of immigrants in "enclave schools" is particularly large in Canada, Greece and Italy.

■ Figure 4.1 ■

Concentration of immigrant students in schools

Percentage of immigrant students in schools where at least half of the students are immigrants

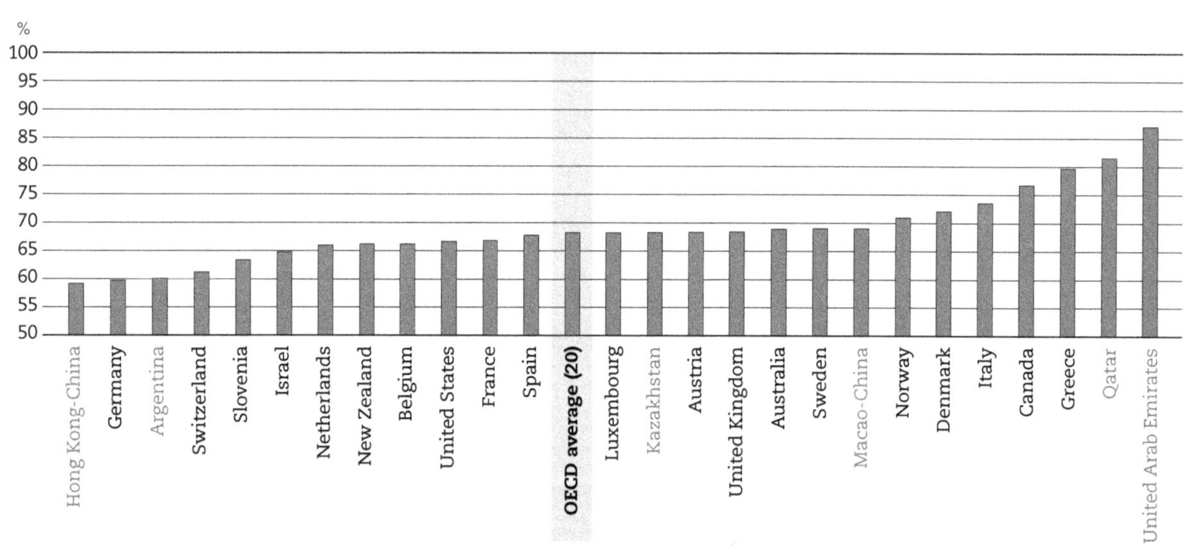

Note: OECD average (20) includes only countries with valid data on schools where at least half of the students are immigrants.

Countries and economies are ranked in ascending order of the the percentage of students with an immigrant background in schools where at least half of the students have an immigrant background.

Source: OECD, PISA 2012 Database.

Underlying data for the figures in this chapter can be found at www.oecd.org/edu/school/Immigrant-Students-Chapter4-Figures.xlsx.

Figure 4.2 shows that, across OECD countries, students who attend schools where the concentration of immigrants is high (i.e. where more than a quarter of students are immigrants) tend to perform worse than those in schools with no immigrant students. The OECD average for the observed difference between these two groups is 18 score points, but after accounting for the socio-economic status of the students and schools, the difference is more than halved, to 5 score points. In fact, Belgium and Greece are the only countries with large immigrant student populations (more than 10%), where the performance gap is large both before and after accounting for socio-economic status (40 and 30 score points, respectively).

Estonia and Portugal have smaller immigrant populations, but the differences in mathematics performance between students in schools with high concentrations of immigrant students and those in schools with no immigrant students are large, even after accounting for the socio-economic status of students and schools. In Germany, Ireland and the Netherlands, large performance differences between these two types of schools are observed before accounting for socio-economic status, but they are no longer observed after taking socio-economic status into account. A similar pattern is observed in Argentina, Finland, Italy and Slovenia, but in these countries the immigrant population is smaller (less than 10%).

In 14 out of 36 countries with comparable data, students in schools with high concentrations of immigrant students perform worse than students in schools with no immigrant students, before accounting for socio-economic disparities. After taking socio-economic status into account, the number of countries/ economies where these students perform worse drops to seven; and in most, the performance gaps are so narrowed, or even halved, that they are practically insignificant. A similar pattern is observed when considering the concentration of students who do not speak the language of assessment at home, although differences in performance are larger.

■ Figure 4.2 ■

Concentration of disadvantage and its effects on student performance

Score-point difference in mathematics performance between schools with high concentrations of immigrant students and those without immigrant students

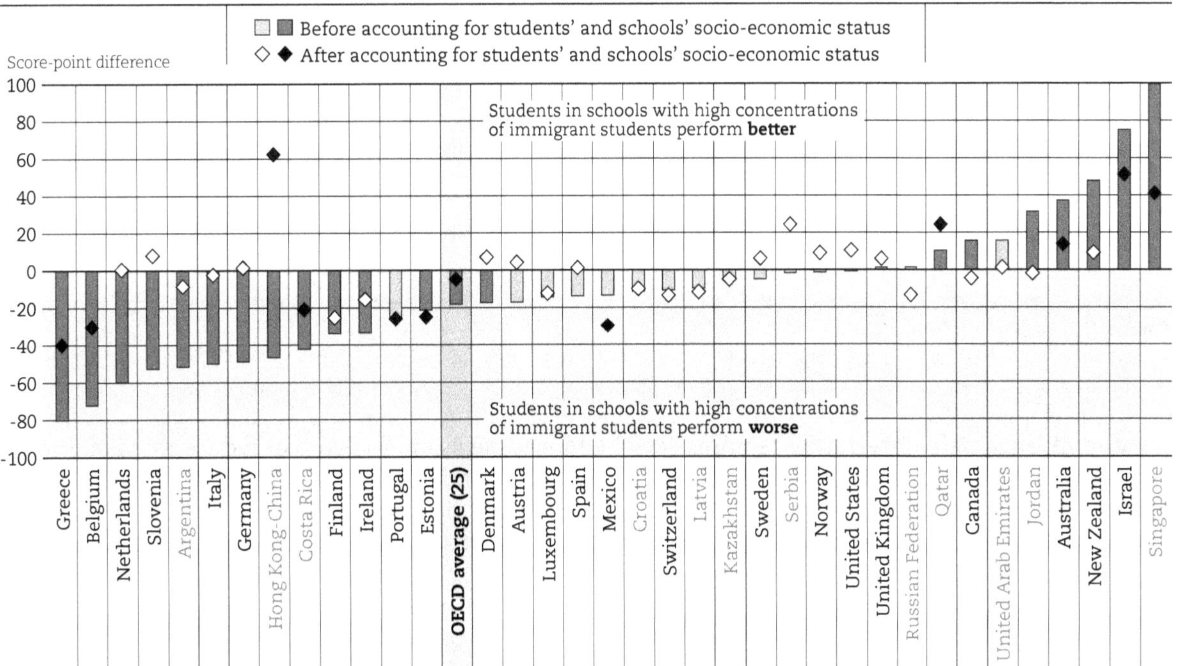

Notes: Statistically significant differences are marked in a darker tone.

Schools with high concentrations of immigrants are defined as those where more than a quarter of students are immigrants.

OECD average (25) includes countries with valid data on the percentage of immigrant students and also considers countries for which data have been withdrawn at the request of the country concerned.

Countries and economies are ranked in ascending order of the score-point difference in mathematics performance between schools with high concentrations of immigrant students and schools without immigrant students, before accounting for students' and schools' socio-economic status.

Source: OECD, PISA 2012 Database.

Underlying data for the figures in this chapter can be found at www.oecd.org/edu/school/Immigrant-Students-Chapter4-Figures.xlsx.

PISA results mirror evidence from other studies indicating that it is the concentration of disadvantage, and not the concentration of immigrants, that has detrimental effects on learning. But differences in socio-economic status only partly explain why many immigrant students perform worse than non-immigrant students. Figure 4.3 shows that the performance gap between these two groups of students shrinks by less than half after accounting for differences in socio-economic status (from 34 to 21 score points across OECD countries with data for 2003 and 2012) and remains significant in most countries. This suggests that countries need to do more than fine-tune their immigrant-selection mechanisms, and that strong and responsive welfare systems can only go so far in helping migrants and their children to flourish in their new communities.

■ Figure 4.3 ■

Reduction in performance gap in mathematics after accounting for students' socio-economic status

Difference in mathematics performance between non-immigrant and immigrant students

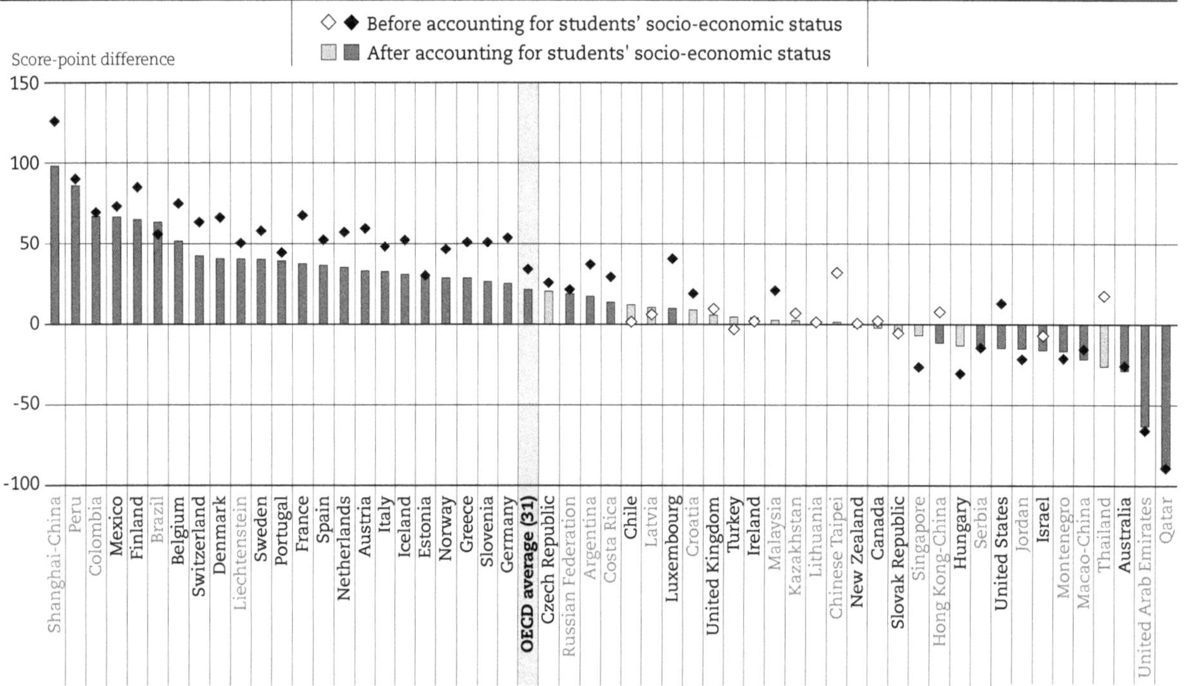

Notes: Statistically significant differences are marked in a darker tone.

OECD average (31) includes only countries with valid data on immigrant children.

Countries and economies are ranked in descending order of the difference in mathematics performance after accounting for students' socio-economic status.

Source: OECD, PISA 2012 Database.

Underlying data for the figures in this chapter can be found at www.oecd.org/edu/school/Immigrant-Students-Chapter4-Figures.xlsx.

Long-term, successful integration requires social and welfare systems that can reduce rates of poverty among migrants and that can guarantee labour market participation among adult immigrants. Integration also depends on the capacity of education systems to act as socialisation mechanisms, both for immigrants and host communities, to foster mutual understanding, respect and trust. Some countries have been able to strengthen the capacity of their education systems to unleash the potential of all immigrant students and create cohesive and vibrant societies. But many education systems struggle to provide the language training necessary for immigrants to succeed in their new communities while ensuring that those immigrants who want to maintain their heritage language also have the opportunity to do so.

Language-related disadvantage

Many immigrant children have to tackle multiple sources of disadvantage if they are to achieve in school in their host country. As described earlier, many immigrant children live in households with fewer resources and worse living conditions than those in which children without an immigrant background live. Often, their parents are poorly educated; but even when they have similar levels of education as other residents, their qualifications may not be recognised in their host country or they may have to work in low-skill jobs because of poor language skills, lack of formal contacts in their host community and/or lack of established pathways into education and the labour market in their host community.

In addition to a lack of economic and cultural resources, many students with an immigrant background face a language barrier. In particular, those students who were not born in the country and migrated at a late age face a particular set of difficulties that stem from the fact that they need to learn in a language in which they are not proficient, with parents who probably are not proficient either. Many migrant parents struggle to ensure that their children become fluent in the language of their host communities so that they can progress through the system and move up the social ladder, while simultaneously maintaining their children's bond with their native country and traditions, a bond that is cemented by their skills in their heritage language.

■ Figure 4.4 ■

Percentage of immigrant students who do not speak the language of assessment at home

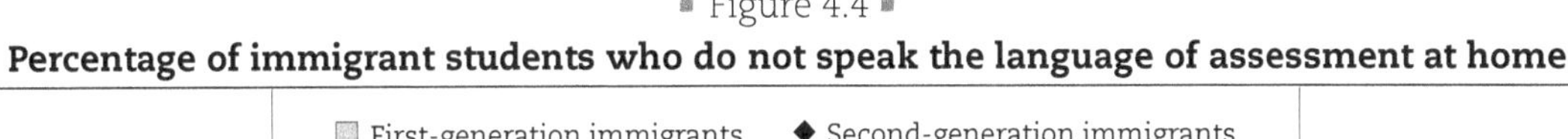

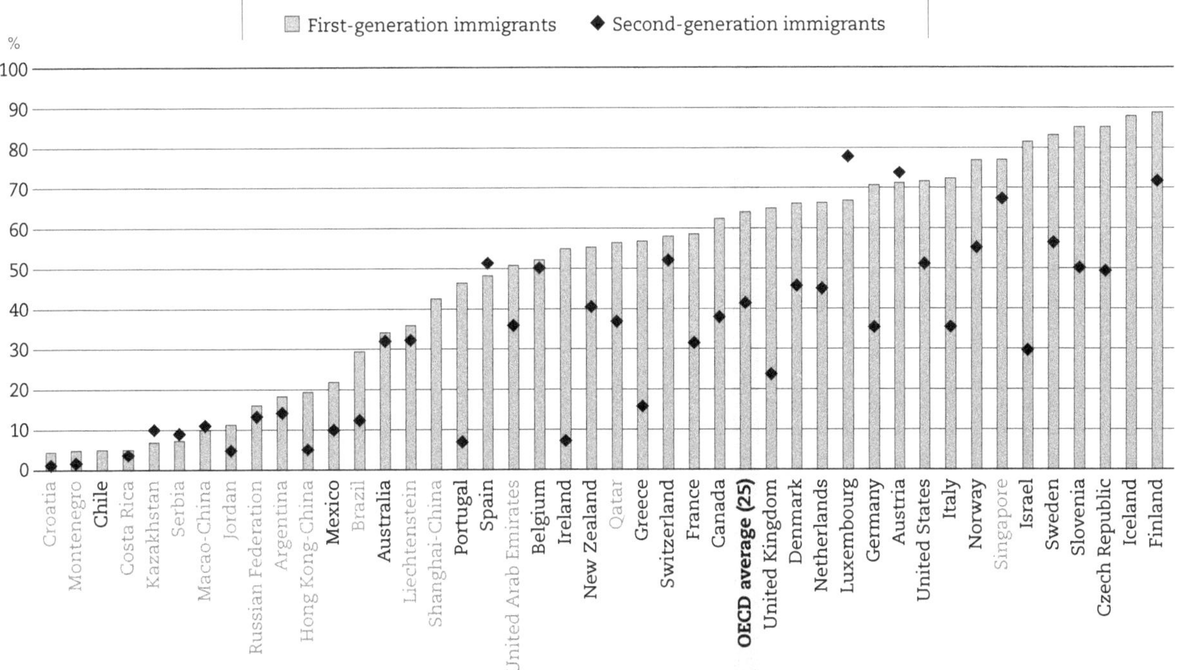

Note: OECD average (25) includes only countries with valid data on first- and second-generation immigrants.

Countries and economies are ranked in ascending order of the percentage of first-generation immigrant students who do not speak the language of assessment at home.

Source: OECD, PISA 2012 Database.

Underlying data for the figures in this chapter can be found at www.oecd.org/edu/school/Immigrant-Students-Chapter4-Figures.xlsx.

Figure 4.4 shows that the language profile of students with an immigrant background varies markedly across PISA-participating countries and economies. On average, 64% of first-generation immigrant students and 41% of second-generation immigrant students speak a language at home that is different from the language of instruction. In the large majority of countries, students who were not born in the country in which they took the PISA test are more likely than students who were born in the country, but to foreign-born parents, to speak a different language at home from the language of assessment.

Over 80% of first-generation immigrants in the Czech Republic, Finland, Iceland, Israel, Slovenia and Sweden speak a different language at home from the language of instruction while less than 10% of first-generation immigrants in Chile, Costa Rica, Croatia, Kazakhstan, Montenegro and Serbia speak a different language at home from the language of instruction (Figure 4.4). The performance gap in reading between first-generation immigrant students and non-immigrant students shrinks considerably in the majority of countries once the language students speak at home is taken into account (Figure 4.5).

■ Figure 4.5 ■

Performance gap in reading and language spoken at home

Difference in reading performance between non-immigrant and immigrant students before and after accounting for the language spoken at home

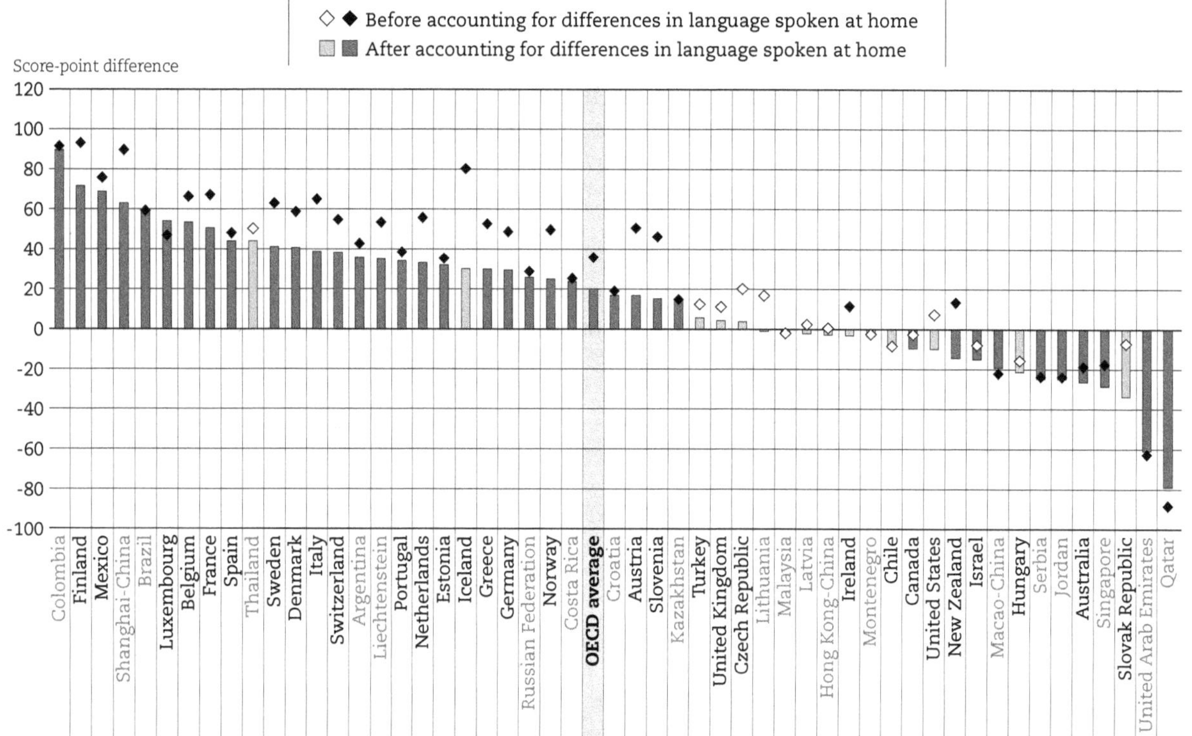

Note: Statistically significant differences are marked in a darker tone.

Countries and economies are ranked in descending order of the difference in reading performance after accounting for the language spoken at home.

Source: OECD, PISA 2012 Database.

Underlying data for the figures in this chapter can be found at www.oecd.org/edu/school/Immigrant-Students-Chapter4-Figures.xlsx.

One way to examine in detail the specific difficulties related to not speaking the same language at home as the language of instruction is to examine these students' performance in the PISA 2012 digital reading test, relative to their performance in the computer-based problem-solving test. Both tests were delivered on a computer and both tests require problem-solving skills. However, the problem-solving assessment used simple language. Thus, by monitoring differences in performance on the two tests among students who speak a language at home that is different from the language of instruction, it is possible to identify the specific disadvantages related to immigrant students' lack of proficiency in the language of the assessment.

Results presented in Figure 4.6 show that among students of similar socio-economic status, those who do not speak the language of instruction at home perform at a lower level in reading than their problem-solving skills would suggest. This is observed in 18 countries and economies with available data. In Brazil, Portugal and Shanghai-China, the performance disadvantage in reading compared to the potential these students show in the problem-solving assessment is larger than 50 score points – the equivalent of almost one-and-a-half years of instruction. Only in Australia, Colombia, Hungary and the United Arab Emirates do students who speak a different language at home from the language of instruction perform at a higher level in the PISA reading assessment than their performance in the problem-solving assessment would suggest.

While these results confirm the specific difficulties these students encounter in reading comprehension, they also reveal these students' great untapped potential. Their problem-solving skills are, in fact, much more developed than would be revealed through more traditional tests. If education systems could provide the language support they need, these students could become considerable assets to their host communities.

■ Figure 4.6 ■

Relative performance in digital reading and language spoken at home

Score-point difference in digital reading between students who are native and students who are non-native language speakers, after accounting for performance in problem solving and socio-economic status

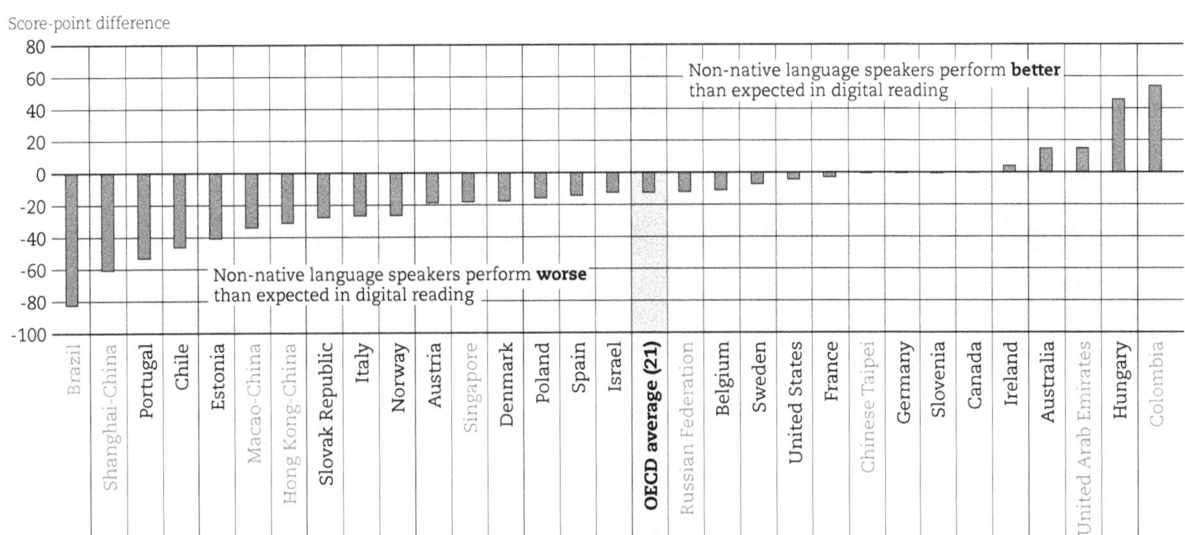

Notes: Relative digital reading performance refers to the score-point difference in digital reading performance between students who, at home, speak the language of assessment (native-language speakers) and those who do not, after accounting for problem-solving performance and socio-economic status.

OECD average (21) includes only countries with valid data for immigrants.

Countries and economies are ranked in ascending order of the score-point difference in relative digital reading performance.

Source: OECD, PISA 2012 Database.

Underlying data for the figures in this chapter can be found at www.oecd.org/edu/school/Immigrant-Students-Chapter4-Figures.xlsx.

■ Figure 4.7 ■

Relative performance in digital reading, by immigrant status

Score-point difference in digital reading between first-generation and second-generation immigrant students, after accounting for problem-solving performance and socio-economic status

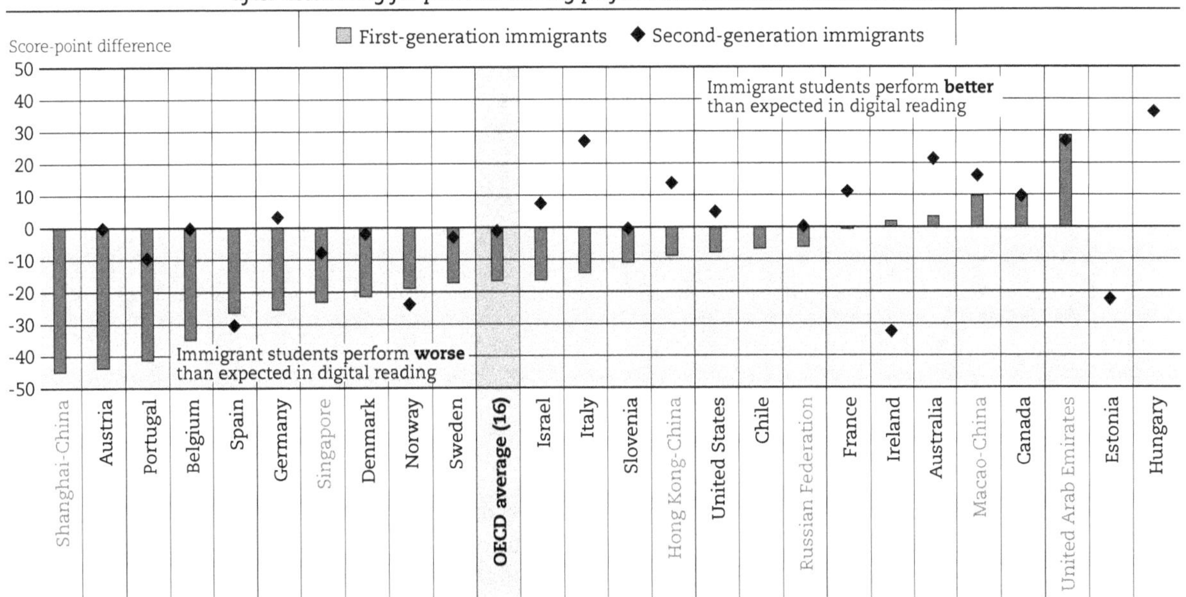

Note: OECD average (16) includes only countries with valid data for immigrants.

Countries and economies are ranked in ascending order of the score-point difference in digital reading performance, relative to performance in problem solving, among first-generation immigrant students.

Source: OECD, PISA 2012 Database.

Underlying data for the figures in this chapter can be found at www.oecd.org/edu/school/Immigrant-Students-Chapter4-Figures.xlsx.

Because of issues related to sample size, it is not possible to disentangle the specific associations between language spoken at home and relative performance in reading among first- and second-generation immigrant students. However, Figure 4.7 shows that among students of similar socio-economic status, relative performance in reading tends to be lower among first-generation students. This suggests that acquiring skills in the language of assessment as early as possible could help immigrant students to succeed in school.

The "late-arrival penalty"

To better capture the specific difficulties with reading comprehension that immigrant students face because of late arrival in their host country, the reading performance of first-generation immigrant students is mapped according to the age at which they immigrated to their host country. Results presented in Figure 4.8 reveal that there are no marked differences in reading proficiency between those who arrived before the age of 5 and those who arrived between the ages of 6 and 11. By contrast, in most OECD countries, immigrant students who arrived at age 12 or older – and have spent at most 4 years in their new country – lag farther behind students in the same grade in reading proficiency than immigrants who arrived at younger ages. In countries with high rates of grade repetition, smaller differences in reading proficiency among immigrant students who arrived when they were older might conceal the fact that these students are more likely to have been held back one or several grades.

▪ Figure 4.8 ▪

Reading proficiency, by immigrant students' age at arrival

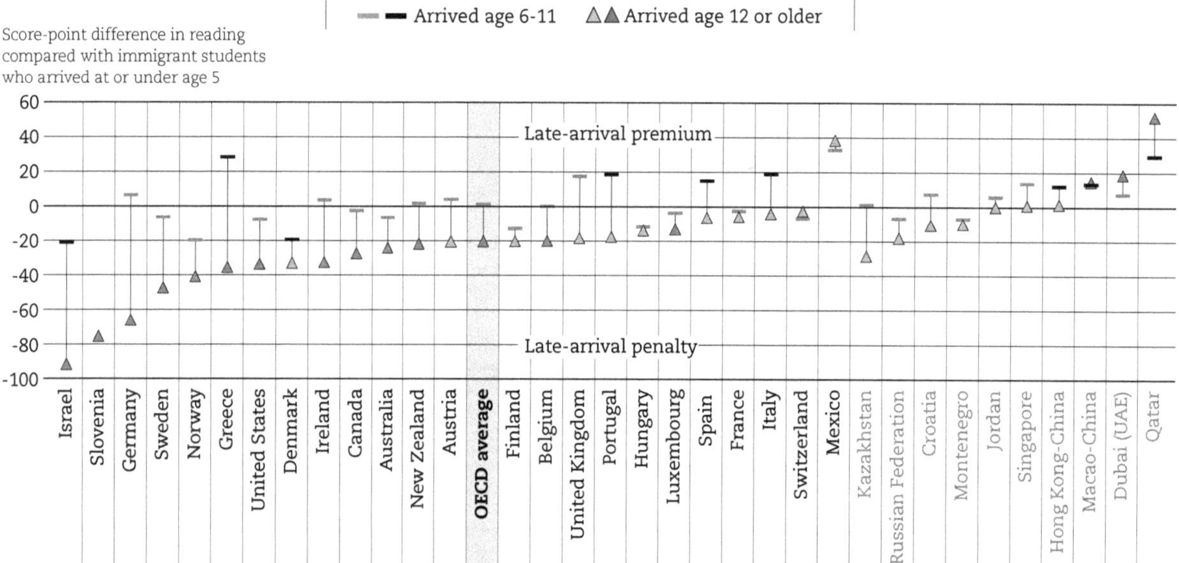

Notes: Only countries/economies with at least 40 observations of immigrant students in the early- and late-arrival categories are included. Statistically significant differences are marked in a darker tone. The differences control for PISA year, gender, and student's grade.
Countries and economies are ranked in descending order of the score-point difference between early and late arrivers.
Sources: OECD (2012), *Untapped Skills: Realising the Potential of Immigrant Students*, Figure 4.1, OECD Publishing, Paris; and Table B4.3, based on analysis by Heath and Kilpi-Jakonen (2012) on PISA pooled data 2003, 2006, 2009.
Underlying data for the figures in this chapter can be found at www.oecd.org/edu/school/Immigrant-Students-Chapter4-Figures.xlsx.

Countries and economies vary markedly in the magnitude of this "late-arrival penalty" for immigrant students. The largest penalties, in descending order, are found in Israel, Slovenia and Germany; while in Dubai (UAE), Macao-China and Qatar, recent immigrants tend to perform better than immigrants who had arrived years before.

Differences in late-arrival penalties across countries and economies tend to reflect the composition of the immigrant populations. Australia, for instance, has a large proportion of immigrants from the United Kingdom who already speak the same language as non-immigrant Australians. As a result, the average late-arrival penalty for immigrants in Australia is smaller than that observed in Germany, for example, where the largest groups of students who were born abroad come from the former Soviet Union, the former Yugoslavia and Turkey, and did not speak German before arriving.

But language may not be the only factor involved. Differences in education and living standards between the origin and destination countries may also play a role. Overall, an analysis of PISA data finds that immigrant students are particularly at risk of suffering a late-arrival penalty if they arrived at lower secondary school age from less-developed countries where the home language is not the same as their new language of instruction. These students have to quickly acquire language skills and catch up with the higher levels of attainment achieved by their peers, all while coping with the difficulties of adjusting to a new school and social environment.

▪ Figure 4.9 ▪

Language penalty and age at arrival

Relationship between PISA reading score and age at arrival in selected destination countries, by immigrants' country of origin

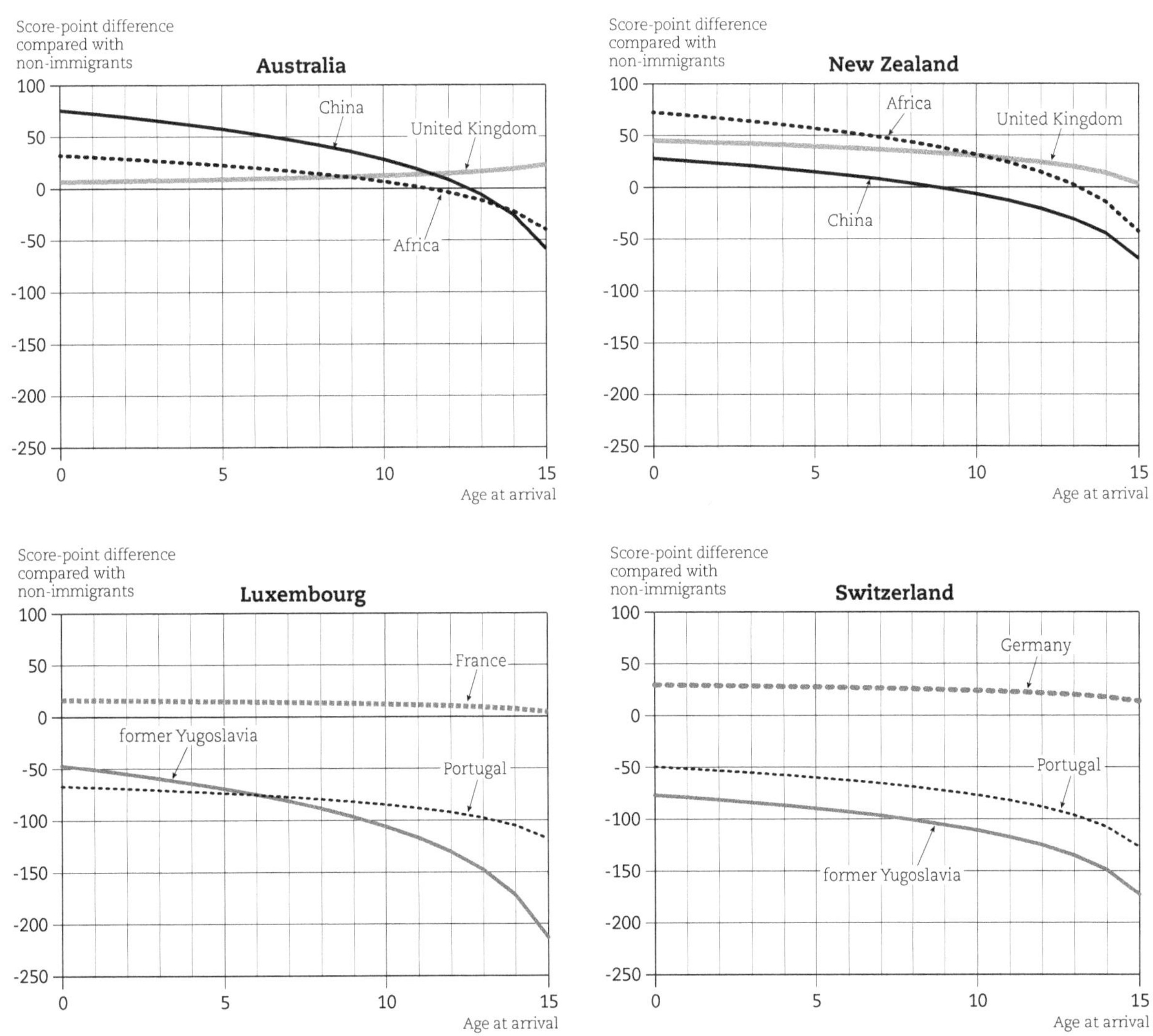

Note: All estimates control for PISA year, gender and student's grade.

Sources: OECD (2012), *Untapped Skills: Realising the Potential of Immigrant Students*, OECD Publishing, Paris, Figure 4.3, based on analysis of PISA pooled data 2003, 2006, 2009 by Heath and Kilpi-Jakonen (2012). Only immigrant groups with more than 100 observations are shown.
Underlying data for the figures in this chapter can be found at www.oecd.org/edu/school/Immigrant-Students-Chapter4-Figures.xlsx.

Figure 4.9, which presents age-at-arrival profiles of the major immigrant groups in selected countries, confirms the difficulty of overcoming language barriers. Take Australia and New Zealand: British students who immigrate to these countries do not suffer a late-arrival penalty. In contrast, children who were born in China but immigrated to Australia or New Zealand suffer steep late-arrival penalties. The same pattern is seen in European countries. French children arriving in Luxembourg do not suffer a late-arrival penalty; and age at arrival seems to make no difference to the reading performance among German students who immigrate to Switzerland. In contrast, 15-year-old students from Portugal and the former Yugoslavia who arrived in Luxembourg or Switzerland within the previous few years fare much worse in reading than immigrant students from the same countries who had spent all their school years in their new country.

When considering the reading performance of 15-year-old immigrant students, age at arrival and length of stay are two sides of the same coin. Immigrant students who arrived at or before age five learned to read and write in their new country, and their families have spent ten or more years in the host country. In contrast, those who arrived when they were already of lower secondary school age had spent several years in a different school system before moving. At the age of 15, these students are still new to the host country. For recent immigrants, lack of familiarity with their new country's language and institutions, as well as insecure living conditions, can result in lower reading performance; but in time, these factors tend to improve.

At the same time, age at arrival has its own effect on reading proficiency. Learning a second (or third) language is more difficult for older children, and the school curriculum tends to be freighted with many more competing demands as students progress from primary to lower secondary school. Unfortunately, given that differences in age at arrival correspond to differences in length of stay, it is impossible for PISA to disentangle the effect on reading performance of students' age at arrival from the effect of how long they have been in their new country.

Participation in language training

In 2012, 16 of the countries and economies participating in PISA administered a special module aimed at capturing students' language training. Results presented in Figure 4.10 show the percentage of students who do not speak the language of the assessment at home and who participate in at least two hours of training per week to improve their skills in the test language. The figure shows that only around 18% of students, on average, participate in at least two hours of language training per week, although in Singapore as many as 57% of immigrant students do.

■ Figure 4.10 ■

Language training at school

Percentage of students who do not speak the language of assessment at home and who participate in at least two hours of training per week to improve their skills in the language of assessment

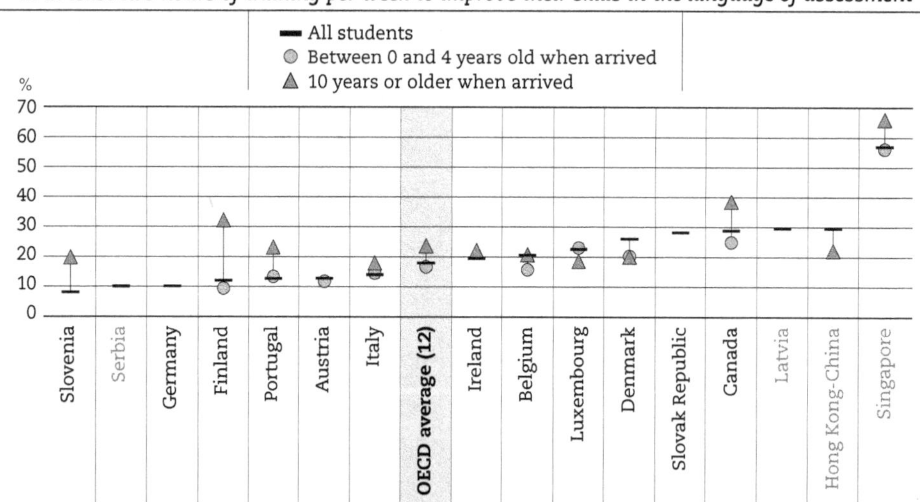

Countries and economies are ranked in ascending order the percentage of all students who participate in language training.
Source: OECD, PISA 2012 Database.
Underlying data for the figures in this chapter can be found at www.oecd.org/edu/school/Immigrant-Students-Chapter4-Figures.xlsx.

■ Figure 4.11 ■

Languages spoken at home by immigrant students and reading performance

After accounting for socio-economic status

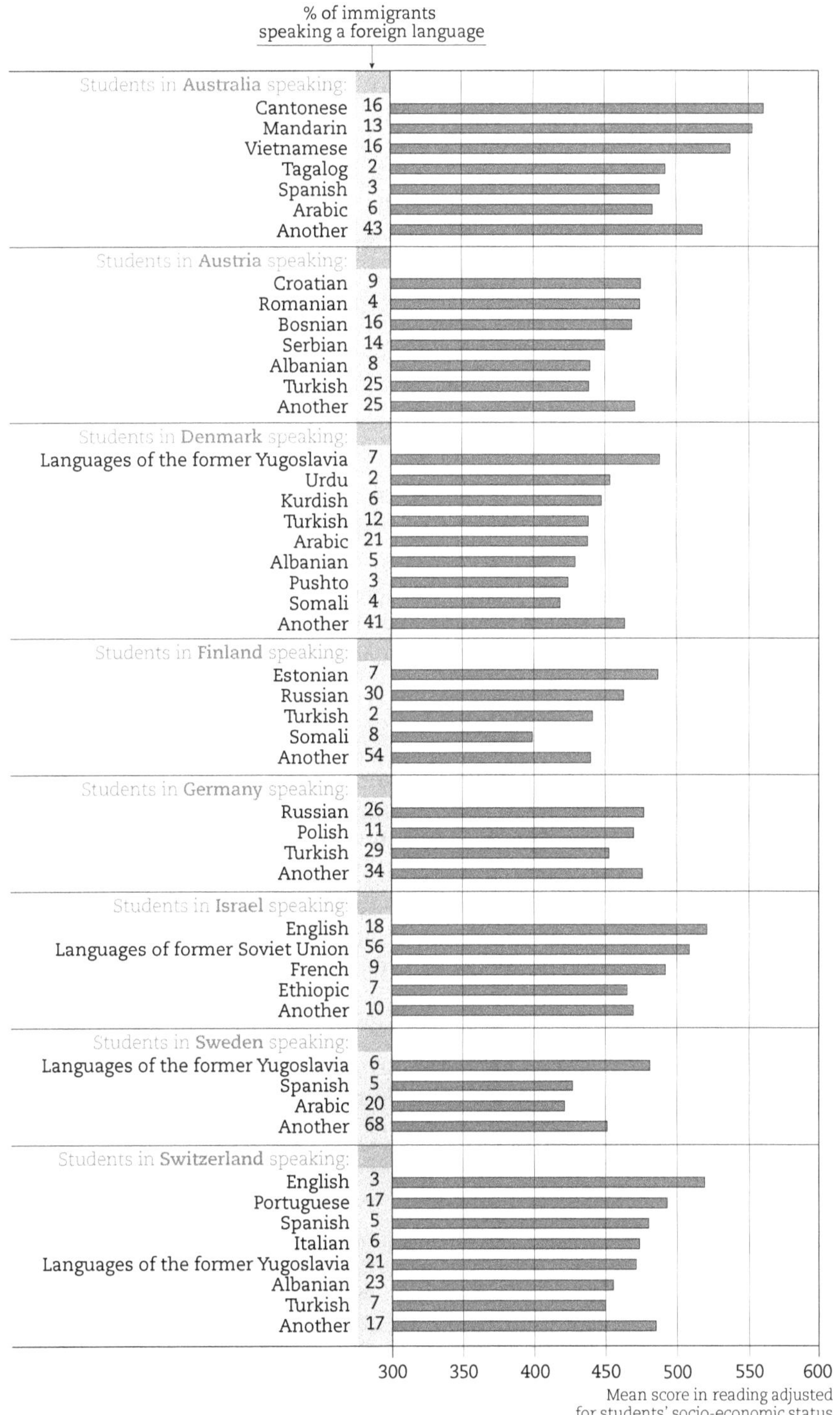

Notes: Estimates are based on pooled PISA data for 2009 and 2012, and are available only for students in countries where detailed information on the language spoken at home is collected.

Reading scores have been adjusted for differences in students' socio-economic status. They should be interpreted as the performance that would be observed if all students with an immigrant background, who speak, at home, a language different from the language of assessment, had the same socio-economic status.

Source: OECD, PISA 2009 and 2012 Databases.

Underlying data for the figures in this chapter can be found at www.oecd.org/edu/school/Immigrant-Students-Chapter4-Figures.xlsx.

However, many countries provide different training opportunities, depending on the age at which students migrated into the country. This suggests that countries clearly recognise that children who arrive in a new country after the age of 10 may have specific needs for language training. In Singapore, 66% of students who arrived after the age of 10 participate in at least two hours of training per week to improve their skills in the test language. In Canada, 38% and in Finland, 32% of students who arrived after the age of 10 participate in such courses.

Providing adequate language training to students who speak a language at home that is different from the language of instruction has different implications for different education systems. First, the number of different language minorities that are present in a country varies greatly. Second, some countries host immigrants whose native languages are farther/closer to the linguistic family tree of the language spoken in the country, thus immigrants will need more/less time and greater/less support to become proficient speakers.

For a selected number of countries with available data on the heritage language spoken by immigrant students, Figure 4.11 displays the languages that students speak as well as their performance in the PISA reading assessment (which was administered in the host-country language). The figure highlights that the language profile of students who speak a language at home that is different from the language of assessment differs markedly across countries.

For example, in Germany, 89% of students who do not speak German at home speak one of the following three languages: Polish, Russian or Turkish. Putting in place targeted language training in countries with few heritage languages is easier than doing the same in countries with larger numbers of heritage languages since most of the students who need such language training share the same heritage language. By contrast, in Sweden, only 32% of students who do not speak Swedish at home speak Spanish, Arabic or one of the languages of the former Yugoslavia – the three main language groups spoken by non-Swedish-speaking students in Sweden.

Maintaining proficiency in the heritage language

Many immigrant students and their families aspire to become proficient in the language spoken in their host communities but fear weakening their linguistic roots. Bilingualism and multilingualism can improve students' capacity for learning, promote understanding between cultures and increase employability. But the heritage language also plays an important cultural role: it is at the heart of immigrants' culture and traditions. Many immigrants rely on the formal and informal help of communities of other immigrants from the same country of origin. Continuing to speak their heritage language can be a way for some immigrants to access formal and informal networks of other immigrants.

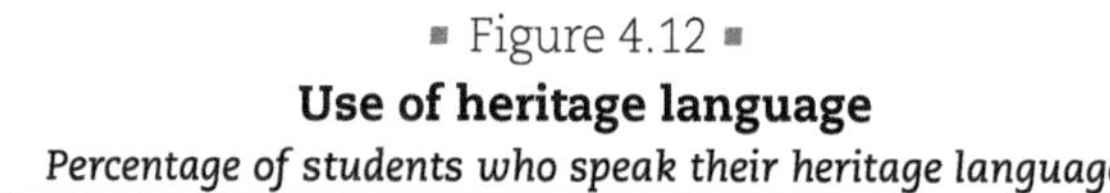

▪ Figure 4.12 ▪

Use of heritage language

Percentage of students who speak their heritage language

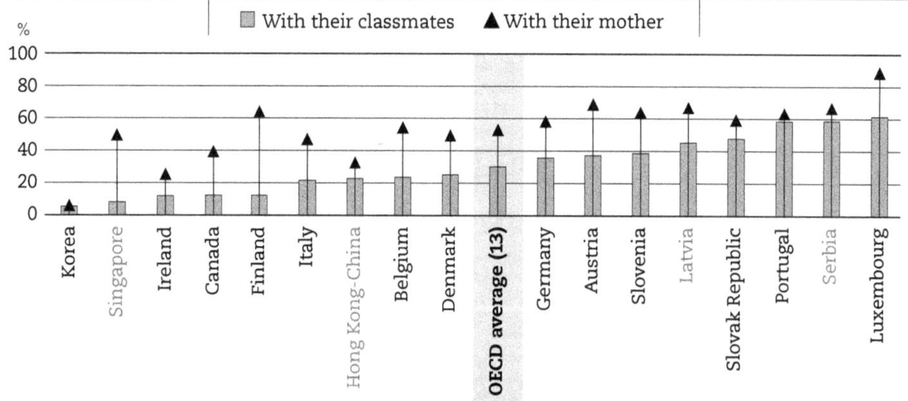

Note: The sample is restricted to those students whose native language is different from the language of assessment.

Countries and economies are ranked in ascending order of the percentage of students who mostly speak their heritage language with their classmates.

Source: OECD, PISA 2012 Database.

Underlying data for the figures in this chapter can be found at www.oecd.org/edu/school/Immigrant-Students-Chapter4-Figures.xlsx.

Figure 4.12 reveals that around 53% of immigrant students whose native language is different from the language of the PISA test speak their heritage language with their mother. In Luxembourg, nearly nine in ten (89%) of these students speak their heritage language with their mother, while in Austria, Finland, Latvia, Portugal, Serbia and Slovenia, more than six in ten do.

The figure also shows that large minorities of students use their heritage language when speaking with their classmates. In Austria, Germany, Latvia, Luxembourg, Portugal, Serbia, the Slovak Republic and Slovenia, more than one in three students do. While these results suggest that many non-native language students can maintain their heritage language by practicing it with their classmates, they also imply that many migrant children are concentrated in particular schools, often those that suffer from socio-economic disadvantage.

Some education systems help immigrant students to build their skills in their heritage language and offer instruction in that language. Figure 4.13 shows that, on average, one in ten students who are not native speakers of the language used in the PISA assessment can attend classes taught in their heritage language; in Portugal and Singapore, more than one in four of these students attend such classes.

■ Figure 4.13 ■

Percentage of immigrant students who are instructed in school subjects in their heritage language

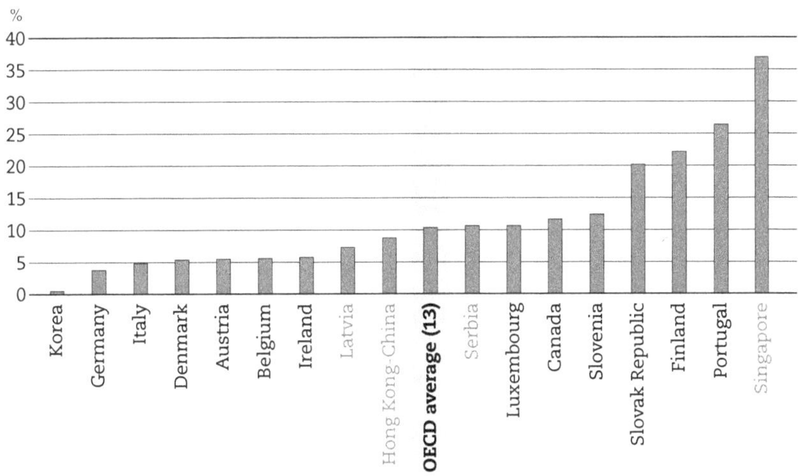

Countries and economies are ranked in ascending order the percentage of students who are taught in their heritage language.
Source: OECD, PISA 2012 Database.
Underlying data for the figures in this chapter can be found at www.oecd.org/edu/school/Immigrant-Students-Chapter4-Figures.xlsx.

Attendance at pre-primary education

One of the ways in which education systems can help to integrate immigrant children into their new communities is to encourage their enrolment in pre-primary education programmes. Early entrance into these programmes helps all students to be better prepared to enter and succeed in formal schooling; but these programmes may be particularly beneficial for immigrant children, as they expose these children to the host community's language, habits and social milieu.

Figure 4.14 shows that in most countries, participation in pre-primary programmes among immigrant students is considerably lower than it is among students without an immigrant background. In some countries, this may be due to a resistance to pre-primary education programmes on the part of immigrant parents, possibly because they had little or no experience of these types of programmes in their country of origin. In other countries, these differences reflect a broader socio-economic divide: PISA finds that socio-economically disadvantaged 15-year-old students are considerably less likely than their more advantaged peers to have attended pre-primary education.

■ Figure 4.14 ■

Attendance at pre-primary education and immigrant background

Difference between immigrant and non-immigrant students in the likelihood of having attended pre-primary education

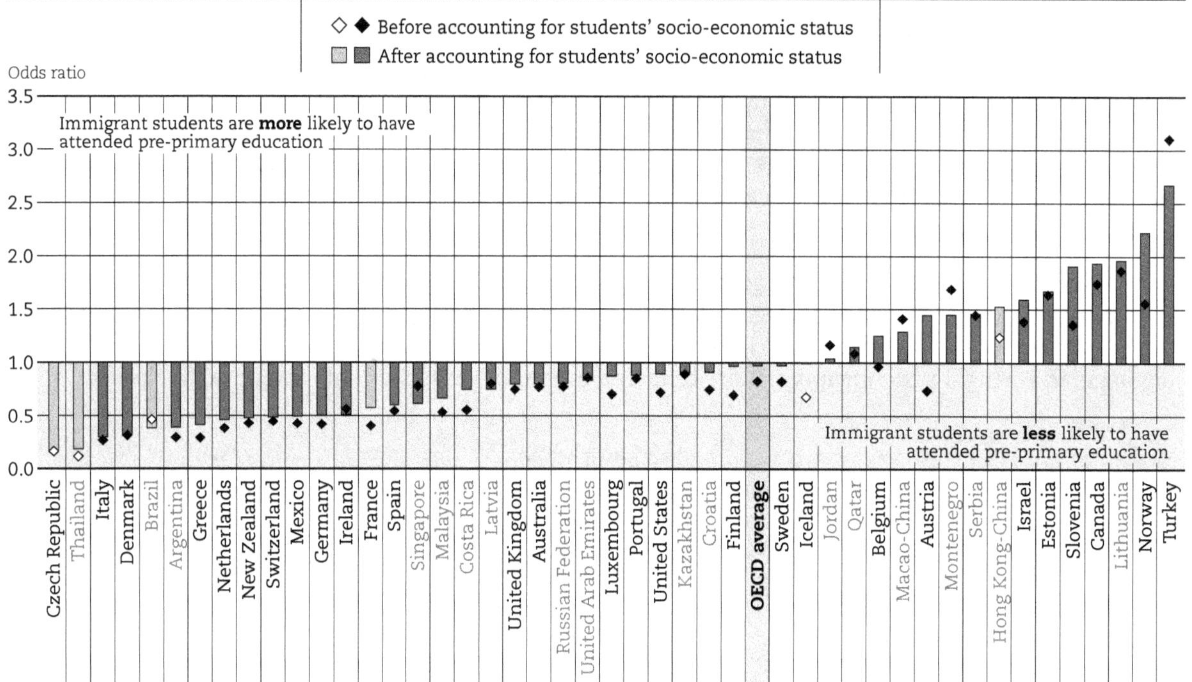

How to read the graph

A value of 2 for the odds ratio means that first-generation immigrant students are twice as likely as non-immigrant students to have attended pre-primary education. Similarly, a value of 0.5 for the odds ratio means that first-generation immigrant students are half as likely as non-immigrant students to have attended pre-primary education.

Notes: Statistically significant differences are marked in a darker tone.

Immigrant students are defined in the analysis as the children of foreign-born parents and the foreign-born students who arrived in the country where the test was conducted when they were three years old or younger. Only students with valid values on the PISA *index of economic, social and cultural status* are included in the analysis.

Countries and economies are ranked in ascending order of the difference between immigrant students and non-immigrant students in the likelihood of having attended pre-primary education, after accounting for students' socio-economic status.

Source: OECD, PISA 2012 Database.

Underlying data for the figures in this chapter can be found at www.oecd.org/edu/school/Immigrant-Students-Chapter4-Figures.xlsx.

Figure 4.15 indicates that, on average across OECD countries, immigrant students who reported that they had attended pre-primary education programmes score 49 points higher in the PISA reading assessment than immigrant students who reported that they had not participated in such programmes. Immigrant students are, on average, 18% less likely than students with no immigrant background to have attended pre-primary education. The participation gap is mostly explained by differences in socio-economic status between the two groups, but there are large differences across countries. For example, in Italy, children of immigrants are 3.4 times less likely than children with no immigrant background to attend pre-primary schooling, after accounting for socio-economic status.

Opportunity to learn, grade repetition and tracking

Differences in the quality of instruction and in the depth of curricula across countries of origin and destination can also lead to gaps in readiness to learn advanced material. But apart from these differences, the high concentration of immigrant students in disadvantaged schools might explain why these students are not familiar with certain material, particularly mathematical concepts. Immigrant students are often concentrated in schools characterised by high turnover rates for teachers, less learning time and low-quality educational resources. Thus these students are less likely to be able to overcome their initial disadvantages.

■ Figure 4.15 ■

Reading performance of immigrant students, by attendance at pre-primary education

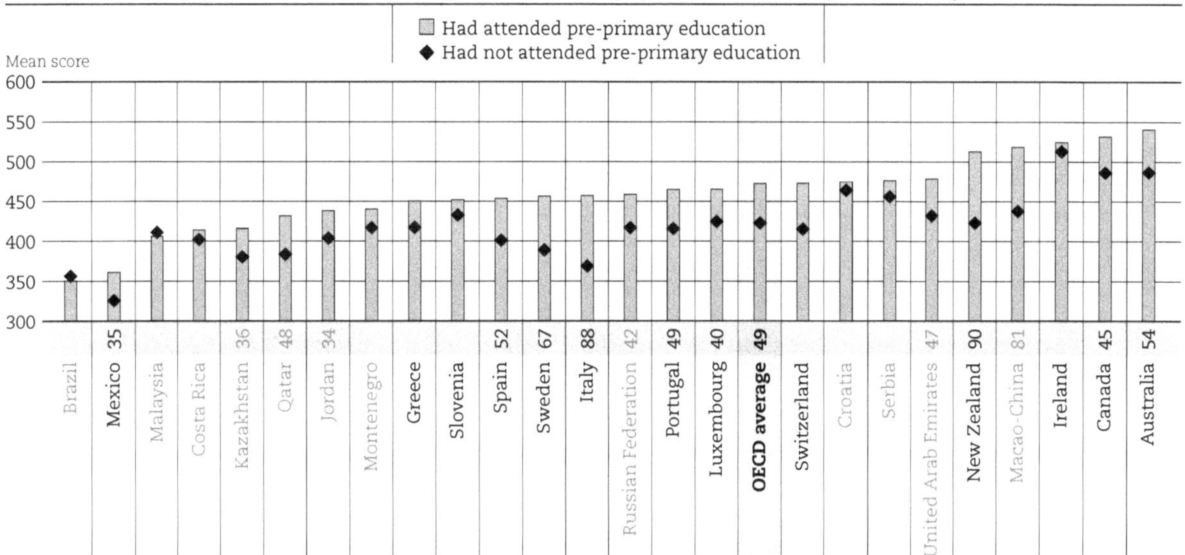

Note: Statistically significant score-point differences in reading performance between immigrant students who had attended pre-primary education and those who had not are shown next to the country/economy name.

Countries and economies are ranked in ascending order of the reading score of immigrant students who had attended pre-primary education.

Source: OECD, PISA 2012 Database.

Underlying data for the figures in this chapter can be found at www.oecd.org/edu/school/Immigrant-Students-Chapter4-Figures.xlsx.

■ Figure 4.16 ■

Familiarity with mathematics, by immigrant background

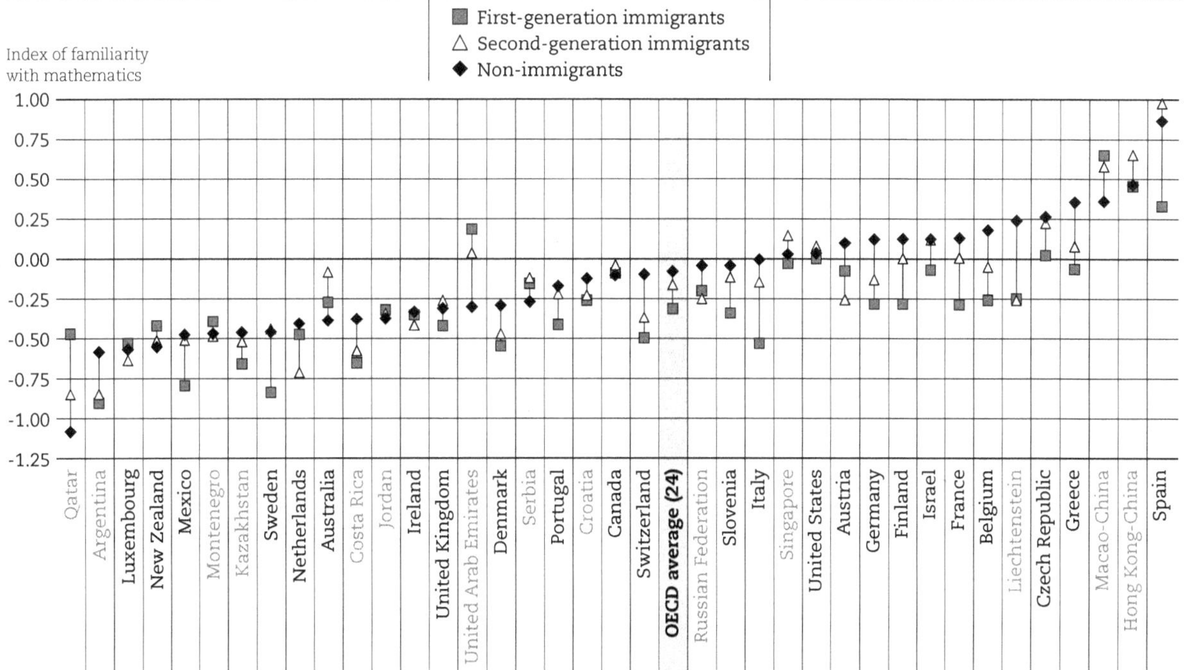

Note: The *index of familiarity with mathematics* is based on student responses to 13 items measuring students' perceived familiarity with mathematics concepts (such as exponential functions, divisor, quadratic function, etc.). The index is corrected for overclaiming (or signal detection) using information from student responses to three non-existent pseudo-concepts (e.g. proper number).

OECD average (24) includes only countries with valid data on first- and second- generation immigrants.

Countries and economies are ranked in ascending order of the index of familiarity with mathematics *for non-immigrant students.*

Source: OECD, PISA 2012 Database.

Underlying data for the figures in this chapter can be found at www.oecd.org/edu/school/Immigrant-Students-Chapter4-Figures.xlsx.

Figure 4.16 shows that immigrant students are much less familiar than non-immigrant students with the mathematical concepts that they are expected to learn in secondary education (i.e. linear equations, exponential functions, divisors, quadratic functions, etc.). In most countries, second-generation immigrant students reported higher levels of knowledge of mathematics than first-generation immigrant students, suggesting that late arrival might reduce the opportunities of being exposed to mathematics content, or increase the mismatch between what was learned in the country of origin and what is learned in the destination country. Immigrant students are also likely to have spent considerable time out of school as they were making their way from their country of origin to their host country. Figure 4.17 shows that at least one in six immigrant students who attend school in an OECD country lost more than two months of school at least once in their life.

■ Figure 4.17 ■

Students who lost more than two months of schooling, by immigrant background

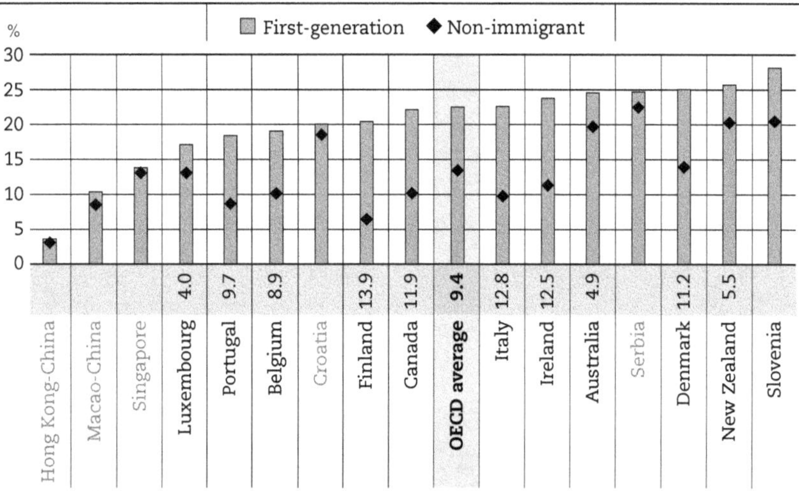

Note: Statistically significant differences between first-generation immigrant and non-immigrant students are shown next to the country/economy name.

Countries and economies are ranked in ascending order of the percentage of first-generation immigrant students.

Source: OECD, PISA 2012 Database.

Underlying data for the figures in this chapter can be found at www.oecd.org/edu/school/Immigrant-Students-Chapter4-Figures.xlsx.

■ Figure 4.18 ■

Teachers' needs for professional development for teaching in a multicultural setting

Percentage of lower secondary teachers who indicated that they have a high level of need for professional development in the area of teaching in a multicultural or multilingual setting

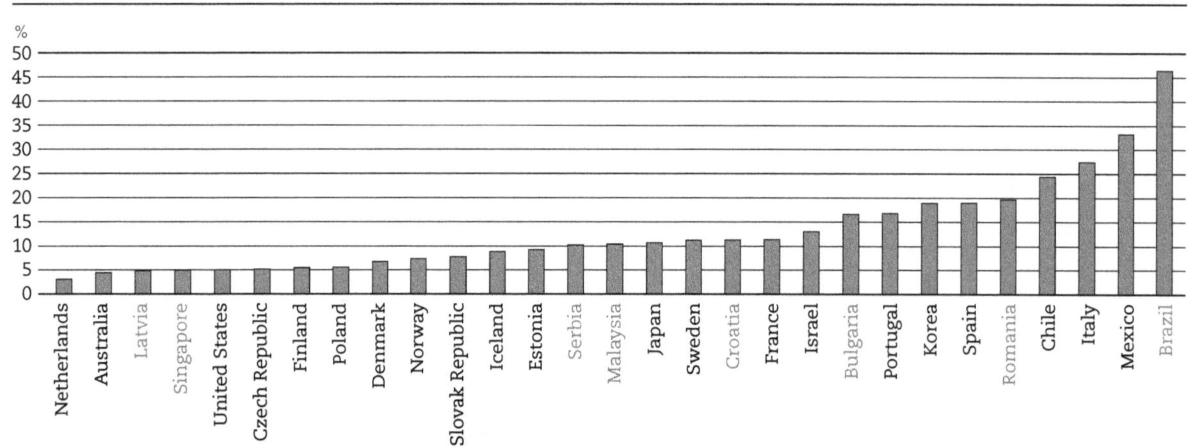

Countries are ranked in ascending order of the percentage of lower secondary teachers.

Source: OECD, TALIS 2013 Database.

Underlying data for the figures in this chapter can be found at www.oecd.org/edu/school/Immigrant-Students-Chapter4-Figures.xlsx.

Teachers and school administrators face the challenge of teaching increasingly multiethnic and multilingual classes, where students differ not only in their background knowledge, but also in the strategies they use to approach and solve problems. For example, mathematics teachers can choose among many different representations of the algorithm of division, and this choice is often culture-specific. Teachers who are not fully aware of these differences in approaches to mathematical problems or who "play down" cultural differences, arguing for general notions of ability and equity (Abreu, 2005), are ill-equipped to build on their students' knowledge and experiences. Indeed, many teachers recognise that handling cultural diversity in class is difficult and requires preparation.

Figure 4.18 shows that large proportions of teachers in several countries feel they need more professional development in the area of teaching in a multicultural or multilingual setting. This feeling of unpreparedness is notable in Latin American countries and in the European countries that recently saw rapid increases in the linguistic and cultural diversity in schools, such as Italy and Spain.

Ethnic heterogeneity is not *per se* a hindrance to learning in the classroom. More and more schools have started to recognise that minority groups have something to contribute to the classroom. On average across OECD countries, only 4% of students are in schools whose principal reported that ethnic heterogeneity is a serious obstacle to learning (Figure 4.19).

Figure 4.19 shows that, within countries, there are large differences in schools' preparedness to handle multilingualism and multiculturalism, and thus in their perception of ethnic heterogeneity as a liability rather than as a resource for learning. Unsurprisingly, principals of socio-economically disadvantaged schools are much more likely than principals of advantaged schools to report that ethnic diversity hinders learning. This difference reflects the concentration of immigrant students – those with arguably the largest learning and linguistic deficits – in poor schools and also indicates that disadvantaged schools need more support to start viewing ethnic differences as a learning resource.

Education systems also differ in the strategies they follow to address the diversity in students' academic abilities. A traditional solution is to sort students by ability, mostly through grade repetition. In theory, grade repetition gives struggling students more time to master the curriculum. But grade repetition is not only linked to students' socio-economic status, it is has also been shown to be costly for education systems (OECD, 2013).

Figure 4.20 shows that immigrant students are 3.3 times more likely than non-immigrant students to repeat a grade either in primary or secondary school, on average across OECD countries. Differences in grade repetition between immigrant and non-immigrant students are particularly large in countries that host relatively high percentages of humanitarian migrants, such as Finland and Sweden. And immigrant students are found to be more likely to repeat grades even after accounting for their performance in mathematics and reading and their socio-economic status.

These results invite further analysis of how "social representations" of immigrants might influence teachers' expectations for their students. Experimental studies have found that teachers react to demographic characteristics of their students, and that sharing common characteristics affects teacher-student relations through a variety of active (e.g. overt bias) and passive (role model effects, students' fear of stereotypes) effects (Dee, 2005, Lavy 2008). In addition, as a result of grade repetition, many immigrant students may be older than their classmates, which could create problems for their social integration into groups of peers.

Tracking is another education policy that can affect immigrant students' progress through compulsory schooling. Early tracking of students into academic or vocational courses tends to increase inequalities in the system, because students from socio-economically disadvantaged backgrounds are more likely to end up in "lower" tracks. This effect has been observed both in education systems that sort students into different schools and in school systems that sort students into different courses within the same school (Chmielewski, 2014).

■ Figure 4.19 ■

Attitudes towards ethnic diversity in schools

Percentage of students in schools whose principal reported that ethnic diversity hinders learning

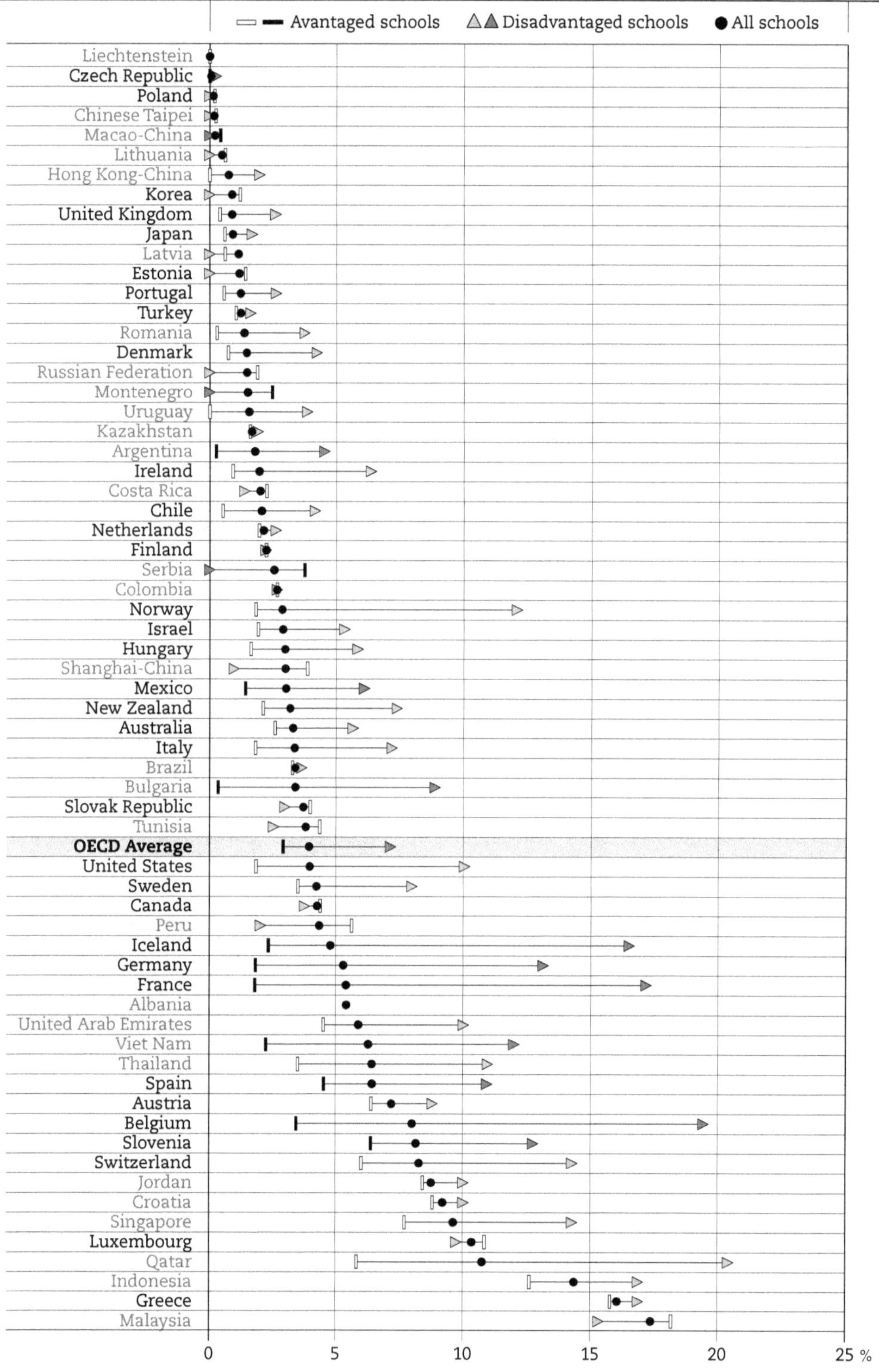

Notes: Disadvantaged (advantaged) schools are defined as those schools where the average PISA *index of economic, social and cultural status* is statistically significantly below (above) the average for the country.

Statistically significant differences between advantaged and disadvantaged schools are marked in a darker tone.

Countries and economies are ranked in ascending order of the percentage of students in disadvantaged schools whose principal reported that ethnic diversity hinders learning very much.

Source: OECD, PISA 2012 Database.

Underlying data for the figures in this chapter can be found at www.oecd.org/edu/school/Immigrant-Students-Chapter4-Figures.xlsx.

■ Figure 4.20 ■

Grade repetition and immigrant background

Difference between first-generation immigrant and non-immigrant students in the likelihood of having repeated a grade

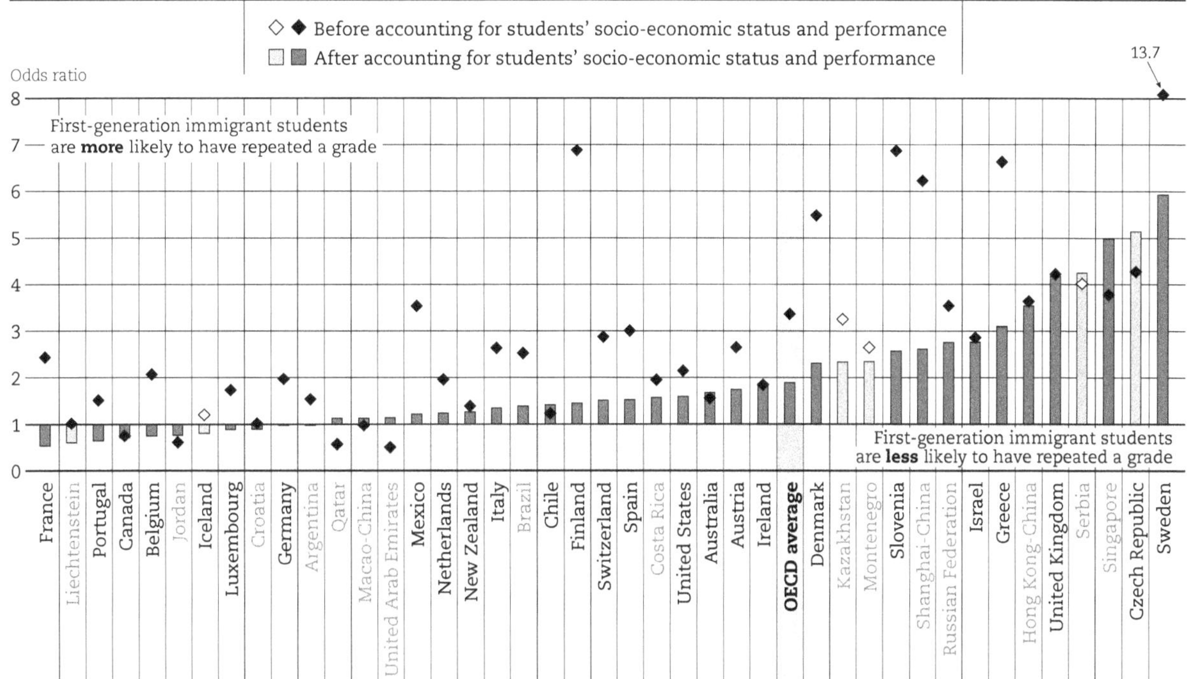

How to read the graph

A value of 2 for the odds ratio means that first-generation immigrant students are twice as likely as non-immigrant students to have repeated a grade. Similarly, a value of 0.5 for the odds ratio means that first-generation immigrant students are half as likely as non-immigrant students to have repeated a grade.

Notes: Statistically significant differences are marked in a darker tone.

Only students with valid values on the PISA *index of economic, social and cultural status* are included in the analysis.

Countries and economies are ranked in ascending order the difference between first-generation immigrant students and non-immigrant students in the likelihood of having repeated a grade, after accounting for students' socio-economic status and performance in mathematics and reading.

Source: OECD, PISA 2012 Database.

Underlying data for the figures in this chapter can be found at www.oecd.org/edu/school/Immigrant-Students-Chapter4-Figures.xlsx.

Early tracking can put immigrant students at a significant disadvantage, even after accounting for their prior academic achievement (Oakes, 2005). Immigrant parents are likely to be unfamiliar with the education system of the host country and thus may not know how to choose the programme that would best suit their child. Even fully informed parents might fail to have their children enrolled in academic tracks if negative expectations or stereotypes about immigrant students are deeply entrenched in the host society. Research has shown that children of immigrants in Germany are less likely to receive a teacher recommendation for an academic track, and this difference cannot be attributed to differences in test scores or general intelligence alone (Ludemann and Schwert, 2010).

Figure 4.21 shows that, in some countries, immigrant students are more likely than non-immigrant students to be enrolled in vocational programmes, after accounting for socio-economic status and performance in reading and mathematics, while in other countries they are less likely to be enrolled in these programmes. In Chile (where immigrants represent a small proportion of the student population, and where students are sorted into different programmes at the relatively late age of 16), the Russian Federation and the United Kingdom, immigrant students are considerably more likely than non-immigrant students to be enrolled in such programmes. Socio-economic status and cognitive differences explain a large part of the greater likelihood that immigrant students will be enrolled in vocational programmes. The data do not seem to support the hypothesis that immigrant students have stronger preferences for work-oriented study streams. Rather, their lower socio-economic status and knowledge gaps make them back away from the race to academic degrees at the starting line.

The systematic tracking of disadvantaged immigrants into vocational tracks and less-demanding courses not only limits the academic skills these students might acquire, but also creates an additional barrier to entry into high-status, professional occupations. Many employers still distinguish among prospective employees based on the school attended and the degree earned. Early tracking is particularly troubling in those education systems where students cannot easily change tracks after their initial choice.

■ Figure 4.21 ■

Vocational track and immigrant status

Difference between first-generation immigrant and non-immigrant students in the likelihood of being enrolled in a vocational track

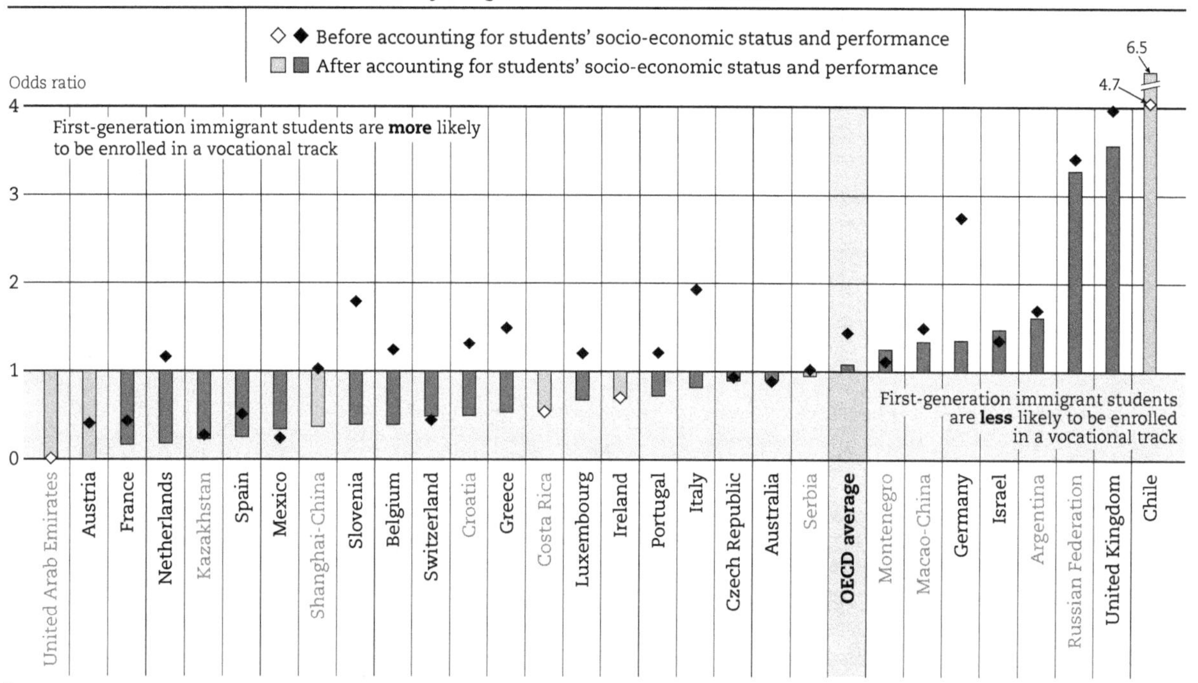

How to read the graph

A value of 2 for the odds ratio means that first-generation immigrant students are twice as likely as non-immigrant students to be enrolled in a vocational track. Similarly, a value of 0.5 for the odds ratio means first-generation immigrant students are half as likely as non-immigrant students to be enrolled in a vocational track.

Note: Statistically significant differences are marked in a darker tone.

Countries and economies are ranked in ascending order of the difference between first-generation immigrant and non-immigrant students in the likelihood of being enrolled in a vocational track, after accounting for student's socio-economic status and performance in mathematics and reading.

Source: OECD, PISA 2012 Database.

Underlying data for the figures in this chapter can be found at www.oecd.org/edu/school/Immigrant-Students-Chapter4-Figures.xlsx.

References

Abreu, G. de (2005), "Cultural identities in the multiethnic mathematical classroom", in M. Bosch (ed.), *Proceedings of the Fourth Congress of the European Society for Research in Mathematics Education*, pp. 1131-1140, Sant Feliu de Guíxols, Spain.

Chmielewski, A.K. (2014), "An international comparison of achievement inequality in within- and between-school tracking systems", *American Journal of Education*, Vol. 120/3, pp. 293-324.

Dee, T.S. (2005), "A teacher like me: Does race, ethnicity or gender matter?", *American Economic Review*, Vol. 95/2.

Lavy, V. (2008), "Do gender stereotypes reduce girls' or boys' human capital outcomes? Evidence from a natural experiment", *Journal of Public Economics*, Vol. 92/10, pp. 2083-2105.

Ludemann, E. and **G. Schwerdt** (2010), "Migration background and educational tracking: Is there a double disadvantage for second-generation immigrants?" *CESifo Working Paper Series*, No. 3256, CESifo Group, Munich.

Oakes, J. (2005), *Keeping Track: How Schools Structure Inequality*, 2nd edition, Yale University Press, New Haven and London.

OECD (2013), *PISA 2012 Results: What Makes Schools Successful (Volume IV): Resources, Policies and Practices*, PISA, OECD Publishing, Paris, http://dx.doi.org/10.1787/9789264201156-en.

Schneeweis, N. (2006), "How should we organize schooling to further children with migration background?", *Working Paper*, No. 0620, Department of Economics, Johannes Kepler University, Linz.

Schnepf, S.V. (2004), "How different are immigrants? A cross-country and cross-survey analysis of educational achievement", *IZA Discussion Paper*, No. 1398, IZA, Bonn.

Chapter 5
Aspirations of Immigrant Parents and Children

When students and their parents hold high, but realistic, expectations for their futures, they tend to invest more in their learning and to receive the support they need to be able to achieve their goals. This chapter examines immigrant parents' aspirations for their children's further education and immigrant students' aspirations for their own careers.

Note regarding data from Israel

The statistical data for Israel are supplied by and are under the responsibility of the relevant Israeli authorities. The use of such data by the OECD is without prejudice to the status of the Golan Heights, East Jerusalem and Israeli settlements in the West Bank under the terms of international law.

Many migrants decide to leave their country as a way to improve their and, particularly, their children's economic condition and well-being. Even though many immigrants face hardships and difficult living conditions, most have an ambition to succeed that in most cases matches, and in some cases even surpasses, the aspirations of families in their host country. Many immigrants are determined to make the most of any opportunity that arises from the sacrifices they made by immigrating.

Immigrant parents' aspirations for their children

Figure 5.1 reveals that the parents of immigrant students in Belgium, Germany and Hungary are more likely to expect that their children will earn a tertiary degree than the parents of students without an immigrant background. This is remarkable, given that immigrant students in these countries do not perform as well as, and their families are more disadvantaged than, non-immigrant students.

When comparing students of similar socio-economic status, the difference between immigrant and non-immigrant students in their parents' educational expectations for them grows considerably larger. In Belgium, Germany, Hong Kong-China and Hungary, the parents of immigrant students hold much higher educational expectations for their children than the parents of similarly disadvantaged non-immigrant students. And this result holds when the comparison group is students with similar performance and socio-economic status.

The figure also shows that, when considering families of similar socio-economic status, parents of immigrant students in Italy and Mexico tend to hold lower educational expectations for their children than parents of students who do not have an immigrant background. These disparities may be due to differences among the immigrant groups settling in various countries, and the value different cultures ascribe to education qualifications. However, and more unsettling, these disparities may reflect the different barriers immigrant students face during their progress through education and the opportunities available to highly skilled immigrants in different countries. If, for example, immigrant students struggle at school and the returns to education are lower for immigrants, then parents may be less likely to expect their children to pursue a tertiary education.

■ Figure 5.1 ■

Parents' expectations for their child's education, by immigrant status

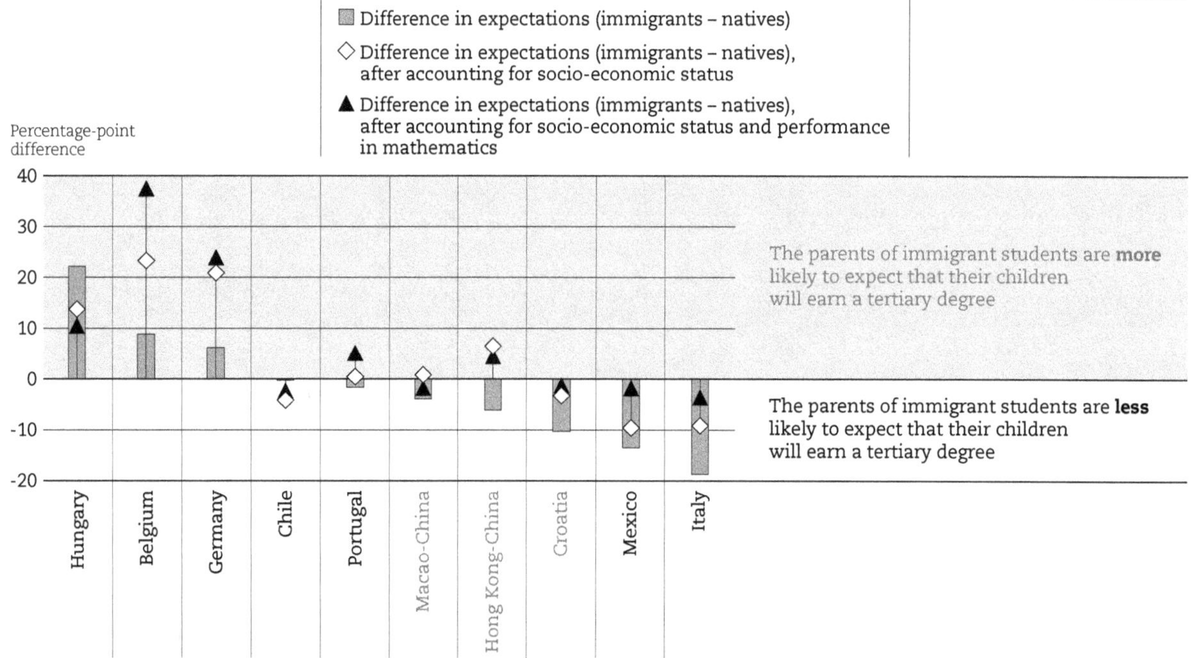

Countries and economies are ranked in descending order of the percentage-point difference between students with and students without an immigrant background whose parents expect them to complete a tertiary degree (ISCED level 5A or 6).

Source: OECD, PISA 2012 Database.

Underlying data for the figures in this chapter can be found at www.oecd.org/edu/school/Immigrant-Students-Chapter5-Figures.xlsx.

Table 5.4 (see Annex) shows that the foreign-born parents of students who were born in the country in which they sat the PISA test hold particularly ambitious educational expectations for their children, possibly because these children face fewer barriers and less disruption than the children who were themselves subject to displacement. In Belgium, Germany, Hong Kong-China and Hungary, foreign-born parents of students who were born in the country in which they sat the PISA are considerably more likely than parents of students without an immigrant background, but are of similar socio-economic status, to expect their children to earn a tertiary degree. In Italy and Mexico, this difference in parents' expectations only pertains to first-generation immigrant students.

Parents' expectations are strongly and positively associated with students' academic performance, such that better-performing students tend to have parents who hold more ambitious expectations for them (OECD, 2013). The association between parents' expectations and academic achievement might reflect both the fact that parents whose children perform at high levels in mathematics tend to hold more ambitious expectations of them, but also that parents' expectations and, presumably, their encouragement and support, have a positive impact on students' achievement.

Results presented in Figure 5.1 therefore suggest that immigrant students in some countries find – at home – the emotional support they need to deal with the many difficulties arising from their immigrant status, including language barriers, a lack of understanding of social norms and cultural traditions in the host community, a lack of strong and extensive social networks based on kinship and on non-kinship relations forged across multiple generations.

Immigrant students' aspirations

In PISA 2006, students were asked to report what job they expected to hold at the age of 30. In 15 countries and economies, students with an immigrant background were more likely to hold ambitious career expectations than students without an immigrant background; in 25 countries and economies, immigrant students held career expectations that were similar to those held by non-immigrant students. Only in Croatia, Italy, Luxembourg and Slovenia did students with an immigrant background hold less ambitious expectations than their non-immigrant peers. But these differences do not reflect the fact that immigrant students generally come from less socio-economically advantaged households. When comparing students of similar socio-economic status and academic performance, the gap grows considerably larger. It is significant in as many as 19 of the 44 countries and economies with available data (Figure 5.2).

Students who hold ambitious – yet realistic – expectations about their educational prospects are more likely to put effort into their learning and make better use of the education opportunities available to them to achieve their goals. Therefore, educational expectations, in part, become self-fulfilling prophecies. When comparing students with similar levels of skills, and similar attitudes towards school, those who expect to graduate from university are more likely than those who do not hold such expectations to eventually earn a university degree (OECD, 2012).

Countries and economies vary widely in the extent to which their students expect to graduate from university. In 9 of the 21 participating countries and economies, over 50% of 15-year-old students expect to complete a university degree. In Korea, as many as four out of five students expect to do so. Between 2003 and 2009, many of the countries and economies with available data saw a substantial increase in the percentage of 15-year-olds who expect to earn a university degree (OECD, 2012).

However, countries vary widely in whether students' skills match their expectations and whether other factors, such as their immigrant status, is related to students' educational expectations. Previous analyses of PISA 2009 data revealed that in many of the countries and economies with available data, boys and socio-economically disadvantaged students are less likely than girls and advantaged students to expect to graduate from university, even when they perform at the same level. To the extent that such inequalities in expectations constitute a barrier to eventual enrolment and graduation, they represent a potentially great waste of human capital and skills.

■ Figure 5.2 ■

Students' expectations to work as professionals and managers, by immigrant background

Based on PISA 2006 data

■ Gap between immigrant and non-immigrant students
◆ Gap between immigrant and non-immigrant students, after accounting for socio-economic status
△ Gap between immigrant and non-immigrant students, after accounting for socio-economic status and performance

Percentage-point difference

Immigrant students are **more** likely to expect to work as professionals and managers

Immigrant students are **less** likely to expect to work as professionals and managers

Country/economy	Percentage of immigrant students who expect to work in professional and managerial occupations
United Kingdom	73
Canada	73
Australia	68
New Zealand	67
Finland	56
Ireland	73
Lithuania	77
Sweden	52
Norway	62
France	52
United States	71
Netherlands	52
Denmark	48
Austria	42
Spain	67
Switzerland	37
Portugal	65
OECD average (29)	**57**
Jordan	87
Azerbaijan	85
Argentina	72
Israel	75
Latvia	58
Montenegro	55
Liechtenstein	32
Chinese Taipei	65
Macao-China	64
Mexico	81
Belgium	57
Hong Kong-China	54
Brazil	59
Serbia	49
Germany	31
Turkey	79
Russian Federation	61
Estonia	49
Czech Republic	40
Croatia	36
Greece	55
Kyrgyzstan	64
Luxembourg	55
Slovenia	49
Hungary	37
Italy	50
Iceland	51

Notes: Professional occupations are occupations defined under ISCO-08 major occupational classifications 1 and 2.

OECD average (29) includes only those countries with valid data for immigrant students.

Countries and economies are ranked in descending order of the percentage-point difference between students with and students without an immigrant background in students' expectations to work as professionals or managers at the age of 30.

Source: OECD, PISA 2006 Database.

Underlying data for the figures in this chapter can be found at www.oecd.org/edu/school/Immigrant-Students-Chapter5-Figures.xlsx.

■ Figure 5.3 ■

Openness to problem solving, by immigrant background

Percentage of students who reported that they like solving complex problems

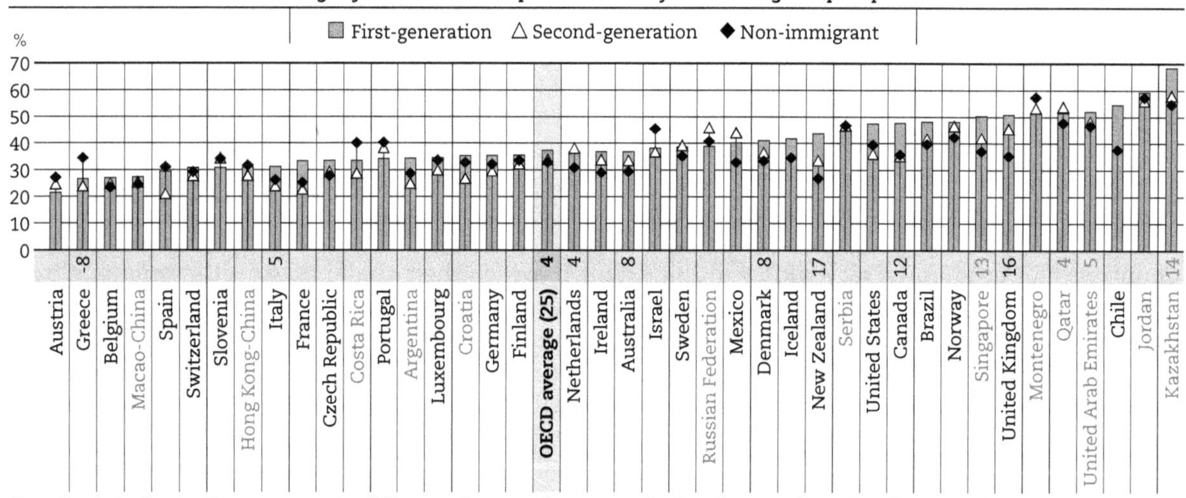

Note: Statistically significant score-point differences between first-generation immigrant and non-immigrant students who reported that they like solving complex problems are shown next to the country/economy name.

OECD average (25) includes only those countries with valid data for first-generation and second-generation immigrants.

Countries and economies are ranked in ascending order of the percentage of first-generation immigrant students who reported that they like solving complex problems.

Source: OECD, PISA 2012 Database.

Underlying data for the figures in this chapter can be found at www.oecd.org/edu/school/Immigrant-Students-Chapter5-Figures.xlsx.

Despite the considerable challenges they face, many immigrant students do succeed in school, a testament to the great drive, motivation and openness that they and their families possess. For example, Figure 5.3 shows that a higher percentage of first-generation immigrant students than of students without an immigrant background reported that they like to solve complex problems. On average across OECD countries, around 33% of students without an immigrant background reported that they like to solve complex problems, similar to the percentage of second-generation immigrant students (33%), but lower than the 36% of first-generation immigrant students who so reported. In Australia, Canada, Denmark, Ireland, Italy, Kazakhstan, New Zealand, Qatar, Singapore, the United Arab Emirates and the United Kingdom, first-generation immigrant students are more likely to report that they like to solve complex problems, while in Greece first-generation immigrant students are less likely to report so.

Moreover, strategic selection policies are blind to immigrants' potential to flourish. With the right mix of social welfare and education policies, immigrants might become invaluable resources for their host communities.

This report presents ample evidence that the link between the level of skills acquired before immigration and performance in the destination country is strong, but not unbreakable, and that supporting disadvantaged immigrants can yield large benefits. While immigrants often face cultural and social barriers that compound the effects of socio-economic disadvantage, PISA data show that in Australia, Israel and the United States, the share of socio-economically disadvantaged students who perform among the top quarter of all PISA students is larger among immigrant students than among non-immigrant students (Figure 5.4). These highly motivated students, who managed to overcome the double disadvantage of poverty and an immigrant background, have the potential to make exceptional contributions to their host countries. As the world grapples with increases in complexity and uncertainty, some immigrant students and the communities that helped them thrive are a source of inspiration about how our societies can become more cohesive and resilient.

■ Figure 5.4 ■

Resilience of immigrant students

Percentage of disadvantaged students performing among the top quarter of all students in mathematics, by immigrant status

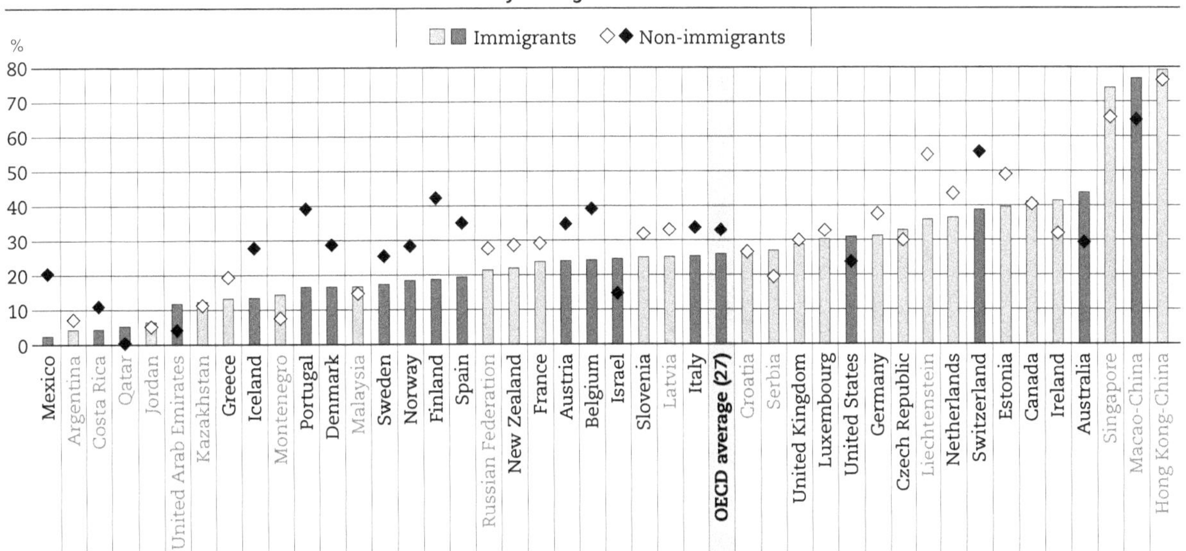

Notes: The graph shows the percentage of immigrant and non-immigrant students who are in the bottom quarter of the PISA *index of economic, social and cultural status* in the country of assessment, and who perform among the top quarter of students in all countries, after accounting for socio-economic status.

OECD average (27) includes only countries with valid data on non-immigrant students.

Statistically significant percentage-point differences between immigrant and non-immigrant students are marked in a darker tone.

Countries and economies are ranked in ascending order of the percentage of students with an immigrant background.

Source: OECD, PISA 2012 Database.

Underlying data for the figures in this chapter can be found at www.oecd.org/edu/school/Immigrant-Students-Chapter5-Figures.xlsx.

References

OECD (2013), *PISA 2012 Results: Ready to Learn (Volume III): Students' Engagement, Drive and Self-Beliefs*, PISA, OECD Publishing, Paris, http://dx.doi.org/10.1787/9789264201170-en.

OECD (2012), *Grade Expectations: How Marks and Education Policies Shape Students' Ambitions*, PISA, OECD Publishing, Paris, http://dx.doi.org/10.1787/9789264187528-en.

Chapter 6
Education Policies to Help Integrate Immigrant Students

This chapter details a number of education policies that have proven to be particularly effective in helping immigrant students to integrate into their new schools and communities. Some of these policies can be implemented immediately, as new immigrant students arrive; some help to reinforce already successful integration policies.

As the previous chapters make clear, education systems can play a significant role in helping immigrant students to integrate into their new communities. This part of the report, which draws on material from an earlier OECD working paper (Nusche, 2009), describes various education policies that have proven to be particularly effective in this regard. The responses fall into three categories: high-impact responses that countries can adopt relatively quickly; high-impact responses that may take longer to put in place; and other responses that reinforce the integration of immigrant students into an education system. The nine specific actions related to these three types of responses are illustrated in Figure 6.1 and examined in detail below.

Immediate policy responses

- Provide sustained language support, within regular classrooms, as soon as it becomes feasible.
- Encourage immigrant parents to enrol their young children in high-quality early childhood education.
- Build the capacity of all schools attended by immigrant students.

High-impact, medium-term responses

- Avoid concentrating students with an immigrant background in disadvantaged schools.
- Avoid ability grouping, early tracking and grade repetition.
- Provide extra support and guidance to immigrant parents.

Responses to strengthen integration

- Support innovation and experimentation, evaluate results and target funding to what works.
- Demonstrate the value of cultural diversity.
- Monitor progress.

▪ Figure 6.1 ▪
Policy responses

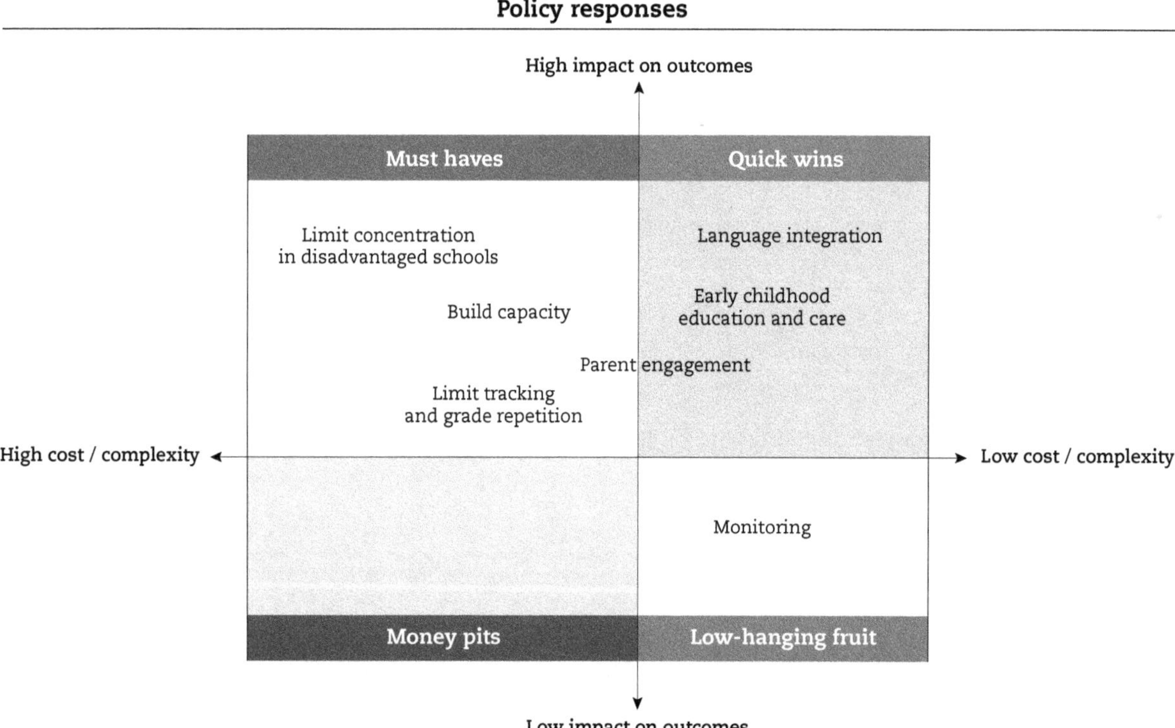

Immediate policy responses

Provide sustained language support, within regular classrooms, as soon as it becomes feasible

Language skills are essential for most learning processes, including listening, reading, writing and interacting with teachers and peers. Any student who does not master the language of instruction is at a significant disadvantage at school. Cross-country data from PISA show that students with an immigrant background who do not speak the language of instruction at home score the equivalent of one year of schooling behind students without an immigrant background on the PISA assessment. Those immigrant students who do speak the language of instruction at home are about six months behind.

Even when students with an immigrant background have learned basic communication and literacy skills, they are still at a greater risk of failure in school than their peers. Research indicates that while it takes children approximately two years to develop "communicative" language skills, it can take up to seven years for students to become proficient in the "academic" language used in school environments (Cummins, 1979). Systematic and ongoing language support is therefore necessary at all levels of education.

An OECD review of policies affecting immigrant students' achievement found that countries with relatively small performance gaps between students with an immigrant background and their non-immigrant peers had provided sustained and time-intensive language support in primary and secondary school. By contrast, countries with a large gap between these two groups of students tend to provide less systematic support (OECD, 2006, 2010).

Successful language-support programmes generally have certain features in common: sustained language support across grade levels; centrally developed curricula; teachers who are specifically trained in second-language teaching; assessment of individual students' needs and progress; early language interventions and parental involvement in language stimulation; a focus on academic language and integration of language and content learning; and appreciation of different mother tongues (OECD, 2010).

Avoid "pull-out" programmes

Some countries immediately place newly arrived immigrant children into mainstream classrooms and provide additional language support, if needed. In other countries, children are placed in special preparatory classes before transferring to mainstream education (OECD, 2006). Some host countries do not allow children with an immigrant background to enter mainstream classes until they can demonstrate proficiency in the host language (Sirin and Rogers-Sirin, 2015).

Combining language and content learning as soon as it becomes feasible has proven to be most effective in integrating children with an immigrant background into education systems. While language assistance is important, it should be in addition to, rather than instead of, regular instruction – regardless of the age of the student or how long ago he or she arrived in the host country (OECD, 2010).

"Pull-out programmes" are generally unsuccessful both in developing strong language skills and in supporting transitions into mainstream classes because they tend to reduce the amount of teaching time devoted to the main curriculum. Thus immigrant students fall even further behind their non-immigrant peers. Students who participate in these programmes can also wind up being stigmatised, and they are often taught by less-qualified teachers (Karsten, 2006).

Research has also shown that it is neither necessary nor desirable to postpone teaching of the main curriculum until students fully master the language of instruction (Watts-Taffe and Truscott, 2000). Language development and cognitive development are interconnected, and language learning seems to work best when learners use language for meaningful purposes (Au, 1998).

One way to integrate language and academic learning is to develop curricula for second-language learning. Another is to ensure close co-operation between language teachers and classroom teachers, an approach that is widely used in countries that seem most successful in educating immigrant students, such as Australia, Canada and Sweden (Christensen and Stanat, 2007).

Language classes can also be provided in addition to regular curriculum classes. This is particularly valuable during school holidays, when some students with an immigrant background may not have many opportunities to speak in the language of the host country. In Estonia, for example, schools receive additional resources to provide immigrant students with weekly tuition in the Estonian language and acculturation courses outside regular teaching time (Magi and Nestor, 2014).

Support mainstream teachers in developing children's language skills

In a series of OECD country reviews on immigrant education, teachers often reported that they did not have the diagnostic skills and tools to assess their immigrant students' linguistic and cognitive capacities (OECD, 2010). Thus, practical tools, such as assessment kits, that are age- and culturally appropriate can help teachers to identify the language-support needs of each student.

Some countries require language screening for all children well before they enter primary school, while others assess children with an immigrant background when they first enter the education system. Screening for language proficiency not only informs teachers about individual students' needs, but also informs education authorities at the district or system level, and can be used as a basis for distributing additional funding to schools (Mengering, 2005).

Denmark, for example, introduced a mandatory assessment of language development for all 3-year-olds that aims to diagnose possible language problems before children start school (OECD, 2015a). In Germany, several *Lander* introduced screening processes to identify pre-school children in need of additional language support (Bertschi-Kaufmann et al., 2006; OECD, 2007, 2014). Ireland developed guidelines for language assessment, with assessment tool kits and intercultural education guidelines for pedagogy to integrate language learning and content learning (OECD, 2010).

Second-language development should be covered in both initial and in-service teacher training. In Finland, the National Core Curriculum for Instruction Preparing Immigrants for Basic Education was introduced in 2009 to support students with an immigrant background who were not proficient in the Finnish or Swedish languages. The curriculum is differentiated according to age, learning capabilities and background to support students' balanced development and integration into society. Austria developed a national curriculum framework for early language learning in kindergarten and standards for second-language learning (OECD, 2010).

Encourage immigrant parents to enrol their young children in high-quality early childhood education

PISA consistently shows that students who had attended at least one year of pre-primary education perform better on the assessment than students who had not. Immigrant students, in particular, benefit greatly from these types of programmes. Yet in some countries, immigrant students are less likely than their non-immigrant peers to be enrolled (see Chapter 4 for a discussion of possible reasons for this lack of participation).

Improve access to pre-primary education

In most OECD countries, access to pre-primary education has been expanded to include immigrant children. Most of these programmes are offered free of charge to disadvantaged students. Germany, for example, set a strategic goal in its National Action Plan on Integration (2011) to facilitate access to early learning, care and education in day-care facilities and day nurseries for children (OECD, 2015b).

In the United States, many states have tried to increase immigrant enrolment in these programmes as part of wider efforts to expand pre-school options among disadvantaged communities. To improve access, some states have created or expanded public pre-school systems, which supplement and complement the federal Head Start and Early Head Start programmes (Crosnoe, 2013).

Both national and municipal governments in Norway have made special efforts to support equality of participation, particularly for low-income and minority-language families. Initiatives include fee reductions or exemptions, as well as pilot programmes providing up to four hours per day of kindergarten free for children aged 3 to 5. This scheme is expected to be extended to all 4-5 year-olds from low-income families across Norway (OECD, 2015c).

Reach out to families

OECD countries raise parents' awareness of the value of early learning in several ways, including through home visits, recruiting culturally appropriate and trained specialists, providing learning resources and information to families, launching awareness campaigns, and training pre-primary teachers and staff to work with culturally and linguistically diverse children (OECD, 2014).

The Parent-Child Home Programme in the United States is an early childhood literacy, parenting and school-readiness programme. The programme provides two years of twice-weekly visits to families with children between the ages of 16 months and 4 years that are living in poverty or isolation, have limited opportunities for education and poor language and literacy skills, and/or are confronted with other obstacles to healthy development and success in education. The programme employs early literacy specialists from the community they serve, sharing both the language and culture of the families with whom they work. In addition to leading weekly activities to stimulate parent-child interaction and help the child to acquire the mainstream language, the specialist also connects the families to other community resources, such as health and medical facilities and other education programmes. On completion of the programme, families are assisted in enrolling their child in a centre-based, pre-school programme. In Ireland, partnerships between pre-primary programmes and community services have proven to be effective in supporting harder-to-reach families, such as Roma and travelling families.

Facilitating mothers' involvement in school and pre-school not only benefits their children, it can also help to integrate mothers themselves, as it improves their language skills and participation in community life (OECD, 2014). The programme "Home Instruction for Parents of Pre-school Youngsters" has helped connect educationally disadvantaged parents with the labour market and improved their children's education outcomes in several OECD countries. Another example of an effective way to activate immigrant parents is Denmark's "District Mothers" programme, through which immigrant mothers are trained to visit and advise other women in their neighbourhood on education and job search.

Monitor the quality of, and attendance at, pre-primary programmes

Monitoring the quality and impact of pre-primary education systems is not a well-developed practice across OECD countries. Monitoring processes tend to focus more on compliance with regulations than on the quality of service delivery or assessing how well children's needs are being identified and met (OECD, 2015d).

However, a few OECD countries have developed systems to benchmark and monitor children's progress, including children from different socio-economic and ethnic groups. Some countries use school entry tests as a means to focus on child development and to provide information on how young children are progressing. Australia, for example, uses a national adaptation of the Early Development Instrument (EDI). The EDI, originally developed in Ontario, Canada, is a measure of children's development as they enter school. Teachers complete a checklist measuring children's physical health and well-being, social competence, emotional maturity, language and cognitive skills, and communication skills and general knowledge. The results are aggregated to the group level (school, neighbourhood, city) to provide a population-based measure of children's development (OECD, 2015d).

In Norway, data on children's development is gathered across the health and education sectors. This information provides data on children who do not participate and their language development at ages two and four. Some municipalities use this information to increase participation rates, especially for children with an immigrant background (OECD, 2015d).

Build the capacity of all schools

The quality of teaching is the most important school variable shaping student learning outcomes, regardless of students' socio-economic status and other background factors (OECD, 2005, 2013). Yet, while immigrant and disadvantaged students stand to benefit the most from high-quality teaching, they are often the least likely to receive it (Field et al., 2007). Research has shown that teacher preferences may direct the more qualified and more experienced teachers to schools enrolling mostly non-immigrant students (Hanushek et al., 2001; Bénabou, 2003; Karsten et al., 2006). In France, for example, the share of young, inexperienced teachers and the rates of teacher turnover are much higher in the education priority zones (ZEP) than the national average (Bénabou, 2003).

According to principals' reports, disadvantaged schools in OECD countries have lower student-teacher ratios but have less-experienced and -qualified teachers (OECD, 2012c). Reducing class size can be a costly and often ineffective way to lift student outcomes. However, disadvantaged children have been shown to do better in school when they are in smaller classes in the early years (i.e. kindergarten to third grade) (Hanushek, 2000; Krueger, 2000). But these positive effects are relatively small in comparison to the effects of having high-quality teachers (Rivkin et al., 2000).

To build the capacity of all schools to provide high-quality education for students with an immigrant background, it is essential to support school leadership, attract teachers to schools in need, strengthen teaching capacity, and tap the new supply of trained immigrant teachers.

Support school leadership

School leadership plays a key role in adapting school environments to the specific mix of students and local circumstance (Pont et al., 2008; OECD, 2015c). Common features of successful leadership in challenging schools have been found to include a culture of high expectations, a belief that all students can achieve, irrespective of context or background, alignment of others to a shared vision and values, distributed leadership, staff development and community building (Mulford et al., 2008).

Despite the increasing diversity of student bodies, school leaders in most countries have no formal training on diversity, intercultural pedagogy or language development. Thus, they may lack the awareness, knowledge and skills necessary to guide the teachers they work with in providing quality support to students with a range of different learning needs. Diversity training for school leaders could be embedded in whole-school professional development programmes.

In addition, few countries are able to demonstrate effective policies for recruiting and retaining highly effective leaders to the lowest-performing and most disadvantaged schools. Having good working conditions and systemic support is key to attracting and retaining competent leaders in disadvantaged schools. In the United Kingdom, one targeted programme allows for more flexibility in pay for school leaders to reward and attract good leaders. This programme provides special financial incentives for exceptional school leaders working in schools that find it difficult to attract talented principals (www.gov.uk/government/policies/improving-the-quality-of-teaching-and-leadership).

Other incentives, such as career progression, can also attract high-calibre candidates. These are sometimes a more powerful influence than higher pay. In Korea, for example, becoming a school leader in a low-performing, disadvantaged school is highly regarded by the profession, and these appointees are recognised as among the best performers (OECD, 2012a).

Attract teachers to schools in need

Some governments provide additional funding to teachers in "challenging" schools in the form of higher salaries or better working conditions. Such funding schemes are intended to reduce teacher turnover rates and attract high-quality teachers to schools serving disadvantaged, immigrant and ethnic minority students. Overall, there is some evidence that higher salaries for teachers in challenging schools may contribute to raising teachers' satisfaction and attracting high-quality teachers to these schools. But the evidence also indicates that such salary increases would need to be substantial to make a difference to teacher turnover rates (Hanushek et al., 1999; 2001).

Other actions that have been taken to recruit and retain high-quality teachers into disadvantaged schools have included: aligning initial and in-service teacher education with disadvantaged schools' needs, to ensure that teachers have the skills and knowledge they need to work in these schools; providing mentoring for beginning teachers working in these schools; and designing adequate career incentives, in addition to any financial incentives (OECD, 2012a).

In Korea, all teachers are held to high standards, which contributes to the country's high levels of performance and equitable distribution of teachers. Disadvantaged students in Korea are more likely than advantaged students to be taught by high-quality mathematics teachers, as measured by characteristics such as full certification, a mathematics or mathematics education major, and at least three years of experience.

Multiple incentives are offered to candidates who work in high-need schools. Incentives include additional pay, smaller classes, less instructional time, additional credit towards future promotion to administrative positions, and the ability to choose the next school where the teacher works (Schleicher, 2014).

Strengthen teaching capacity

Some 45% of teachers who participated in the OECD Teaching and Learning International Survey (TALIS) in 2008 reported a high or moderate need for professional development in the area of teaching in a multicultural setting (OECD, 2009; Jensen, 2010). By 2013, a larger proportion of teachers so reported (see Chapter 4).

Teaching students from a wide range of cultural, socio-economic and linguistic backgrounds takes a complex set of skills that many teachers may not have acquired through formal training. Most OECD countries now have requirements for teacher training institutions to include topics associated with intercultural education in initial teacher training (Eurydice, 2004). However, these institutions are at least partially free to determine their own curricula; generally they are not provided with any clear instructions as to how to offer intercultural training.

In the United Kingdom, a whole-school professional development programme introduced by the Department for Children, Schools and Families to raise the confidence and expertise of primary teachers to support their bilingual students produced promising results. Qualitative case-study evidence shows that teachers and teaching assistants gained confidence in their abilities, and bilingual students developed higher expectations for themselves, became more confident, asked more questions and became more focused (White et al., 2006).

In Norway, funding was provided for the period 2013-17 to develop competence in multicultural issues across the education sector. Employees, managers and owners of kindergartens, as well as staff of schools and teacher-training institutions, all benefit (OECD, 2015c).

Tap the new supply of trained immigrant teachers

While hiring teachers with an immigrant background will not, and should not, be relied upon as the sole strategy to ensure effective teaching for immigrant children, increasing the share of minority and immigrant teachers may have a positive influence on immigrant students' learning experiences and sense of belonging. However, some countries do not permit new immigrants to work as teachers because of regulations on public service occupations (Sirin and Rogers-Sirin, 2015).

Countries that wish to reverse a growing disparity between an increasingly diverse student population and a largely homogeneous teacher workforce have adopted initiatives to hire more teachers from ethnic minority or immigrant backgrounds. Such initiatives are often based on the belief that teachers of the same ethnic or racial background may serve as role models, enhancing the self-confidence and motivation of immigrant students, ultimately leading to improved education outcomes (Clewell and Villegas, 1998; Carrington and Skelton, 2003). However, the empirical evidence of this positive effect is tentative, at best (OECD, 2009).

In England and Wales, the Teacher Training Agency introduced measures to attract more ethnic minorities to the profession. These measures included targeted advertising, mentoring schemes, "taster" courses, training bursaries, and setting recruitment targets for initial teacher training institutions (Carrington and Skelton, 2003).

High-impact, medium-term responses

Avoid concentrating immigrant students in disadvantaged schools

Countries have used three main ways to address the concentration of immigrant and other disadvantaged students in particular schools. The first is to attract and retain other students, including more advantaged students. The second is to better equip immigrant parents with information on how to select the best school for their child. The third is to limit the extent to which advantaged schools can select students on the basis of their family background.

Make schools attractive to non-immigrant and advantaged students

Studies have shown that it is mostly advantaged, non-immigrant families who exercise school choice. In Denmark, for example, research suggests that since public school choice was introduced in the 1990s, segregation has increased because non-immigrant students tend to choose schools with fewer immigrant and disadvantaged students (Bloem and Diaz, 2007). Rangvid (2007) shows that native Danes tend to "opt out" of local schools when the proportion of immigrants is at or above 35%. But Schneeweis (2015) did not find evidence of non-immigrant "flight" in Austrian schools with relatively large concentrations of immigrant students.

Making schools with diverse student populations attractive to non-immigrant students is one way to avoid the flight of non-immigrant students where it does or may occur. For example, schools with special curricula that are appealing to students across socio-economic groups can be placed in relatively disadvantaged areas. In the United States, such "magnet schools" offering special mathematics, science and/or art curricula have existed since the 1970s (Heckman, 2008). They aim to provide high-quality education in an integrated learning environment. Generally, transport is provided for children, mostly from advantaged, white families, to be brought to these schools outside their catchment areas.

Other initiatives focus on raising the quality of existing schools with large proportions of immigrant students. In Switzerland, where growing numbers of middle-class families were leaving inner-city districts with ethnically diverse populations, the education authorities responded by introducing an area-wide model of quality assurance in multiethnic schools (Gomolla, 2006). The Quality in Multiethnic Schools programme offers extra resources and professional support to schools where at least 40% of students have an immigrant background. Among other things, the project explicitly aims to raise the standards of education in these schools to attract more non-immigrant and middle-class students (Gomolla, 2006).

Help immigrant parents to choose a school for their children

Language barriers, resource constraints, lower levels of education or lack of knowledge of the host country's school system may hinder immigrant parents' capacity to enrol their children in the most appropriate schools. These factors may be compounded by practical obstacles to access, such as a lack of transportation, concerns about security, operating hours of schools, and workplace arrangements (André-Bechely, 2007). Even when buses are provided, free of charge, to bring children to their schools of choice, immigrant parents may be less likely to opt out of neighbourhood schools.

Some jurisdictions have made concerted efforts to help parents who might not otherwise be confident in choosing a school for their child, including by having schools produce materials to promote their particular programmes and organising information and enrolment sessions for parents (Godwin et al., 2006).

Some policies try to influence the preferences of non-immigrant and immigrant parents simultaneously. In Denmark, Copenhagen city authorities introduced the Copenhagen Model for Integration to reduce segregation in the city's schools (Bloem and Diaz, 2007). The model sought to expand school choice for immigrant students. Schools with a predominantly non-immigrant student population tried to attract immigrant students by providing specific preparation and training for teachers and guaranteeing that an integration specialist or a translator from an ethnic minority would be employed at the school. Similarly, schools with large proportions of immigrant students tried to reach out to Danish parents to encourage them to enrol their child through various publicity campaigns. Schools collaborated with kindergartens to persuade parents to choose their local school.

Manage schools' selection criteria

School choice rarely means that parents have complete freedom to choose the school their child will attend. As school places are limited, the schools that are perceived to be of the highest quality are likely to attract more applicants than they have places available. If oversubscribed schools are allowed to give preference to better-performing students or to those who live near the school, school choice can reinforce segregation.

Several studies suggest that school-choice plans should use simple lotteries to select among the applicants for oversubscribed schools in order to promote more diverse student populations (Godwin et al, 2006).

Education systems can also consider providing financial incentives for oversubscribed schools to enrol immigrant students (Field et al., 2007). For example, funding for schools could be weighted according to the socio-demographic characteristics of the student population, as is done, for example, in the Netherlands (OECD, 2008).

Avoid ability grouping, early tracking and grade repetition

As discussed in Chapter 4, ability grouping, early tracking and grade repetition have adverse effects on student achievement, particularly for immigrant students.

Tracking students into different types of school programmes, such as vocational or academic, seems to be especially harmful for immigrant students when it occurs at an early age. Early separation from mainstream students may not allow immigrant students to develop the linguistic and culturally relevant skills needed to perform well at school. One study (Entorf and Lauk, 2006) finds that separating students into different tracks at an early age amplifies the learning differences between non-immigrant and immigrant students that already existed before they were separated into different tracks. In addition, assessing students' capabilities can be particularly difficult for teachers when students have endured traumatic events, as is the case for many immigrants and asylum seekers. Educators who do not understand the impact of such trauma may fail to recognise behavioural and cognitive difficulties that are trauma-related. In these cases, such difficulties can be misdiagnosed as learning disabilities or mental health problems (Sirin and Rogers-Sirin, 2015). It is essential, then, that immigrant students are given sufficient time to develop their full potential before they are assigned to different tracks.

Policies to reduce the use of grade repetition have been introduced in a few countries. For example, France reduced repetition rates by 11.1 percentage points between 2003 and 2012. The country now intends to use grade repetition only in exceptional cases (OECD 2013). In the French Community of Belgium, the Take-off project (2012) was developed to reduce the use of grade repetition by providing remedial pedagogical tools for schools (OECD, 2015b).

Provide extra support and guidance to immigrant parents

As PISA and many other studies show, students are better learners when their parents are involved in their education, and particularly when their parents value reading (Jeynes, 2005, 2007; Fan and Chen, 2001; Desforges and Abouchaar, 2003; Schofield, 2006; OECD, 2012b). While immigrant parents often have high aspirations for their children, they may face multiple obstacles to becoming involved in their child's schooling, including language barriers, insufficient understanding of how schools in the host country function, and lack of time or money to invest in their child's education. They may also feel alienated and unwelcome, especially if their child has encountered discrimination or abuse (Sirin and Rogers-Sirin, 2015). Communities and schools that host immigrants need to find ways to communicate with immigrant parents who may have widely different levels of education, language skills and understanding of the school system.

Undertake home visits

The aim of home visits is to encourage parents to participate in educational activities with their children. This approach is widely used at the pre-school level. For example, as part of Germany's National Action Plan on Integration (2011), the federal government helps difficult-to-reach parents organise their children's path through education through its model project, Education Bridges – the Qualifications of Parents for Better Educational Opportunities in Immigrant Families (OECD, 2015b).

These programmes can benefit from the active involvement of migrant families. For example, the "regional work posts for the promotion of migrant children" in Essen, Germany, train migrant mothers to run local groups of other migrant mothers through which they can communicate ways to improve their children's education. The idea behind this is to strengthen the skills of both the mothers and their children (OECD 2007).

Partnerships with non-governmental organisations are particularly effective for providing guidance to hard-to-reach groups. "Syria Bright Future", for example, specifically targets refugee families. This organisation provides tailored education and mental health support services for Syrian refugee children in Jordan. Its aim is to help the entire family function better in the face of extreme hardship.

Employ school liaison staff

In some countries, schools have appointed special professionals to ensure that schools and students' families can communicate with each other. Liaison activities include providing support to families that want to improve their children's performance at school, and improving access to social and medical services (OECD, 2010).

In New Zealand, the Pasifika Education Plan (2013-17) includes actions to strengthen the relationship between education institutions and Pasifika communities as a way to improve Pasifika students' achievement (OECD, 2015b).

Encourage parental involvement in school activities

Schools can reach out to parents to encourage them to participate in school-based activities. In Austria, for example, some states offer programmes to involve parents with kindergartens and schools, including language courses for mothers at the schools. The aim is to familiarise mothers with their child's learning environment and help them to meet other parents and teaching staff. Free childcare is provided during the lessons for children who are too young to be in school or kindergarten (Nusche et al., 2010).

Research indicates that parental-involvement programmes are most effective when targeted in specific subject areas. In a review of family influence on literacy in the United States, Sheldon and Epstein (2005a) find that 22 out of 23 targeted reading programmes that taught parents how to become involved in reading and language activities with their children produced significant gains in student performance in these areas. Many of the students who participated in the studies were from ethnic minority or immigrant groups.

Strengthen integration efforts

Support innovation and experimentation, evaluate results and target funding to what works

Countries often allocate additional resources, in the form of funding or teaching staff, to schools or districts enrolling large proportions of immigrant students. This is because immigrant students are more likely to be enrolled in schools located in disadvantaged areas (see Chapter 4) and additional resources may be necessary to bring these schools up to par with average schools (OECD 2005; Darling-Hammond, 2000; Pugin, 2007).

However, targeted funding can have unintended consequences, including signalling that the school targeted is of lower quality. In the education priority zones (ZEP) in France, for example, a decline in school enrolments was found to be due both to depopulation of ZEP areas and to middle-class parents avoiding ZEP schools (Bénabou et al., 2003).

Provide extra resources to students who need it most

A targeted approach to funding can provide additional support for at-risk students and also encourage schools to be more receptive to enrolling such students. In England, the Pupil Premium provides additional funding to schools to improve the performance of disadvantaged students. It targets students who have received free school meals at any point in the preceding six years. The funding targets primary and secondary school children, and was recently extended to cover early childhood education (OECD, 2015b). Schools have autonomy over how the funding is used. In addition, each year, about 500 "Pupil Premium Awards", ranging from GBP 1 000 to GBP 250 000 are distributed to the schools that have improved the performance of their disadvantaged students the most (www.pupilpremiumawards.co.uk).

Since many immigrants are also disadvantaged, allocating additional resources to schools with large proportions of disadvantaged students is likely to benefit many immigrant students as well.

Direct funding to local authorities

In many OECD countries, large proportions of immigrant students are clustered in certain, generally disadvantaged, areas. Thus some funding strategies also target more general conditions of disadvantage, such as high unemployment, in addition to student-based criteria. By allocating resources for immigrant education to more local authorities, such as school districts or municipalities, the funding can then be used to support initiatives tailored to the local context.

France's education priority zones (ZEP) target disadvantaged areas specifically. The scheme allocates additional resources to schools within the targeted areas. These resources can be used for a range of purposes, including hiring additional teachers, social workers and health professionals. Schools have discretion over the use of the extra resources. While the additional funding has been spent on a range of actions, such as adding hours of instruction, raising teachers' salaries, promoting the value of reading, providing homework assistance and organising cultural activities, most of this additional funding is directed towards supplementary teachers (90%) and bonuses for teachers (8%) (Schleicher, 2014; OECD, 2008).

It may be advisable to earmark funds allocated to intermediate authorities, to be sure that they are used for immigrant education, rather than for other local priorities. In Sweden, targeted grants given to municipalities were found to have had a positive and significant impact on school spending, while general, untargeted grants had an insignificant or even negative impact (Ahlin and Mork, 2005; Field et al., 2007).

When funding for immigrant education is distributed directly to schools, it is important that further guidance or professional training is provided on how to use the resources effectively. School staff may not know how to fit new initiatives into their school development plans, or they may use the money on programmes that have not been demonstrated to be effective in improving immigrant students' achievement (Karsten, 2006).

Demonstrate the value of cultural diversity

Acknowledge the importance of the heritage language

It is unclear whether it is necessary for children to have a good command of their mother tongue in order to be able to become proficient in the language of instruction. Still, countries may want to support heritage-language education as an important goal in itself. Valuing immigrant students' mother tongue can be an essential component of intercultural education, ensuring that immigrant children feel that their cultural and language background is appreciated as much as that of the majority (Brind et al., 2007). It has been argued that learning the mother tongue is an important step towards integration because it helps children to bridge the gap between their home and school. The heritage-language teacher can also play the role of intermediary between families and the school (Driessen, 2005).

However, it is important to offer mother-tongue instruction in addition to, rather than as a substitute for, regular curriculum instruction. In Sweden, for example, minority students who were less well-integrated into their schools were more likely to have participated in mother-tongue instruction than students who were better integrated (Frandji et al., 2009).

Very few countries actually pursue a bilingual approach to education. In the Netherlands, for example, mother-language teaching was abolished in 2004 (Driessen, 2005). The limited use of bilingual approaches in immigrant education may also be due to practical and logistical obstacles. Providing mother-tongue education to all immigrant students can be costly and difficult to implement, especially when many different language groups are present in the country. It can also be difficult to find a sufficient number of qualified teachers and to provide high-quality materials that link mother-tongue instruction to the mainstream curriculum.

Monitor progress

Countries generally either do not collect or do not publish data that make it possible to determine whether school systems are effective or equitable in reaching immigrant students and meeting their learning needs (OCED, 2010). Yet, for any programme that aims to improve student performance, monitoring progress towards that goal is essential. That involves using assessments and evaluations both to identify struggling students and schools and to determine systematically whether the measures used to improve the performance of those students and schools are working. International comparisons can be particularly useful when weighing the relative merits of certain education policies, and countries can learn a great deal from the experience of other countries.

References

Ahlin, A. and **E. Mork** (2005), "Effects of decentralization on school resources", *Working Paper*, No. 2005/5, Institute for Labour Market Policy Evaluation (IFAU), Uppsala.

André-Bechely, L. (2007), "Finding space and managing distance: Public school choice in an urban California district", *Urban Studies*, Vol. 44/7.

Au, K.H. (1998), "Social constructivism and the school literacy learning of students of diverse backgrounds", *Journal of Literacy Research*, Vol. 30.

Bénabou, R., F. Kramarz and **C. Prost** (2005), "Zones d'éducation prioritaire : Quels moyens pour quels résultats? Une évaluation sur la période 1982-1992", *Économie et Statistique*, No. 380, INSEE, Paris.

Bertschi-Kaufmann, A., M. Gyger, U. Kaser, H. Schneider and **J. Weiss** (2006), *Sprachforderung von Migrationskindern im Kindergarten : Literaturstudie erstellt im Auftrag des Departements Bildung, Kultur und Sport des Kantons Aargau (Zusammenfassung)*, University of Applied Sciences and Arts Northwestern Switzerland FHNW, Switzerland.

Bloem, N.S. and **R. Diaz** (2007), "White flight: Integration through segregation in Danish metropolitan public schools", *Humanity in Action*, Team Denmark.

Brind, T., C. Harper and **K. Moore** (2008), *Education for Migrant, Minority and Marginalised Children in Europe,* a report commissioned by the Open Society Institute's Education Support Programme.

Carrington, B. and **C. Skelton** (2003), "Re-thinking 'role models': Equal opportunities in teacher recruitment in England and Wales", *Journal of Education Policy*, Vol. 18/3.

Christensen, G. and **P. Stanat,** (2007), "Language Policies and Practices for Helping Immigrants and Second-Generation Students Succeed", the *Transatlantic Taskforce on Immigration and Integration,* Migration Policy Institute (MPI) and Bertelsmann Stiftung.

Clewell, B.C. and **A.M. Villegas** (1998), "Introduction", *Education and Urban Society*, Vol. 31/1, pp. 3-17.

Crosnoe, R. (2013), *Preparing the Children of Immigrants for Early Academic Success*, Migration Policy Institute, Washington, DC.

Cummins, J. (1979), "Linguistic interdependence and the educational development of bilingual children", *Review Of Educational Research*, Vol. 49/2, pp. 222.251.

Darling-Hammond, L. (2000), "Teacher quality and student achievement: A review of state policy and evidence", *Education Policy Analysis Archives*, Vol. 8/1.

Desforges, C. and **A. Abouchaar** (2003), "The impact of parental involvement, parental support and family education on pupil achievements and adjustment: A literature review", *Research Report*, No. 4333, Department for Education and Skills, London.

Driessen, G. (2005), "From cure to curse: The rise and fall of bilingual education programs in the Netherlands", in J. Sohn (ed.), *The Effectiveness of Bilingual School Programs for Immigrant Children*, Programme on Intercultural Conflicts and Societal Integration (AKI), Social Science Research Center Berlin (WZB), Berlin.

Entorf, H. and **M. Lauk** (2006), "Peer effects, social multipliers and migration at school: An international comparison", *HWWI Research Paper*, Hamburg Institute of International Economics, Hamburg.

Eurydice (2004), *Integrating Immigrant Children into Schools in Europe*, European Commission, Brussels.

Fan, X. and **M. Chen** (2001), "Parental involvement and students' academic achievement: A meta-analysis", *Educational Psychology Review*, Vol. 13/1.

Field, S., M. Kuczera and **B. Pont** (2007), *No More Failures: Ten Steps to Equity in Education*, Education and Training Policy, OECD Publishing, Paris, http://dx.doi.org/10.1787/9789264032606-en.

Frandji, D., J-M Pincemin, M. Demeuse, D. Greger and **J-Y. Rochex** (2009), *Comparaison des politiques d'Éducation prioritaire en Europe*, Rapport scientifique, Vol.1.

Godwin, R.K., S.M. Leland, A.D. Baxter and **S. Southworth** (2006), "Sinking *Swann*: Public school choice and the resegregation of Charlotte's public schools", *Review of Policy Research*, Vol. 23/5.

Gomolla, M. (2006), "Tackling the underachievement of learners from ethnic minorities: A comparison of recent policies of school improvement in Germany, England and Switzerland", *Current Issues in Comparative Education*, Vol. 9/1.

Hanushek, E.A. (2000) "Evidence, politics, and the class size debate", The Class Size Policy Debate, *Working Paper*, No. 121, Economic Policy Institute, Washington DC.

Hanushek, E.A., J.F. Kain and **S.G. Rivkin** (2001), "Why public schools loose teachers", *NBER Working Paper Series*, No. 8599.

Hanushek, E.A., J.F. Kain and **S.G. Rivkin** (1999), "Do higher salaries buy better teachers?", *Working Paper*, No. 7082, National Bureau of Economic Research, Cambridge, MA.

Heckman, J. (2008), *Education and the Integration of Migrants*, NESSE Analytical Report 1 for EU Commission DG Education and Culture, EFMS, Bamberg.

Jensen, B. (2010), "The OECD Teaching and Learning International Survey (TALIS) and teacher education for diversity", in OECD (2010), *Educating Teachers for Diversity: Meeting the Challenge*, Educational Research and Innovation, OECD Publishing, Paris, http://dx.doi.org/10.1787/9789264079731-en.

Jeynes, W.H. (2007), "The relationship between parental involvement and urban secondary school student achievement: A meta-analysis", *Urban Education*, Vol. 42/1.

Jeynes, W.H. (2005), "A meta-analysis of the relation of parental involvement to urban elementary school student academic achievement", *Urban Education*, Vol. 40/ 3.

Karsten, S. (2006), "Policies for disadvantaged children under scrutiny: The Dutch policy compared with policies in France, England, Flanders and the USA", *Comparative Education*, Vol. 42/2.

Krueger, A.B. (2000), "Understanding the magnitude and effect of class size on student achievement", The Class Size Policy Debate, *Working Paper*, No. 121, Economic Policy Institute, Washington, DC.

Magi, E. and **M. Nestor** (2014), "Students with different mother tongue and cultural backgrounds in Estonian schools: Attention, awareness and support at the school level", Praxis Center for Policy Studies, Tallinn.

Mengering, F. (2005), "Barenstark – Empirische Ergebnisse der Berliner Sprachstandserhebung an Kindern im Vorschulalter", Zeitschrift fur Erziehungswissenschaft, Vol. 8/2.

Mulford, B. et al. (2008), "Successful principalship of high-performance schools in high poverty communities", *Journal of Educational Administration*, Vol. 46/3.

Nusche, D. (2009), "What works in migrant education? A review of evidence and policy options", *OECD Education Working Papers*, No. 22, OECD Publishing, Paris, http://dx.doi.org/10.1787/227131784531.

Nusche, D., C. Shewbridge and **C. Lamhauge Rasmussen** (2010), *OECD Reviews of Migrant Education: Austria 2010*, OECD Reviews of Migrant Education, OECD Publishing, Paris, http://dx.doi.org/10.1787/9789264086180-en.

OECD (2015a), *International Migration Outlook 2015*, OECD Publishing, Paris. http://dx.doi.org/10.1787/migr_outlook-2015-en.

OECD (2015b), *Education Policy Outlook 2015: Making Reforms Happen*, OECD Publishing, Paris, http://dx.doi.org/10.1787/9789264225442-en.

OECD (2015c), *Early Childhood Education and Care Policy Review: Norway*, OECD, Paris, www.oecd.org/norway/Early-Childhood-Education-and-Care-Policy-Review-Norway.pdf.

OECD (2015d), *Starting Strong IV: Monitoring Quality in Early Childhood Education and Care*, OECD Publishing, Paris, http://dx.doi.org/10.1787/9789264233515-en.

OECD (2014), *International Migration Outlook 2014*, OECD Publishing, Paris, http://dx.doi.org/10.1787/migr_outlook-2014-en.

OECD (2013), *PISA 2012 Results: What Makes Schools Successful (Volume IV)? Resources, Policies and Practices*, PISA, OECD Publishing, Paris, http://dx.doi.org/10.1787/9789264201156-en.

OECD (2012a), *Equity and Quality in Education: Supporting Disadvantaged Students and Schools*, OECD Publishing, http://dx.doi.org/10.1787/9789264130852-en.

OECD (2012b), *Let's Read Them a Story! The Parent Factor in Education*, OECD Publishing, Paris, http://dx.doi.org/10.1787/9789264176232-en.

OECD (2010), *Closing the Gap for Immigrant Students: Policies, Practice and Performance*, OECD Reviews of Migrant Education, OECD Publishing, Paris, http://dx.doi.org/10.1787/9789264075788-en.

OECD (2009), *Creating Effective Teaching and Learning Environments: First Results from TALIS*, TALIS, OECD Publishing, Paris, http://dx.doi.org/10.1787/9789264068780-en.

OECD (2008), *Jobs for Immigrants (Vol. 2) Labour Market Integration in Belgium, France, the Netherlands and Portugal*, OECD Publishing, Paris, http://dx.doi.org/10.1787/9789264055605-en.

OECD (2007), *Jobs for Immigrants (Vol. 1) Labour Market Integration in Australia, Denmark, Germany and Sweden*, OECD Publishing, Paris, http://dx.doi.org/10.1787/9789264033603-en.

OECD (2006), *Where Immigrant Students Succeed: A Comparative Review of Performance and Engagement in PISA 2003*, PISA, OECD Publishing, Paris, http://dx.doi.org/10.1787/9789264023611-en.

OECD (2005), *Teachers Matter: Attracting, Developing and Retaining Effective Teachers*, Education and Training Policy, OECD Publishing, Paris, http://dx.doi.org/10.1787/9789264018044-en.

Pont, B., D. Nusche and **H. Moorman** (2008), *Improving School Leadership, Volume 1: Policy and Practice*, OECD Publishing, Paris, http://dx.doi.org/10.1787/9789264044715-en.

Pugin, V. (2007), "La politique d'éducation prioritaire : bilans et perspectives", *Millénaire*, Centre Ressources et Perspectives du Grand Lyon, Lyon.

Rangvid, B.S. (2007), "School choice, universal vouchers and native flight out of local public schools", *Working Paper*, May 2007/3, AKF, Danish Institute of Governmental Research, Copenhagen.

Rivkin, S.G., E.A. Hanushek and **J.F. Kain** (2000), "Teachers, schools and academic achievement", *Working Paper*, No. 6691, National Bureau of Economic Research, Cambridge, MA.

Scheldon, S.B. and **J.L. Epstein** (2005a), "School programs of family and community involvement to support children's reading and literacy development across the grades", in J. Flood and P. Anders (eds.), *Literacy Development of Students in Urban Schools: Research and Policy*, International Reading Association, Newark, DE.

Schleicher, A. (2014), *Equity, Excellence and Inclusiveness in Education: Policy Lessons from Around the World*, International Summit on the Teaching Profession, OECD Publishing, Paris, http://dx.doi.org/10.1787/9789264214033-en.

Schneeweis, N. (2015), "Immigrant concentration in schools: Consequences for native and migrant students", *Labour Economics*, Vol. 35.

Schofield, J.W., K. Alexander, R. Bangs and **B. Schauenburg** (2006), "Migration background, minority-group membership and academic achievement: Research evidence from social, educational, and developmental psychology", *AKI Research Review*, No. 5, Programme on Intercultural Conflicts and Societal Integration (AKI), Social Science Research Center, Berlin.

Sirin, S.R. and **L. Rogers-Sirin** (2015), *The Educational and Mental Health Needs of Syrian Refugee Children*, Migration Policy Institute, Washington, DC.

Watts-Taffe, S. and **D.M. Truscott** (2000), "Using What we know about language and literacy development for ESL students in the mainstream classroom", *Language Arts*, Vol. 77/3.

White, K., K. Lewis and **F. Fletcher-Campbell** (2006), "Raising the achievement of bilingual learners in primary schools: Evaluation of the pilot/programme", *DfES Research Report*, No. 758, Department for Education and Skills, London.

ANNEX

Selected data tables on immigrant students

Notes regarding Cyprus

Note by Turkey: The information in this document with reference to "Cyprus" relates to the southern part of the Island. There is no single authority representing both Turkish and Greek Cypriot people on the Island. Turkey recognises the Turkish Republic of Northern Cyprus (TRNC). Until a lasting and equitable solution is found within the context of the United Nations, Turkey shall preserve its position concerning the "Cyprus issue".

Note by all the European Union Member States of the OECD and the European Union: The Republic of Cyprus is recognised by all members of the United Nations with the exception of Turkey. The information in this document relates to the area under the effective control of the Government of the Republic of Cyprus.

Note regarding data from Israel

The statistical data for Israel are supplied by and are under the responsibility of the relevant Israeli authorities. The use of such data by the OECD is without prejudice to the status of the Golan Heights, East Jerusalem and Israeli settlements in the West Bank under the terms of international law.

[Part 1/1]

Table 1.1 **Trends in the number of immigrants**

Percentage of students

	PISA 2003				PISA 2012				Change between 2003 and 2012 (PISA 2012 - PISA 2003)			
	First-generation		Second-generation		First-generation		Second-generation		First-generation		Second-generation	
	%	S.E.	%	S.E.	%	S.E.	%	S.E.	% dif.	S.E.	% dif.	S.E.
OECD												
Australia	11.0	(0.7)	11.7	(0.6)	10.3	(0.4)	12.4	(0.6)	-0.7	(0.8)	0.7	(0.8)
Austria	9.2	(0.7)	4.1	(0.5)	5.6	(0.6)	10.9	(0.7)	**-3.6**	(0.9)	**6.8**	(0.8)
Belgium	5.5	(0.6)	6.3	(0.6)	7.3	(0.6)	8.0	(0.6)	**1.8**	(0.9)	**1.7**	(0.8)
Canada	10.9	(0.8)	9.2	(0.5)	13.0	(0.7)	16.6	(0.8)	**2.2**	(1.1)	**7.4**	(1.0)
Chile	m	m	m	m	0.7	(0.1)	0.2	(0.1)	m	m	m	m
Czech Republic	0.8	(0.1)	0.5	(0.1)	1.9	(0.2)	1.4	(0.3)	**1.0**	(0.3)	**0.9**	(0.3)
Denmark	3.0	(0.4)	3.5	(0.6)	3.0	(0.2)	6.1	(0.5)	0.0	(0.4)	**2.7**	(0.8)
Estonia	m	m	m	m	0.7	(0.2)	7.5	(0.5)	m	m	m	m
Finland	1.8	(0.2)	0.0	(0.0)	1.9	(0.2)	1.5	(0.1)	0.1	(0.3)	**1.5**	(0.1)
France	3.5	(0.5)	10.8	(1.1)	5.0	(0.5)	10.0	(0.8)	**1.5**	(0.7)	-0.8	(1.4)
Germany	8.5	(0.7)	6.9	(0.8)	2.8	(0.3)	10.6	(0.7)	**-5.7**	(0.8)	**3.7**	(1.0)
Greece	6.9	(0.7)	0.5	(0.1)	6.3	(0.6)	4.3	(0.4)	-0.6	(0.9)	**3.8**	(0.5)
Hungary	2.2	(0.2)	0.1	(0.0)	0.8	(0.2)	1.0	(0.2)	**-1.4**	(0.3)	**0.9**	(0.2)
Iceland	0.8	(0.2)	0.2	(0.1)	2.8	(0.3)	0.7	(0.1)	**2.0**	(0.4)	**0.5**	(0.2)
Ireland	2.5	(0.3)	1.0	(0.2)	8.5	(0.7)	1.7	(0.2)	**6.0**	(0.7)	**0.7**	(0.3)
Israel	m	m	m	m	5.6	(0.6)	12.7	(0.8)	m	m	m	m
Italy	1.7	(0.2)	0.4	(0.1)	5.5	(0.3)	2.0	(0.2)	**3.8**	(0.3)	**1.6**	(0.2)
Japan	0.1	(0.0)	0.0	(0.0)	0.1	(0.0)	0.2	(0.1)	0.1	(0.1)	**0.2**	(0.1)
Korea	0.0	c	0.0	(0.0)	0.0	(0.0)	0.0	(0.0)	0.0	(0.0)	0.0	(0.0)
Luxembourg	17.4	(0.5)	15.8	(0.6)	17.3	(0.5)	28.7	(0.6)	-0.1	(0.7)	**12.9**	(0.8)
Mexico	1.8	(0.2)	0.5	(0.1)	0.8	(0.1)	0.5	(0.1)	**-1.0**	(0.2)	0.0	(0.1)
Netherlands	3.9	(0.4)	7.1	(1.1)	2.7	(0.4)	8.1	(0.9)	-1.2	(0.6)	1.1	(1.4)
New Zealand	13.3	(0.7)	6.6	(0.7)	16.8	(1.0)	9.6	(0.8)	**3.6**	(1.2)	**3.0**	(1.0)
Norway	3.4	(0.4)	2.3	(0.4)	4.8	(0.5)	4.7	(0.6)	**1.4**	(0.7)	**2.5**	(0.7)
Poland	0.0	(0.0)	0.0	(0.0)	0.0	(0.0)	0.2	(0.1)	0.0	(0.0)	**0.1**	(0.1)
Portugal	2.7	(1.1)	2.3	(0.4)	3.6	(0.5)	3.3	(0.4)	0.9	(1.2)	1.0	(0.6)
Slovak Republic	0.3	(0.1)	0.6	(0.2)	0.3	(0.1)	0.4	(0.1)	0.0	(0.1)	-0.2	(0.2)
Slovenia	m	m	m	m	2.2	(0.2)	6.5	(0.4)	m	m	m	m
Spain	2.8	(0.4)	0.6	(0.1)	8.4	(0.5)	1.5	(0.2)	**5.6**	(0.6)	**0.9**	(0.2)
Sweden	5.9	(0.7)	5.7	(0.5)	6.2	(0.5)	8.7	(0.6)	0.3	(0.8)	**3.0**	(0.8)
Switzerland	11.1	(0.6)	8.9	(0.5)	6.8	(0.4)	17.5	(0.7)	**-4.3**	(0.7)	**8.5**	(0.8)
Turkey	0.5	(0.1)	0.5	(0.2)	0.2	(0.1)	0.7	(0.2)	-0.3	(0.2)	0.2	(0.3)
United Kingdom	m	m	m	m	7.3	(0.8)	5.7	(0.5)	m	m	m	m
United States	6.1	(0.4)	8.3	(0.7)	6.8	(0.8)	14.8	(1.4)	0.7	(0.9)	**6.5**	(1.6)
OECD average 2003	4.7	(0.1)	3.9	(0.1)	5.2	(0.1)	6.4	(0.1)	**0.4**	(0.1)	**2.5**	(0.1)
Partners												
Albania	m	m	m	m	0.2	(0.1)	0.1	(0.1)	m	m	m	m
Argentina	m	m	m	m	1.5	(0.2)	2.4	(0.3)	m	m	m	m
Brazil	0.2	(0.1)	0.6	(0.2)	0.4	(0.1)	0.4	(0.1)	0.2	(0.1)	-0.2	(0.2)
Bulgaria	m	m	m	m	0.2	(0.1)	0.4	(0.2)	m	m	m	m
Colombia	m	m	m	m	0.1	(0.1)	0.2	(0.0)	m	m	m	m
Costa Rica	m	m	m	m	2.1	(0.3)	3.5	(0.7)	m	m	m	m
Croatia	m	m	m	m	3.7	(0.4)	8.4	(0.5)	m	m	m	m
Hong Kong-China	20.4	(1.3)	22.9	(0.9)	14.2	(1.0)	20.5	(0.8)	**-6.2**	(1.6)	**-2.4**	(1.2)
Indonesia	0.1	(0.0)	0.2	(0.1)	0.1	(0.0)	0.1	(0.0)	0.0	(0.1)	-0.1	(0.1)
Jordan	m	m	m	m	2.8	(0.3)	10.5	(0.6)	m	m	m	m
Kazakhstan	m	m	m	m	6.5	(1.2)	9.6	(1.0)	m	m	m	m
Latvia	1.1	(0.2)	8.3	(0.8)	0.4	(0.1)	4.3	(0.5)	**-0.8**	(0.2)	**-3.9**	(1.0)
Liechtenstein	9.4	(1.6)	7.6	(1.3)	13.5	(2.2)	20.1	(2.3)	4.0	(2.7)	**12.5**	(2.6)
Lithuania	m	m	m	m	0.2	(0.1)	1.5	(0.3)	m	m	m	m
Macao-China	18.2	(1.4)	57.9	(1.5)	15.4	(0.4)	49.7	(0.7)	-2.8	(1.4)	**-8.2**	(1.7)
Malaysia	m	m	m	m	0.1	(0.0)	1.7	(0.3)	m	m	m	m
Montenegro	m	m	m	m	3.1	(0.3)	2.7	(0.2)	m	m	m	m
Peru	m	m	m	m	0.2	(0.1)	0.3	(0.1)	m	m	m	m
Qatar	m	m	m	m	34.6	(0.4)	17.2	(0.4)	m	m	m	m
Romania	m	m	m	m	0.1	(0.0)	0.0	(0.0)	m	m	m	m
Russian Federation	7.0	(0.5)	6.4	(0.5)	3.2	(0.4)	7.7	(0.6)	**-3.8**	(0.7)	1.3	(0.8)
Serbia	m	m	m	m	1.9	(0.3)	6.6	(0.6)	m	m	m	m
Shanghai-China	m	m	m	m	0.6	(0.1)	0.3	(0.1)	m	m	m	m
Singapore	m	m	m	m	12.4	(0.7)	5.9	(0.3)	m	m	m	m
Chinese Taipei	m	m	m	m	0.1	(0.0)	0.4	(0.1)	m	m	m	m
Thailand	0.0	(0.0)	0.1	(0.1)	0.0	(0.0)	0.7	(0.4)	0.0	(0.0)	0.5	(0.4)
Tunisia	0.1	(0.0)	0.2	(0.1)	0.1	(0.0)	0.4	(0.1)	0.0	(0.1)	0.2	(0.1)
United Arab Emirates	m	m	m	m	31.6	(1.0)	23.2	(0.7)	m	m	m	m
Uruguay	0.4	(0.1)	0.4	(0.1)	0.3	(0.1)	0.2	(0.1)	-0.1	(0.2)	-0.2	(0.1)
Viet Nam	m	m	m	m	0.0	(0.0)	0.1	(0.1)	m	m	m	m

Notes: Changes between 2003 and 2012 that are statistically significant are indicated in bold.

OECD average 2003 includes only OECD countries with comparable data since PISA 2003.

Results presented in this table can differ from those reported in *PISA 2012 Results (Volume II)* because they are computed including students without data on the PISA *index of economic, social and cultural status.*

Source: OECD, PISA 2012 Database.

Underlying data for the tables can be found at www.oecd.org/edu/school/Immigrant-Students-Tables.xlsx.

[Part 1/3]

Table 2.1 **Immigrant students' performance in reading, mathematics and problem solving**

		Mathematics				
		Non-immigrant		Second-generation		First-generation	
		Mean score	S.E.	Mean score	S.E.	Mean score	S.E.
OECD	**Australia**	502	(1.5)	537	(5.2)	516	(3.7)
	Austria	516	(2.7)	458	(5.3)	454	(8.5)
	Belgium	529	(2.2)	460	(6.5)	445	(6.7)
	Canada	522	(1.8)	513	(4.6)	527	(5.2)
	Chile	424	(3.1)	c	c	423	(13.3)
	Czech Republic	500	(2.7)	461	(21.0)	481	(12.4)
	Denmark	508	(2.2)	447	(4.0)	428	(5.3)
	Estonia	524	(2.0)	496	(6.2)	c	c
	Finland	523	(1.9)	453	(4.9)	425	(7.7)
	France	507	(2.8)	448	(6.7)	424	(10.3)
	Germany	528	(3.2)	476	(5.7)	455	(11.4)
	Greece	459	(2.6)	415	(7.7)	405	(7.2)
	Hungary	478	(3.1)	522	(15.2)	c	c
	Iceland	497	(1.8)	c	c	436	(9.6)
	Ireland	503	(2.3)	503	(12.0)	499	(4.9)
	Israel	469	(4.7)	480	(8.4)	467	(7.6)
	Italy	490	(2.1)	461	(7.4)	435	(3.3)
	Japan	538	(3.6)	c	c	c	c
	Korea	554	(4.6)	c	c	c	c
	Luxembourg	510	(1.7)	470	(2.5)	469	(4.1)
	Mexico	416	(1.3)	359	(9.9)	333	6.3
	Netherlands	531	(3.4)	474	(9.2)	471	(9.7)
	New Zealand	502	(2.7)	489	(6.9)	507	(5.3)
	Norway	496	(2.9)	457	(9.4)	440	(6.2)
	Poland	518	(3.6)	c	c	c	c
	Portugal	492	(3.8)	445	(10.0)	450	(8.2)
	Slovak Republic	484	(3.3)	c	c	c	c
	Slovenia	506	(1.1)	463	(5.3)	430	(10.4)
	Spain	491	(1.7)	457	(8.5)	436	(4.8)
	Sweden	490	(2.3)	445	(5.3)	410	(7.3)
	Switzerland	548	(3.0)	489	(3.8)	471	(5.7)
	Turkey	449	(4.8)	476	(35.4)	c	c
	United Kingdom[1]	498	(3.0)	480	(7.5)	490	(11.5)
	United States	486	(3.6)	478	(6.5)	463	(9.0)
	OECD average[2]	501	(0.5)	465	(1.6)	453	(1.5)
Partners	Albania	394	(2.0)	c	c	c	c
	Argentina	391	(3.5)	357	(9.2)	351	(9.4)
	Brazil	391	(1.9)	334	(16.4)	337	(17.6)
	Bulgaria	442	(3.9)	c	c	c	c
	Colombia	378	(2.9)	c	c	c	c
	Costa Rica	409	(2.9)	374	(14.1)	389	(9.6)
	Croatia	474	(3.6)	456	(5.0)	453	(10.2)
	Hong Kong-China	566	(3.8)	569	(4.1)	543	(5.2)
	Indonesia	376	(4.0)	c	c	c	c
	Jordan	387	(2.8)	408	(5.1)	415	(8.9)
	Kazakhstan	433	(3.1)	440	(8.2)	407	(5.8)
	Latvia	492	(2.8)	487	(8.0)	c	c
	Liechtenstein	552	(5.4)	504	(12.1)	498	(14.2)
	Lithuania	480	(2.7)	472	(8.3)	c	c
	Macao-China	529	(2.1)	546	(1.8)	541	(3.0)
	Malaysia	423	(3.2)	404	(9.1)	c	c
	Montenegro	410	(1.2)	436	(8.1)	427	(8.4)
	Peru	370	(3.6)	c	c	c	c
	Qatar	335	(1.1)	388	(2.1)	442	(1.5)
	Romania	445	(3.7)	c	c	c	c
	Russian Federation	485	(3.2)	467	(4.9)	457	(7.9)
	Serbia	449	(3.4)	471	(7.0)	439	(13.1)
	Shanghai-China	615	(3.2)	c	c	510	(14.6)
	Singapore	570	(1.6)	609	(6.4)	590	(4.3)
	Chinese Taipei	562	(3.3)	c	c	c	c
	Thailand	428	(3.3)	412	(56.6)	c	c
	Tunisia	389	(3.9)	c	c	c	c
	United Arab Emirates	400	(2.4)	443	(2.9)	483	(2.9)
	Uruguay	411	(2.6)	c	c	c	c
	Viet Nam	512	(4.8)	c	c	c	c

Note: First-generation immigrant students are foreign-born students whose parents were also foreign born. Second-generation immigrant students are students who were born in the country of assessment but whose parents are foreign born.

Results presented in this table can differ from those reported in *PISA 2012 Results (Volume II)* because they are computed including students without data on the PISA *index of economic, social and cultural status.*

1. Only England participated in the problem-solving assessment.

2. OECD average includes only countries with valid data for first- and second-generation immigrant students.

Source: OECD, PISA 2012 Database.

Underlying data for the tables can be found at www.oecd.org/edu/school/Immigrant-Students-Tables.xlsx.

[Part 2/3]

Table 2.1 **Immigrant students' performance in reading, mathematics and problem solving**

		Reading					
		Non-immigrant		Second-generation		First-generation	
		Mean score	S.E.	Mean score	S.E.	Mean score	S.E.
OECD	Australia	511	(1.6)	538	(4.4)	520	(3.8)
	Austria	499	(2.7)	451	(5.9)	443	(9.4)
	Belgium	522	(2.1)	466	(6.9)	443	(8.0)
	Canada	526	(2.0)	527	(4.1)	530	(5.2)
	Chile	442	(2.9)	c	c	456	(15.8)
	Czech Republic	494	(2.8)	474	(19.1)	474	(12.2)
	Denmark	504	(2.5)	454	(3.3)	427	(8.1)
	Estonia	521	(2.1)	487	(5.6)	c	c
	Finland	529	(2.3)	465	(5.7)	413	(8.7)
	France	518	(3.2)	464	(8.4)	425	(12.5)
	Germany	522	(2.9)	481	(5.9)	445	(11.7)
	Greece	484	(3.4)	450	(11.0)	419	(7.9)
	Hungary	489	(3.1)	522	(14.0)	c	c
	Iceland	488	(1.9)	c	c	393	(11.4)
	Ireland	525	(2.6)	518	(13.8)	513	(5.2)
	Israel	489	(4.9)	502	(9.2)	484	(9.9)
	Italy	497	(1.9)	457	(7.5)	422	(4.2)
	Japan	540	(3.6)	c	c	c	c
	Korea	536	(3.9)	c	c	c	c
	Luxembourg	511	(2.1)	463	(2.7)	467	(3.9)
	Mexico	426	(1.4)	375	(11.0)	337	6.9
	Netherlands	519	(3.3)	465	(9.5)	460	(13.0)
	New Zealand	518	(2.9)	496	(8.2)	509	(4.9)
	Norway	512	(3.2)	481	(8.7)	444	(8.3)
	Poland	519	(3.1)	c	c	c	c
	Portugal	493	(3.7)	460	(12.8)	450	(7.9)
	Slovak Republic	464	(4.1)	c	c	c	c
	Slovenia	486	(1.2)	450	(5.0)	410	(9.2)
	Spain	495	(1.7)	448	(10.2)	447	(4.7)
	Sweden	496	(3.1)	457	(6.6)	400	(9.3)
	Switzerland	524	(2.5)	473	(3.9)	459	(5.5)
	Turkey	477	(4.2)	482	(29.6)	c	c
	United Kingdom[1]	504	(3.3)	494	(7.2)	491	(10.8)
	United States	502	(3.9)	502	(4.7)	480	(9.6)
	OECD average[2]	501	(0.5)	465	(1.6)	453	(1.5)
Partners	Albania	395	(3.1)	c	c	c	c
	Argentina	399	(3.6)	357	(12.1)	356	(15.6)
	Brazil	410	(2.0)	348	(21.3)	353	(12.3)
	Bulgaria	441	(5.7)	c	c	c	c
	Colombia	405	(3.4)	c	c	c	c
	Costa Rica	443	(3.4)	413	(12.6)	424	(11.0)
	Croatia	487	(3.4)	474	(5.9)	457	(10.1)
	Hong Kong-China	546	(3.2)	554	(4.1)	534	(5.1)
	Indonesia	397	(4.1)	c	c	c	c
	Jordan	403	(3.1)	428	(5.6)	423	(7.8)
	Kazakhstan	395	(2.7)	394	(7.1)	361	(6.1)
	Latvia	489	(2.4)	488	(8.7)	c	c
	Liechtenstein	534	(5.2)	491	(12.4)	464	(13.8)
	Lithuania	479	(2.5)	455	(11.3)	c	c
	Macao-China	495	(1.8)	517	(1.5)	518	(2.6)
	Malaysia	400	(3.3)	407	(12.1)	c	c
	Montenegro	424	(1.3)	442	(8.4)	413	(10.4)
	Peru	387	(4.3)	c	c	c	c
	Qatar	347	(1.2)	401	(2.4)	453	(1.7)
	Romania	438	(4.0)	c	c	c	c
	Russian Federation	480	(3.1)	448	(5.9)	457	(9.6)
	Serbia	446	(3.5)	476	(7.3)	450	(11.5)
	Shanghai-China	571	(2.8)	c	c	502	(13.0)
	Singapore	540	(1.6)	581	(6.0)	546	(4.5)
	Chinese Taipei	525	(3.0)	c	c	c	c
	Thailand	443	(2.9)	391	(38.9)	c	c
	Tunisia	405	(4.5)	c	c	c	c
	United Arab Emirates	410	(2.5)	454	(3.3)	487	(3.1)
	Uruguay	414	(3.0)	c	c	c	c
	Viet Nam	509	(4.4)	c	c	c	c

Note: First-generation immigrant students are foreign-born students whose parents were also foreign born. Second-generation immigrant students are students who were born in the country of assessment but whose parents are foreign born.

Results presented in this table can differ from those reported in *PISA 2012 Results (Volume II)* because they are computed including students without data on the PISA *index of economic, social and cultural status*.

1. Only England participated in the problem-solving assessment.
2. OECD average includes only countries with valid data for first- and second-generation immigrant students.

Source: OECD, PISA 2012 Database.

Underlying data for the tables can be found at www.oecd.org/edu/school/Immigrant-Students-Tables.xlsx.

[Part 3/3]

Table 2.1 **Immigrant students' performance in reading, mathematics and problem solving**

		Computer problem solving					
		Non-immigrant		Second-generation		First-generation	
		Mean score	S.E.	Mean score	S.E.	Mean score	S.E.
OECD	Australia	524	(1.9)	537	(4.8)	524	(4.0)
	Austria	516	(3.6)	465	(6.0)	454	(8.6)
	Belgium	522	(2.5)	438	(7.0)	455	(7.7)
	Canada	532	(2.2)	519	(5.6)	521	(5.9)
	Chile	448	(3.7)	c	c	454	(15.7)
	Czech Republic	510	(3.2)	477	(20.6)	482	(11.5)
	Denmark	505	(2.9)	436	(7.6)	424	(7.6)
	Estonia	519	(2.5)	489	(7.3)	c	c
	Finland	526	(2.3)	461	(5.7)	426	(8.2)
	France	523	(3.5)	464	(8.7)	432	(10.3)
	Germany	523	(3.4)	475	(6.8)	463	(10.6)
	Greece	m	m	m	m	m	m
	Hungary	459	(4.0)	482	(14.7)	c	c
	Iceland	m	m	m	m	m	m
	Ireland	501	(3.4)	493	(14.1)	487	(5.6)
	Israel	452	(5.7)	481	(9.4)	460	(10.7)
	Italy	514	(4.1)	493	(10.1)	451	(10.5)
	Japan	553	(3.1)	c	c	c	c
	Korea	562	(4.3)	c	c	c	c
	Luxembourg	m	m	m	m	m	m
	Mexico	m	m	m	m	m	m
	Netherlands	520	(4.0)	450	(9.7)	440	(15.8)
	New Zealand	m	m	m	m	m	m
	Norway	510	(3.0)	467	(17.1)	446	(8.7)
	Poland	482	(4.4)	c	c	c	c
	Portugal	498	(3.6)	459	(10.5)	475	(8.0)
	Slovak Republic	485	(3.5)	c	c	c	c
	Slovenia	481	(1.4)	453	(5.5)	383	(13.9)
	Spain	482	(4.0)	458	(15.2)	440	(6.9)
	Sweden	501	(3.2)	461	(5.8)	417	(9.1)
	Switzerland	m	m	m	m	m	m
	Turkey	455	(4.0)	489	(28.6)	c	c
	United Kingdom[1]	523	(4.0)	474	(8.5)	503	(10.3)
	United States	512	(3.8)	503	(6.9)	487	(11.4)
	OECD average[2]	509	(0.8)	473	(2.3)	459	(2.2)
Partners	Albania	m	m	m	m	m	m
	Argentina	m	m	m	m	m	m
	Brazil	428	(4.5)	c	c	c	c
	Bulgaria	405	(5.0)	c	c	c	c
	Colombia	400	(3.5)	c	c	c	c
	Costa Rica	m	m	m	m	m	m
	Croatia	467	(4.0)	458	(6.0)	469	(8.5)
	Hong Kong-China	545	(4.7)	544	(3.7)	519	(5.1)
	Indonesia	m	m	m	m	m	m
	Jordan	m	m	m	m	m	m
	Kazakhstan	m	m	m	m	m	m
	Latvia	m	m	m	m	m	m
	Liechtenstein	m	m	m	m	m	m
	Lithuania	m	m	m	m	m	m
	Macao-China	538	(1.8)	545	(1.7)	535	(3.0)
	Malaysia	424	(3.5)	417	(8.6)	c	c
	Montenegro	406	(1.2)	439	(9.6)	412	(8.7)
	Peru	m	m	m	m	m	m
	Qatar	m	m	m	m	m	m
	Romania	m	m	m	m	m	m
	Russian Federation	490	(3.6)	485	(5.9)	476	(8.7)
	Serbia	474	(3.2)	480	(7.1)	473	(14.5)
	Shanghai-China	538	(3.2)	c	c	437	(13.8)
	Singapore	561	(1.4)	592	(5.4)	567	(4.3)
	Chinese Taipei	535	(2.9)	c	c	c	c
	Thailand	m	m	m	m	m	m
	Tunisia	m	m	m	m	m	m
	United Arab Emirates	376	(3.4)	424	(3.8)	459	(3.7)
	Uruguay	405	(3.4)	c	c	c	c
	Viet Nam	m	m	m	m	m	m

Note: First-generation immigrant students are foreign-born students whose parents were also foreign born. Second-generation immigrant students are students who were born in the country of assessment but whose parents are foreign born.

Results presented in this table can differ from those reported in *PISA 2012 Results (Volume II)* because they are computed including students without data on the PISA *index of economic, social and cultural status.*

1. Only England participated in the problem-solving assessment.

2. OECD average includes only countries with valid data for first- and second-generation immigrant students.

Source: OECD, PISA 2012 Database.

Underlying data for the tables can be found at www.oecd.org/edu/school/Immigrant-Students-Tables.xlsx.

[Part 1/2]

Change between 2003 and 2012 in the relationship between mathematics performance and immigrant background

Table 2.2 ***Results based on students' self-reports***

		Non-immigrant					
		PISA 2003		PISA 2012		Change between 2003 and 2012 (PISA 2012 – PISA 2003)	
		Mean score	S.E.	Mean score	S.E.	Score dif.	S.E.
OECD	Australia	527	(2.1)	502	(1.5)	**-25**	(2.6)
	Austria	515	(3.3)	516	(2.7)	1	(4.3)
	Belgium	545	(2.5)	529	(2.2)	**-17**	(3.3)
	Canada	537	(1.6)	522	(1.8)	**-15**	(2.4)
	Czech Republic	523	(3.2)	500	(2.7)	**-23**	(4.2)
	Denmark	520	(2.5)	508	(2.2)	**-12**	(3.4)
	Finland	546	(1.9)	523	(1.9)	**-23**	(2.6)
	France	520	(2.4)	507	(2.8)	**-13**	(3.6)
	Germany	525	(3.5)	528	(3.2)	2	(4.8)
	Greece	449	(3.9)	459	(2.6)	**10**	(4.7)
	Hungary	491	(3.0)	478	(3.1)	**-13**	(4.3)
	Iceland	517	(1.4)	497	(1.8)	**-20**	(2.3)
	Ireland	503	(2.4)	503	(2.3)	-1	(3.4)
	Italy	468	(3.0)	490	(2.1)	**23**	(3.7)
	Japan	535	(4.0)	538	(3.6)	4	(5.4)
	Korea	543	(3.2)	554	(4.6)	**11**	(5.6)
	Luxembourg	507	(1.3)	510	(1.7)	3	(2.1)
	Mexico	392	(3.6)	416	(1.3)	**24**	(3.8)
	Netherlands	551	(3.0)	531	(3.4)	**-20**	(4.5)
	New Zealand	528	(2.6)	502	(2.7)	**-26**	(3.7)
	Norway	499	(2.3)	496	(2.9)	-3	(3.7)
	Poland	491	(2.5)	518	(3.6)	**27**	(4.4)
	Portugal	470	(2.9)	492	(3.8)	**23**	(4.8)
	Slovak Republic	499	(3.2)	484	(3.3)	**-16**	(4.6)
	Spain	487	(2.4)	491	(1.7)	4	(2.9)
	Sweden	517	(2.2)	490	(2.3)	**-28**	(3.2)
	Switzerland	543	(3.3)	548	(3.0)	5	(4.4)
	Turkey	425	(6.7)	449	(4.8)	**24**	(8.2)
	United States	490	(2.8)	486	(3.6)	-3	(4.6)
	OECD average 2003	506	(0.6)	502	(0.5)	**-3**	(0.8)
Partners	Brazil	359	(4.7)	391	(1.9)	**32**	(5.1)
	Hong Kong-China	557	(4.5)	566	(3.8)	9	(5.9)
	Indonesia	363	(4.0)	376	(4.0)	**13**	(5.7)
	Latvia	484	(3.8)	492	(2.8)	7	(4.7)
	Liechtenstein	545	(5.0)	552	(5.4)	8	(7.4)
	Macao-China	528	(5.9)	529	(2.1)	2	(6.2)
	Russian Federation	472	(4.4)	485	(3.2)	**14**	(5.4)
	Thailand	419	(3.0)	428	(3.3)	**9**	(4.5)
	Tunisia	360	(2.5)	389	(3.9)	**29**	(4.7)
	Uruguay	423	(3.2)	411	(2.6)	**-11**	(4.2)

Notes: Values that are statistically significant are indicated in bold.
OECD average 2003 includes only OECD countries with comparable data since PISA 2003.
Only countries and economies with comparable data from PISA 2003 and PISA 2012 are shown.
Results presented in this table can differ from those reported in *PISA 2012 Results (Volume II)* because they are computed including students without data on the PISA *index of economic, social and cultural status.*
Source: OECD, PISA 2012 Database.
Underlying data for the tables can be found at www.oecd.org/edu/school/Immigrant-Students-Tables.xlsx.

[Part 2/2]

Table 2.2 Change between 2003 and 2012 in the relationship between mathematics performance and immigrant background

Results based on students' self-reports

	Second-generation immigrants						First-generation immigrants					
	PISA 2003		PISA 2012		Change between 2003 and 2012 (PISA 2012 – PISA 2003)		PISA 2003		PISA 2012		Change between 2003 and 2012 (PISA 2012 – PISA 2003)	
	Mean score	S.E.	Mean score	S.E.	Score dif.	S.E.	Mean score	S.E.	Mean score	S.E.	Score dif.	S.E.
OECD												
Australia	522	(4.7)	537	(5.2)	**16**	(7.0)	525	(4.9)	516	(3.7)	-9	(6.2)
Austria	459	(8.8)	458	(5.3)	-1	(10.2)	452	(6.0)	454	(8.5)	3	(10.4)
Belgium	454	(7.5)	460	(6.5)	6	(9.9)	437	(10.8)	445	(6.7)	9	(12.7)
Canada	543	(4.3)	513	(4.6)	**-30**	(6.3)	530	(4.7)	527	(5.2)	-3	(7.1)
Czech Republic	c	c	461	(21.0)	m	m	500	(14.5)	481	(12.4)	-19	(19.0)
Denmark	449	(11.2)	447	(4.0)	-2	(11.9)	455	(10.1)	428	(5.3)	**-27**	(11.4)
Finland	c	c	453	(4.9)	m	m	474	(10.6)	425	(7.7)	**-49**	(13.1)
France	472	(6.1)	448	(6.7)	**-24**	(9.1)	448	(15.0)	424	(10.3)	-24	(18.2)
Germany	432	(9.1)	476	(5.7)	**44**	(10.8)	454	(7.5)	455	(11.4)	0	(13.6)
Greece	c	c	415	(7.7)	m	m	402	(6.3)	405	(7.2)	3	(9.6)
Hungary	c	c	522	(15.2)	m	m	488	(10.8)	c	c	m	m
Iceland	c	c	c	c	m	m	c	c	436	(9.6)	m	m
Ireland	474	(19.2)	503	(12.0)	29	(22.6)	509	(11.8)	499	(4.9)	-10	(12.8)
Italy	461	(21.2)	461	(7.4)	-1	(22.5)	441	(14.3)	435	(3.3)	-6	(14.6)
Japan	c	c	c	c	m	m	c	c	c	c	m	m
Korea	c	c	c	c	m	m	c	c	c	c	m	m
Luxembourg	476	(3.3)	470	(2.5)	-7	(4.1)	462	(3.7)	469	(4.1)	7	(5.5)
Mexico	333	(29.3)	359	(9.9)	26	(30.9)	292	(12.7)	333	(6.3)	**41**	(14.2)
Netherlands	492	(10.3)	474	(9.2)	-18	(13.8)	472	(8.4)	471	(9.7)	-2	(12.8)
New Zealand	496	(8.4)	489	(6.9)	-7	(10.9)	523	(4.9)	507	(5.3)	**-16**	(7.3)
Norway	460	(11.7)	457	(9.4)	-3	(15.0)	438	(9.3)	440	(6.2)	2	(11.2)
Poland	c	c	c	c	m	m	c	c	c	c	m	m
Portugal	440	(14.7)	445	(10.0)	6	(17.8)	383	(22.0)	450	(8.2)	**68**	(23.5)
Slovak Republic	432	(27.2)	c	c	m	m	c	c	c	c	m	m
Spain	450	(18.4)	457	(8.5)	7	(20.3)	440	(12.4)	436	(4.8)	-5	(13.3)
Sweden	483	(9.8)	445	(5.3)	**-38**	(11.1)	425	(9.6)	410	(7.3)	-15	(12.0)
Switzerland	484	(5.0)	489	(3.8)	5	(6.3)	453	(6.1)	471	(5.7)	**18**	(8.3)
Turkey	c	c	476	(35.4)	m	m	385	(28.7)	c	c	m	m
United States	468	(7.6)	478	(6.5)	10	(10.0)	453	(7.5)	463	(9.0)	9	(11.7)
OECD average 2003	466	(3.1)	467	(1.7)	1	(3.4)	453	(2.3)	454	(1.6)	0	(2.8)
Partners												
Brazil	c	c	334	(16.4)	m	m	c	c	337	(17.6)	m	m
Hong Kong-China	570	(4.6)	569	(4.1)	0	(6.2)	516	(5.3)	543	(5.2)	**27**	(7.4)
Indonesia	c	c	c	c	m	m	c	c	c	c	m	m
Latvia	479	(6.6)	487	(8.0)	7	(10.3)	498	(11.8)	c	c	m	m
Liechtenstein	c	c	504	(12.1)	m	m	482	(20.9)	498	(14.2)	16	(25.3)
Macao-China	532	(4.1)	546	(1.8)	**14**	(4.5)	517	(9.2)	541	(3.0)	**24**	(9.7)
Russian Federation	457	(7.2)	467	(4.9)	9	(8.7)	452	(5.9)	457	(7.9)	5	(9.9)
Thailand	c	c	412	(56.6)	m	m	c	c	c	c	m	m
Tunisia	c	c	c	c	m	m	c	c	c	c	m	m
Uruguay	c	c	c	c	m	m	c	c	c	c	m	m

Notes: Values that are statistically significant are indicated in bold.
OECD average 2003 includes only OECD countries with comparable data since PISA 2003.
Only countries and economies with comparable data from PISA 2003 and PISA 2012 are shown.
Results presented in this table can differ from those reported in *PISA 2012 Results (Volume II)* because they are computed including students without data on the PISA *index of economic, social and cultural status*.
Source: OECD, PISA 2012 Database.
Underlying data for the tables can be found at www.oecd.org/edu/school/Immigrant-Students-Tables.xlsx.

[Part 1/3]

Table 2.3 Host country/economy, country of origin and mathematics performance
Results based on students' self-reports

		Percentage of students out of all students in the sample		Performance in mathematics		Performance in mathematics after accounting for socio-economic status within each immigrant group		Performance in mathematics after accounting for socio-economic profile of the host country/economy	
Host country/ economy	Country of origin	%	S.E.	Mean score	S.E.	Mean score	S.E.	Mean score	S.E.
OECD Australia	China	2.3	(0.2)	596	(13.5)	585	(11.6)	584	(11.5)
	India	1.1	(0.1)	563	(8.9)	522	(11.0)	532	(8.0)
	New Zealand	2.3	(0.2)	485	(5.7)	484	(5.3)	486	(4.1)
	Philippines	1.0	(0.1)	517	(9.1)	507	(7.6)	507	(6.5)
	United Kingdom	3.5	(0.2)	525	(4.6)	508	(5.5)	499	(3.0)
	Viet Nam	1.9	(0.2)	548	(6.9)	553	(8.1)	566	(7.0)
Austria	Bosnia and Herzegovina	3.5	(0.4)	462	(8.9)	463	(10.9)	478	(8.6)
	Former Yugoslavia	2.8	(0.3)	435	(8.3)	454	(10.2)	458	(8.2)
	Germany	0.8	(0.2)	554	(16.3)	526	(17.8)	515	(8.9)
	Romania	0.7	(0.2)	510	(23.1)	508	(20.8)	517	(14.2)
	Turkey	3.6	(0.4)	422	(8.6)	464	(11.6)	467	(8.0)
Belgium	African country	5.1	(0.5)	445	(6.6)	453	(6.2)	470	(4.7)
	Eastern European country	1.7	(0.2)	457	(10.0)	461	(9.3)	473	(6.9)
	France	1.7	(0.5)	462	(22.1)	464	(15.0)	480	(9.9)
	Germany	0.3	(0.1)	525	(13.2)	510	(9.1)	508	(9.5)
	Netherlands Antilles	0.7	(0.2)	506	(14.5)	503	(12.3)	515	(9.3)
	Turkey	1.7	(0.3)	432	(13.8)	454	(12.7)	473	(8.9)
	Western European country	1.4	(0.2)	454	(10.6)	459	(10.3)	480	(6.3)
Czech Republic	Slovakia	0.8	(0.2)	458	(23.3)	488	(19.1)	489	(8.7)
	Ukraine	0.7	(0.1)	492	(16.1)	488	(18.5)	502	(12.6)
	Viet Nam	0.5	(0.1)	524	(14.9)	521	(17.0)	532	(24.7)
Denmark	Afghanistan	0.4	(0.1)	444	(11.0)	445	(10.9)	453	(12.3)
	Former Yugoslavia	0.8	(0.1)	459	(8.0)	460	(7.5)	462	(7.3)
	Iraq	1.0	(0.1)	429	(8.5)	433	(8.5)	436	(7.7)
	Lebanon	0.6	(0.1)	423	(7.5)	429	(8.7)	438	(6.5)
	Pakistan	0.7	(0.3)	433	(14.6)	444	(14.4)	446	(12.4)
	Somalia	0.5	(0.1)	406	(9.2)	404	(10.1)	424	(11.8)
	Turkey	1.1	(0.1)	423	(5.7)	428	(7.2)	446	(5.7)
Estonia	Russian Federation	6.2	(0.5)	500	(5.5)	497	(5.6)	507	(4.4)
Finland	Estonia	0.4	(0.0)	467	(8.9)	469	(7.8)	488	(6.5)
	Former Yugoslavia	0.2	(0.0)	445	(10.7)	451	(11.4)	471	(17.3)
	Iraq	0.2	(0.0)	445	(12.8)	455	(13.1)	460	(11.9)
	Russian Federation	0.6	(0.1)	471	(9.1)	469	(9.9)	477	(8.7)
	Somalia	0.4	(0.1)	385	(6.5)	394	(6.7)	402	(6.7)
	Turkey	0.1	(0.0)	428	(21.5)	427	(21.9)	473	(11.6)
Germany	Poland	1.5	(0.2)	505	(13.8)	505	(13.7)	504	(9.5)
	Russian Federation	3.9	(0.4)	489	(8.7)	497	(7.7)	501	(7.5)
	Turkey	3.6	(0.4)	453	(9.4)	472	(11.6)	480	(7.1)

Note: A student's country of origin is determined using the country of birth the student reported for both their father and mother (only students with valid answers for both these variables are included in this analysis). Only students with an immigrant background (first- and second-generation immigrant students) are considered for this analysis. Only those students who reported a specific country of origin (that is, a country "other than the test country") were included in this analysis. If both parents share the same country of birth (different from the test country), then the student's country of origin is the same as his/her parents' country of birth. If they are different, then the father's country of birth is used.

*See note at the beginning of this Annex.

Source: OECD, PISA 2012 Database.

Underlying data for the tables can be found at www.oecd.org/edu/school/Immigrant-Students-Tables.xlsx.

[Part 2/3]

Table 2.3 Host country/economy, country of origin and mathematics performance
Results based on students' self-reports

OECD

Host country/ economy	Country of origin	Percentage of students out of all students in the sample		Performance in mathematics		Performance in mathematics after accounting for socio-economic status within each immigrant group		Performance in mathematics after accounting for socio-economic profile of the host country/economy	
		%	S.E.	Mean score	S.E.	Mean score	S.E.	Mean score	S.E.
Greece	Albania	5.7	(0.5)	407	(7.1)	420	(8.0)	439	(7.0)
	Russian Federation	2.3	(0.4)	405	(12.3)	421	(10.9)	436	(9.0)
Ireland	United Kingdom	2.8	(0.3)	517	(9.3)	505	(9.6)	503	(3.5)
Israel	Ethiopia	1.5	(0.3)	387	(12.8)	386	(24.0)	463	(15.6)
	France	1.2	(0.2)	471	(18.1)	447	(19.0)	463	(14.0)
	Russian Federation	8.0	(0.9)	492	(7.9)	487	(7.3)	484	(6.3)
	South and Central America	0.8	(0.1)	486	(16.7)	465	(14.7)	483	(10.7)
	United States	1.7	(0.4)	521	(9.2)	501	(10.9)	504	(9.1)
Italy	European Union	2.3	(0.2)	440	(6.1)	457	(6.2)	475	(3.7)
Luxembourg	Belgium	2.0	(0.2)	533	(8.3)	524	(10.2)	506	(6.0)
	Cape Verde	2.7	(0.2)	413	(7.6)	426	(12.7)	450	(7.4)
	European Union	3.1	(0.2)	537	(8.6)	491	(11.3)	506	(6.4)
	Former Yugoslavia	4.9	(0.3)	447	(6.8)	453	(7.6)	463	(6.6)
	France	4.0	(0.3)	521	(6.3)	503	(6.3)	501	(4.4)
	Germany	1.7	(0.2)	551	(10.2)	515	(14.3)	510	(5.4)
	Italy	2.0	(0.2)	476	(9.6)	470	(9.0)	466	(6.9)
	Portugal	19.7	(0.5)	442	(2.9)	448	(3.7)	473	(2.7)
Netherlands	Morocco	1.8	(0.3)	456	(14.2)	455	(17.4)	474	(13.4)
	Suriname	0.9	(0.2)	479	(12.0)	478	(11.8)	476	(9.5)
	Turkey	2.8	(0.4)	460	(14.1)	467	(16.5)	482	(12.5)
New Zealand	China	2.3	(0.4)	588	(12.2)	582	(11.7)	581	(10.2)
	Fiji	1.7	(0.2)	465	(13.8)	472	(13.1)	480	(11.7)
	Korea	1.2	(0.2)	586	(14.6)	569	(18.2)	566	(13.8)
	Samoa	2.8	(0.4)	416	(7.6)	433	(12.5)	451	(7.0)
	South Africa	1.7	(0.2)	507	(9.2)	487	(11.4)	494	(9.0)
	United Kingdom	3.5	(0.3)	528	(7.8)	505	(7.8)	515	(4.4)
Portugal	African country (Portuguese-speaking)	3.4	(0.5)	440	(7.7)	469	(8.3)	493	(4.7)
	Brazil	1.0	(0.2)	443	(11.4)	444	(13.3)	471	(9.8)
	Eastern European country (not EU)	0.5	(0.1)	504	(16.1)	507	(14.7)	515	(15.3)
	European Union	0.7	(0.1)	485	(16.3)	488	(16.9)	511	(5.9)
Switzerland	Albania	0.5	(0.1)	417	(17.7)	435	(32.8)	448	(17.3)
	Former Yugoslavia	7.9	(0.5)	472	(5.5)	481	(6.2)	492	(5.0)
	France	0.7	(0.1)	524	(11.3)	508	(12.5)	526	(6.1)
	Germany	1.6	(0.2)	524	(10.3)	489	(19.3)	513	(6.6)
	Italy	1.9	(0.2)	476	(10.0)	483	(8.0)	498	(6.8)
	Portugal	3.1	(0.2)	487	(6.9)	506	(14.8)	521	(6.2)
	Spain	0.6	(0.1)	494	(14.2)	500	(16.5)	515	(10.4)
	Turkey	1.5	(0.2)	462	(12.0)	475	(10.1)	490	(10.5)

Note: A student's country of origin is determined using the country of birth the student reported for both their father and mother (only students with valid answers for both these variables are included in this analysis). Only students with an immigrant background (first- and second-generation immigrant students) are considered for this analysis. Only those students who reported a specific country of origin (that is, a country "other than the test country") were included in this analysis. If both parents share the same country of birth (different from the test country), then the student's country of origin is the same as his/her parents' country of birth. If they are different, then the father's country of birth is used.

*See note at the beginning of this Annex.

Source: OECD, PISA 2012 Database.

Underlying data for the tables can be found at www.oecd.org/edu/school/Immigrant-Students-Tables.xlsx.

[Part 3/3]

Table 2.3 **Host country/economy, country of origin and mathematics performance**
Results based on students' self-reports

	Host country/ economy	Country of origin	Percentage of students out of all students in the sample		Performance in mathematics		Performance in mathematics after accounting for socio-economic status within each immigrant group		Performance in mathematics after accounting for socio-economic profile of the host country/economy	
			%	S.E.	Mean score	S.E.	Mean score	S.E.	Mean score	S.E.
Partners	**Argentina**	Bolivia (Plurinational State of)	1.4	(0.2)	353	(12.3)	368	(33.4)	396	(10.1)
		Paraguay	1.1	(0.3)	360	(13.1)	388	(18.4)	398	(10.9)
	Costa Rica	Nicaragua	4.2	(0.7)	365	(10.2)	393	(12.9)	417	(6.2)
	Croatia	Bosnia and Herzegovina	9.6	(0.6)	457	(5.8)	471	(6.6)	481	(5.1)
		Other former Yugoslavia	1.1	(0.2)	459	(11.8)	475	(14.8)	498	(8.6)
	Cyprus*	Eastern European country	0.8	(0.1)	432	(15.0)	439	(15.9)	445	(8.9)
		Greece	1.4	(0.2)	427	(11.4)	429	(11.0)	431	(7.1)
		Russian Federation	1.6	(0.2)	461	(11.1)	457	(9.7)	460	(8.2)
		United Kingdom	1.0	(0.1)	447	(14.3)	419	(15.6)	438	(6.1)
	Hong Kong-China	China	31.7	(1.4)	562	(3.4)	594	(5.2)	596	(3.7)
		Macao-China	0.8	(0.1)	554	(14.5)	572	(23.4)	578	(12.9)
	Kazakhstan	Russian Federation	12.1	(1.5)	432	(7.0)	442	(6.3)	448	(5.4)
	Latvia	Belarus	0.7	(0.1)	507	(13.7)	508	(11.8)	502	(8.7)
		Russian Federation	1.8	(0.3)	486	(11.4)	485	(10.9)	494	(5.0)
		Ukraine	1.0	(0.3)	496	(20.1)	508	(16.7)	502	(8.5)
	Macao-China	China	57.4	(0.7)	548	(1.4)	570	(2.7)	568	(1.8)
		Hong Kong-China	2.5	(0.3)	526	(8.1)	540	(11.0)	543	(5.8)
		Philippines	1.0	(0.1)	467	(13.1)	478	(12.4)	467	(11.6)
	Montenegro	Bosnia and Herzegovina	1.3	(0.2)	455	(9.7)	453	(9.7)	442	(5.2)
		Serbia	2.9	(0.3)	424	(8.2)	427	(7.5)	426	(3.7)
	Qatar	Egypt	7.0	(0.2)	416	(3.7)	393	(4.8)	397	(3.6)
		Jordan	1.6	(0.1)	411	(9.0)	371	(13.2)	388	(8.0)
		Palestinian Authority	2.3	(0.1)	396	(6.2)	377	(8.1)	375	(5.4)
		Yemen	2.8	(0.2)	349	(4.9)	351	(4.8)	350	(4.4)
	Russian Federation	Other former USSR	8.3	(0.7)	473	(4.6)	477	(4.1)	491	(3.2)
	Serbia	Other former Yugoslavia	7.4	(0.7)	468	(7.2)	481	(6.1)	479	(4.8)

Note: A student's country of origin is determined using the country of birth the student reported for both their father and mother (only students with valid answers for both these variables are included in this analysis). Only students with an immigrant background (first- and second-generation immigrant students) are considered for this analysis. Only those students who reported a specific country of origin (that is, a country "other than the test country") were included in this analysis. If both parents share the same country of birth (different from the test country), then the student's country of origin is the same as his/her parents' country of birth. If they are different, then the father's country of birth is used.

*See note at the beginning of this Annex.

Source: OECD, PISA 2012 Database.

Underlying data for the tables can be found at www.oecd.org/edu/school/Immigrant-Students-Tables.xlsx.

[Part 1/2]

Table 2.4 **Sense of belonging at school and happiness at school, by immigrant background**

		Percentage of students who feel like they belong at school							
		Non-immigrants		Second-generation immigrants		First-generation immigrants		Difference between the first-generation and non-immigrant students	
		%	S.E.	%	S.E.	%	S.E.	% dif.	S.E.
OECD	Australia	76.9	(0.6)	82.2	(1.4)	81.2	(1.4)	**4.2**	(1.6)
	Austria	86.3	(0.9)	85.4	(1.9)	83.0	(3.1)	-3.3	(3.0)
	Belgium	69.6	(0.8)	62.5	(2.4)	59.8	(3.3)	**-9.8**	(3.2)
	Canada	77.1	(0.6)	81.5	(1.3)	82.3	(1.4)	**5.3**	(1.5)
	Chile	87.7	(0.6)	c	c	77.1	(9.7)	-10.6	(9.7)
	Czech Republic	78.4	(1.1)	69.0	(8.5)	67.0	(8.1)	-11.4	(7.8)
	Denmark	78.1	(0.9)	71.5	(2.7)	74.6	(3.1)	-3.5	(3.2)
	Estonia	81.3	(0.9)	79.7	(2.7)	c	c	c	c
	Finland	84.4	(0.7)	87.1	(3.2)	82.8	(2.8)	-1.6	(3.2)
	France	48.5	(1.1)	39.5	(3.0)	43.1	(4.5)	-5.3	(4.6)
	Germany	84.9	(0.8)	79.4	(2.6)	74.7	(5.5)	-10.2	(5.6)
	Greece	89.0	(0.7)	88.2	(5.2)	88.1	(2.5)	-1.0	(2.6)
	Hungary	85.0	(0.7)	77.5	(7.1)	c	c	c	c
	Iceland	88.5	(0.6)	c	c	81.4	(4.8)	-7.2	(4.8)
	Ireland	80.9	(0.8)	69.2	(6.8)	71.1	(2.8)	**-9.7**	(2.8)
	Israel	90.9	(0.6)	90.2	(1.8)	86.9	(2.7)	-4.0	(2.7)
	Italy	77.8	(0.5)	74.2	(3.2)	69.1	(2.2)	**-8.7**	(2.2)
	Japan	84.0	(0.6)	c	c	c	c	c	c
	Korea	76.4	(1.1)	c	c	c	c	c	c
	Luxembourg	81.0	(0.7)	73.1	(1.4)	66.1	(2.1)	**-14.9**	(2.3)
	Mexico	91.7	(0.3)	79.2	(5.9)	89.2	(2.9)	-2.5	(3.0)
	Netherlands	84.6	(1.1)	85.2	(2.2)	82.1	(4.4)	-2.5	(4.5)
	New Zealand	76.6	(1.0)	87.1	(2.4)	81.6	(1.9)	**5.0**	(2.2)
	Norway	87.5	(0.6)	88.9	(2.7)	79.2	(3.9)	**-8.2**	(4.1)
	Poland	76.0	(0.8)	c	c	c	c	c	c
	Portugal	91.7	(0.6)	87.1	(3.3)	80.5	(4.8)	**-11.2**	(4.8)
	Slovak Republic	77.8	(0.9)	c	c	c	c	c	c
	Slovenia	83.6	(0.7)	83.3	(3.0)	79.0	(6.0)	-4.6	(6.1)
	Spain	93.7	(0.4)	94.1	(2.1)	87.6	(1.8)	**-6.1**	(1.8)
	Sweden	79.1	(1.0)	78.7	(2.6)	72.1	(3.2)	**-6.9**	(3.3)
	Switzerland	83.3	(0.9)	81.7	(1.6)	76.7	(2.4)	**-6.7**	(2.4)
	Turkey	84.2	(0.7)	c	c	c	c	c	c
	United Kingdom	78.8	(1.0)	80.8	(3.5)	84.1	(2.8)	5.3	(3.3)
	United States	80.3	(1.0)	80.0	(1.6)	86.8	(3.3)	6.5	(3.4)
	OECD average (25)	81.4	(0.2)	79.2	(0.7)	77.1	(0.7)	**-4.2**	(0.7)
Partners	Albania	94.0	(0.6)	c	c	c	c	c	c
	Argentina	90.4	(0.7)	83.4	(5.7)	91.3	(2.9)	0.9	(3.1)
	Brazil	86.4	(0.5)	68.6	(9.0)	68.4	(9.9)	-18.0	(9.9)
	Bulgaria	82.0	(0.8)	c	c	c	c	c	c
	Colombia	94.2	(0.5)	c	c	c	c	c	c
	Costa Rica	90.9	(0.7)	87.6	(5.7)	87.6	(4.9)	-3.3	(5.0)
	Croatia	88.4	(0.6)	86.6	(2.1)	84.6	(3.1)	-3.8	(3.1)
	Hong Kong-China	74.0	(1.2)	71.9	(2.1)	71.0	(2.3)	-3.0	(2.5)
	Indonesia	92.7	(0.5)	c	c	c	c	c	c
	Jordan	87.2	(0.7)	83.8	(2.0)	84.1	(2.8)	-3.1	(2.8)
	Kazakhstan	88.9	(0.7)	89.4	(1.9)	86.3	(3.2)	-2.6	(3.3)
	Latvia	90.4	(0.7)	83.8	(2.8)	c	c	c	c
	Liechtenstein	96.4	(1.5)	86.0	(4.9)	c	c	c	c
	Lithuania	66.7	(0.9)	70.8	(7.3)	c	c	c	c
	Macao-China	65.1	(1.4)	66.0	(1.2)	65.0	(2.1)	0.0	(2.4)
	Malaysia	81.7	(0.8)	82.7	(5.4)	c	c	c	c
	Montenegro	68.0	(0.9)	59.9	(5.8)	61.2	(5.4)	-6.8	(5.4)
	Peru	86.4	(0.9)	c	c	c	c	c	c
	Qatar	75.4	(0.8)	79.7	(1.1)	81.8	(0.9)	**6.4**	(1.2)
	Romania	66.8	(0.9)	c	c	c	c	c	c
	Russian Federation	81.7	(0.8)	77.8	(2.6)	80.8	(4.8)	-0.9	(4.9)
	Serbia	87.7	(0.7)	88.5	(2.3)	80.7	(5.1)	-7.0	(5.2)
	Shanghai-China	67.5	(1.0)	c	c	c	c	c	c
	Singapore	83.8	(0.7)	82.7	(2.8)	83.8	(1.8)	0.0	(2.0)
	Chinese Taipei	91.1	(0.5)	c	c	c	c	c	c
	Thailand	91.2	(0.5)	c	c	c	c	c	c
	Tunisia	66.0	(1.1)	c	c	c	c	c	c
	United Arab Emirates	83.0	(0.8)	84.9	(1.0)	84.3	(0.8)	1.3	(1.2)
	Uruguay	92.6	(0.5)	c	c	c	c	c	c
	Viet Nam	82.7	0.8	c	c	c	c	c	c

Notes: Values that are statistically significant are indicated in bold.
OECD average (25) includes only countries with valid data on first-generation immigrants.
Source: OECD, PISA 2012 Database.
Underlying data for the tables can be found at www.oecd.org/edu/school/Immigrant-Students-Tables.xlsx.

[Part 2/2]

Table 2.4 Sense of belonging at school and happiness at school, by immigrant background

		Percentage of students who reported feeling happy at school							
		Non-immigrants		Second-generation immigrants		First-generation immigrants		Difference between the first-generation and non-immigrant students	
		%	S.E.	%	S.E.	%	S.E.	%	S.E.
OECD	Australia	78.4	(0.6)	83.0	(1.7)	83.9	(1.4)	**5.5**	(1.5)
	Austria	80.0	(1.0)	78.4	(2.3)	81.6	(3.1)	1.5	(3.1)
	Belgium	84.8	(0.6)	84.7	(1.9)	80.9	(2.5)	-3.9	(2.6)
	Canada	79.4	(0.6)	84.1	(1.3)	85.3	(1.2)	**5.9**	(1.3)
	Chile	85.0	(0.7)	c	c	92.3	(4.3)	7.3	(4.3)
	Czech Republic	63.5	(1.0)	61.2	(8.0)	59.2	(8.4)	-4.4	(8.5)
	Denmark	86.6	(0.7)	82.0	(4.4)	81.6	(3.6)	-4.9	(3.8)
	Estonia	66.9	(1.0)	64.5	(4.3)	c	c	c	c
	Finland	66.7	(1.0)	75.1	(2.8)	72.3	(3.1)	5.6	(3.3)
	France	81.2	(0.9)	78.9	(2.2)	81.9	(3.7)	0.7	(3.9)
	Germany	80.8	(0.8)	73.9	(2.9)	73.4	(4.5)	-7.3	(4.4)
	Greece	74.5	(0.9)	74.6	(3.8)	75.5	(2.8)	1.0	(2.8)
	Hungary	80.2	(0.9)	74.9	(8.2)	c	c	c	c
	Iceland	90.7	(0.5)	c	c	88.1	(3.9)	-2.5	(3.9)
	Ireland	82.2	(0.8)	87.7	(5.0)	78.3	(2.7)	-3.9	(2.7)
	Israel	89.4	(0.6)	87.1	(1.8)	81.9	(3.7)	**-7.5**	(3.7)
	Italy	76.1	(0.5)	70.7	(3.9)	70.0	(2.4)	**-6.0**	(2.4)
	Japan	85.4	(0.7)	c	c	c	c	c	c
	Korea	60.4	(1.0)	c	c	c	c	c	c
	Luxembourg	81.1	(0.9)	78.2	(1.3)	80.0	(2.1)	-1.1	(2.4)
	Mexico	91.0	(0.3)	90.4	(3.2)	88.4	(3.0)	-2.6	(3.0)
	Netherlands	82.8	(1.1)	79.6	(4.5)	73.5	(4.5)	-9.3	(4.9)
	New Zealand	79.1	(1.0)	86.7	(2.4)	87.6	(1.5)	**8.5**	(1.8)
	Norway	86.9	(0.9)	91.1	(2.7)	83.9	(3.3)	-3.1	(3.5)
	Poland	68.6	(1.0)	c	c	c	c	c	c
	Portugal	86.7	(0.6)	82.8	(4.0)	78.8	(5.0)	-7.8	(4.8)
	Slovak Republic	64.5	(1.3)	c	c	c	c	c	c
	Slovenia	78.9	(0.9)	74.5	(4.1)	83.1	(4.7)	4.2	(4.7)
	Spain	87.6	(0.4)	89.0	(2.8)	83.7	(1.6)	**-3.9**	(1.6)
	Sweden	85.2	(0.9)	87.5	(2.5)	78.4	(3.1)	**-6.7**	(3.1)
	Switzerland	87.6	(0.7)	87.5	(1.1)	82.8	(2.4)	-4.8	(2.6)
	Turkey	83.4	(0.7)	c	c	c	c	c	c
	United Kingdom	82.8	(0.8)	85.7	(2.7)	85.7	(2.5)	2.9	(2.7)
	United States	79.2	(1.0)	78.4	(2.1)	87.4	(2.4)	**8.2**	(2.8)
	OECD average (25)	81.3	(0.2)	81.3	(0.7)	80.0	(0.7)	-1.3	(0.7)
Partners	Albania	94.1	(0.6)	c	c	c	c	c	c
	Argentina	77.5	(0.9)	67.4	(7.1)	73.2	(8.2)	-4.4	(8.5)
	Brazil	85.3	(0.5)	80.6	(8.9)	62.1	(11.5)	**-23.2**	(11.6)
	Bulgaria	80.3	(0.8)	c	c	c	c	c	c
	Colombia	92.3	(0.5)	c	c	c	c	c	c
	Costa Rica	90.6	(0.8)	91.9	(3.3)	94.9	(2.8)	4.3	(2.9)
	Croatia	87.0	(0.7)	88.0	(1.6)	84.9	(3.4)	-2.2	(3.5)
	Hong Kong-China	87.0	(0.8)	84.9	(1.3)	85.5	(1.9)	-1.5	(2.2)
	Indonesia	95.8	(0.4)	c	c	c	c	c	c
	Jordan	83.8	(0.8)	86.4	(1.9)	83.8	(3.8)	0.0	(4.0)
	Kazakhstan	91.2	(0.8)	88.1	(2.3)	85.8	(2.8)	-5.4	(2.8)
	Latvia	67.7	(1.0)	67.5	(5.4)	c	c	c	c
	Liechtenstein	93.1	(2.3)	68.1	(6.6)	c	c	c	c
	Lithuania	78.1	(0.8)	66.8	(10.7)	c	c	c	c
	Macao-China	82.2	(1.1)	81.3	(1.0)	82.0	(1.5)	-0.2	(1.9)
	Malaysia	91.5	(0.5)	97.8	(2.0)	c	c	c	c
	Montenegro	82.2	(0.8)	72.4	(5.2)	72.4	(5.0)	**-9.8**	(5.0)
	Peru	93.7	(0.5)	c	c	c	c	c	c
	Qatar	70.1	(0.9)	75.5	(1.2)	81.9	(0.9)	**11.8**	(1.3)
	Romania	77.4	(1.0)	c	c	c	c	c	c
	Russian Federation	72.2	(1.2)	71.5	(2.8)	75.8	(4.9)	3.5	(5.1)
	Serbia	81.4	(0.8)	81.0	(2.9)	69.7	(5.0)	**-11.6**	(5.1)
	Shanghai-China	84.7	(0.7)	c	c	c	c	c	c
	Singapore	88.1	(0.7)	85.1	(2.5)	87.5	(2.2)	-0.6	(2.2)
	Chinese Taipei	86.5	(0.6)	c	c	c	c	c	c
	Thailand	93.5	(0.5)	c	c	c	c	c	c
	Tunisia	82.3	(0.9)	c	c	c	c	c	c
	United Arab Emirates	82.1	(1.0)	85.2	(0.9)	85.1	(0.9)	**3.0**	(1.3)
	Uruguay	87.5	(0.6)	c	c	c	c	c	c
	Viet Nam	85.9	(0.7)	c	c	c	c	c	c

Notes: Values that are statistically significant are indicated in bold.
OECD average (25) includes only countries with valid data on first-generation immigrants.
Source: OECD, PISA 2012 Database.
Underlying data for the tables can be found at www.oecd.org/edu/school/Immigrant-Students-Tables.xlsx.

[Part 1/1]

Table 3.1 **Attitudes towards immigration in European countries**

		Immigrants make country worse or better place to live[1]		Change between 2000 and 2012 in attitudes towards immigrants from poorer countries outside of Europe					
				2000		2012		Change between 2000 and 2012 (2012 – 2000)	
		Mean	S.E.	Mean	S.E.	Mean	S.E.	Dif.	S.E.
OECD	**Belgium**	4.72	(0.05)	2.68	(0.04)	2.51	(0.02)	**-0.18**	(0.04)
	Czech Republic	4.22	(0.06)	2.89	(0.05)	3.24	(0.04)	**0.35**	(0.05)
	Denmark	5.98	(0.06)	2.87	(0.04)	2.70	(0.04)	**-0.17**	(0.04)
	Estonia	4.81	(0.05)	m	m	m	m	m	m
	Finland	5.64	(0.05)	2.77	(0.03)	2.74	(0.02)	-0.04	(0.03)
	France	4.44	(0.06)	2.74	(0.04)	2.62	(0.03)	**-0.12**	(0.04)
	Germany	5.38	(0.05)	2.52	(0.02)	2.25	(0.02)	**-0.27**	(0.02)
	Hungary	4.40	(0.05)	3.57	(0.04)	3.65	(0.04)	0.07	(0.04)
	Iceland	6.49	(0.08)	m	m	m	m	m	m
	Ireland	5.45	(0.06)	2.50	(0.03)	2.57	(0.02)	**0.07**	(0.03)
	Israel	4.63	(0.06)	2.92	(0.05)	3.61	(0.03)	**0.69**	(0.05)
	Italy	4.19	(0.10)	2.57	(0.04)	2.49	(0.05)	-0.08	(0.04)
	Netherlands	5.43	(0.05)	2.56	(0.02)	2.53	(0.03)	-0.03	(0.02)
	Norway	5.66	(0.05)	2.36	(0.02)	2.26	(0.02)	**-0.10**	(0.02)
	Poland	5.97	(0.05)	2.79	(0.04)	2.36	(0.03)	**-0.43**	(0.04)
	Portugal	3.88	(0.05)	3.13	(0.05)	3.14	(0.03)	0.00	(0.05)
	Slovak Republic	4.19	(0.07)	m	m	m	m	m	m
	Slovenia	4.81	(0.07)	2.73	(0.04)	2.74	(0.04)	0.01	(0.04)
	Spain	5.31	(0.06)	2.95	(0.05)	2.57	(0.03)	**-0.38**	(0.05)
	Sweden	6.43	(0.06)	2.15	(0.03)	1.93	(0.03)	**-0.22**	(0.03)
	Switzerland	5.38	(0.05)	2.47	(0.03)	2.52	(0.03)	0.05	(0.03)
	United Kingdom	4.74	(0.06)	2.65	(0.03)	2.87	(0.03)	**0.21**	(0.03)
Partners	Albania	5.98	(0.13)	m	m	m	m	m	m
	Bulgaria	5.25	(0.07)	m	m	m	m	m	m
	Lithuania	5.00	(0.06)	m	m	m	m	m	m
	Russian Federation	3.30	(0.06)	m	m	m	m	m	m
	Average	5.07	(0.01)	2.73	(0.01)	2.70	(0.01)	**-0.03**	(0.01)

Note: Values that are statistically significant are indicated in bold.

1. Respondents were asked to use a scale ranging from 0 (worse place to live) to 10 (better place to live). Higher mean values indicate more positive attitudes.

Source: European Social Survey 2000, Round 1; European Social Survey 2012 Round 6.

Underlying data for the tables can be found at www.oecd.org/edu/school/Immigrant-Students-Tables.xlsx.

[Part 1/4]

Concentration of immigrant students in school

Table 4.1 ***Results based on students' self-reports***

		Percentage of students									
		Immigrant students		In schools where the percentage of immigrant students is zero		In schools where the percentage of immigrant students is more than 0% but less than 10% (low concentration)		In schools where the percentage of immigrant students is at or above 10% but less than 25% (medium concentration)		In schools where the percentage of immigrant students is at or above 25% (high concentration)	
		%	S.E.	%	S.E.	%	S.E.	%	S.E.	%	S.E.
OECD	Australia	22.7	(0.7)	15.0	(1.3)	18.2	(1.6)	29.1	(1.9)	37.7	(1.8)
	Austria	16.4	(1.1)	15.1	(2.9)	33.6	(3.9)	29.1	(4.0)	22.2	(2.9)
	Belgium	15.1	(0.9)	17.8	(2.2)	36.6	(2.9)	24.2	(2.4)	21.4	(2.2)
	Canada	29.5	(1.3)	17.9	(1.3)	22.4	(1.6)	16.3	(1.6)	43.3	(1.9)
	Chile	0.9	(0.2)	78.4	(3.1)	21.1	(3.1)	0.5	(0.3)	c	c
	Czech Republic	3.2	(0.4)	60.8	(3.7)	26.9	(3.6)	11.5	(2.1)	0.7	(0.5)
	Denmark	8.9	(0.6)	29.8	(2.8)	41.6	(2.9)	20.9	(2.4)	7.7	(1.3)
	Estonia	8.2	(0.5)	39.7	(2.2)	34.8	(2.1)	12.5	(2.1)	13.1	(2.1)
	Finland	3.3	(0.2)	33.4	(3.0)	58.0	(3.0)	7.5	(0.4)	1.1	(0.2)
	France	w	w	w	w	w	w	w	w	w	w
	Germany	13.1	(0.8)	23.3	(2.7)	27.8	(2.8)	31.3	(3.1)	17.6	(2.4)
	Greece	10.5	(0.8)	19.9	(3.2)	49.8	(3.9)	23.3	(3.0)	7.0	(1.5)
	Hungary	1.7	(0.2)	70.7	(3.5)	27.1	(3.4)	1.8	(1.0)	0.4	(0.3)
	Iceland	3.5	(0.3)	43.2	(0.2)	50.7	(0.2)	5.5	(0.2)	0.6	(0.0)
	Ireland	10.1	(0.7)	14.3	(2.4)	40.5	(3.6)	38.7	(3.9)	6.5	(2.0)
	Israel	18.3	(1.2)	17.0	(1.9)	25.7	(3.5)	29.7	(3.6)	27.7	(3.1)
	Italy	7.5	(0.3)	30.3	(1.5)	46.1	(1.6)	18.0	(1.3)	5.6	(1.1)
	Japan	0.3	(0.1)	90.0	(2.1)	10.0	(2.1)	c	c	c	c
	Korea	0.0	(0.0)	99.3	(0.5)	0.7	(0.5)	c	c	c	c
	Luxembourg	46.4	(0.7)	c	c	0.8	(0.0)	16.0	(0.1)	83.2	(0.1)
	Mexico	1.3	(0.1)	77.2	(1.6)	20.4	(1.5)	2.1	(0.5)	0.3	(0.2)
	Netherlands	10.6	(1.0)	29.7	(3.5)	35.6	(4.0)	22.7	(3.7)	12.0	(2.1)
	New Zealand	26.3	(1.5)	7.4	(1.9)	13.9	(2.5)	41.3	(3.5)	37.3	(3.4)
	Norway	9.4	(0.9)	28.9	(3.5)	37.6	(3.6)	26.2	(3.0)	7.2	(1.7)
	Poland	0.2	(0.1)	95.9	(1.5)	4.0	(1.5)	0.1	(0.1)	c	c
	Portugal	6.9	(0.6)	34.4	(4.5)	42.0	(4.5)	16.5	(2.9)	7.2	(2.3)
	Slovak Republic	0.7	(0.2)	85.2	(2.7)	13.6	(2.7)	1.2	(0.7)	c	c
	Slovenia	8.6	(0.4)	36.0	(0.8)	35.8	(0.5)	19.8	(0.6)	8.4	(0.6)
	Spain	9.9	(0.6)	27.7	(2.4)	35.7	(2.8)	26.6	(2.7)	10.0	(1.7)
	Sweden	14.5	(0.9)	17.6	(2.5)	34.3	(3.1)	28.7	(2.9)	19.4	(2.2)
	Switzerland	24.1	(0.9)	3.9	(1.0)	14.5	(2.1)	41.4	(3.2)	40.2	(3.3)
	Turkey	0.9	(0.2)	83.0	(3.3)	15.0	(3.2)	2.0	(1.3)	c	c
	United Kingdom	12.7	(1.1)	33.1	(2.9)	29.8	(3.1)	20.7	(2.9)	16.4	(2.2)
	United States	21	(2.0)	20	(3.4)	29	(4.1)	17.3	(3.5)	34.2	(3.9)
	OECD average	11.2	(0.1)	40.0	(0.4)	28.5	(0.5)	19.0	(0.4)	18.1	(0.4)
Partners	Albania	0.0	c	0.0	c	0.0	c	0.0	c	0.0	c
	Argentina	3.9	(0.4)	56.4	(3.8)	33.1	(3.7)	7.3	(2.2)	3.2	(0.8)
	Brazil	0.7	(0.1)	86.2	(1.6)	12.3	(1.5)	1.4	(0.5)	0.1	(0.1)
	Bulgaria	0.5	(0.2)	90.3	(2.3)	8.6	(2.2)	1.0	(0.7)	0.1	(0.1)
	Colombia	0.3	(0.1)	91.1	(2.0)	8.9	(2.0)	0.1	(0.1)	c	c
	Costa Rica	5.5	(0.7)	43.7	(3.4)	37.1	(3.4)	16.4	(2.3)	2.8	(1.5)
	Croatia	12.1	(0.8)	11.4	(2.5)	34.7	(3.9)	43.9	(3.9)	10.1	(2.5)
	Cyprus*	8.5	(0.4)	15.9	(0.1)	62.5	(0.2)	14.2	(0.1)	7.4	(0.1)
	Hong Kong-China	34.7	(1.5)	c	c	7.6	(2.9)	18.6	(3.1)	73.7	(3.9)
	Indonesia	0.2	(0.1)	96.9	(1.2)	2.9	(1.1)	0.2	(0.1)	c	c
	Jordan	13.4	(0.7)	20.8	(2.7)	22.8	(2.8)	38.8	(4.0)	17.6	(3.1)
	Kazakhstan	16.1	(1.7)	15.6	(2.6)	32.8	(3.6)	35.4	(3.7)	16.1	(3.4)
	Latvia	4.5	(0.5)	58.9	(3.5)	21.7	(3.2)	16.1	(2.5)	3.2	(1.3)
	Liechtenstein	33.3	(2.9)	c	c	c	c	53.1	(1.0)	46.9	(1.0)
	Lithuania	1.7	(0.3)	79.7	(3.1)	16.3	(3.0)	2.4	(1.1)	1.5	(0.8)
	Macao-China	65.1	(0.6)	c	c	c	c	c	c	100.0	c
	Malaysia	1.7	(0.3)	72.8	(3.2)	21.6	(2.9)	5.6	(1.3)	c	c
	Montenegro	5.8	(0.4)	0.9	(0.2)	77.3	(0.2)	21.7	(0.1)	0.0	(0.0)
	Peru	0.5	(0.1)	88.0	(2.1)	11.2	(2.1)	0.6	(0.4)	0.1	(0.1)
	Qatar	52.0	(0.4)	c	c	3.6	(0.0)	20.8	(0.1)	75.6	(0.1)
	Romania	0.2	(0.1)	94.6	(1.9)	5.4	(1.9)	c	c	c	c
	Russian Federation	10.9	(0.8)	13.8	(2.0)	39.3	(3.2)	40.5	(2.7)	6.3	(2.0)
	Serbia	8.5	(0.8)	27.8	(3.6)	42.1	(4.2)	23.9	(3.0)	6.2	(1.8)
	Shanghai-China	0.9	(0.2)	80.1	(3.2)	18.9	(3.1)	0.9	(0.7)	c	c
	Singapore	18.3	(0.8)	2.1	(0.9)	21.2	(0.1)	58.6	(0.2)	18.1	(0.9)
	Chinese Taipei	0.5	(0.1)	84.8	(2.9)	15.2	(2.9)	c	c	c	c
	Thailand	0.7	(0.4)	96.8	(1.4)	1.5	(1.0)	0.7	(0.7)	1.0	(0.7)
	Tunisia	0.4	(0.1)	89.2	(2.6)	10.8	(2.6)	c	c	c	c
	United Arab Emirates	54.9	(1.4)	2.3	(1.1)	11.1	(1.7)	16.5	(1.9)	70.1	(2.2)
	Uruguay	0.5	(0.1)	88.6	(2.4)	11.0	(2.5)	0.5	(0.4)	c	c
	Viet Nam	0.1	(0.1)	97.2	(1.4)	2.8	(1.4)	c	c	c	c

Notes: This table was calculated considering only students with data on the PISA *index of economic, social and cultural status*. Values that are statistically significant are indicated in bold.

The OECD average is computed considering also the value for countries for which data have been withdrawn at the request of the country concerned.

1. The PISA *index of economic, social and cultural status* (ESCS).

*See note at the beginning of this Annex.

Source: OECD, PISA 2012 Database.

Underlying data for the tables can be found at www.oecd.org/edu/school/Immigrant-Students-Tables.xlsx.

[Part 2/4]

Table 4.1 **Concentration of immigrant students in school**
Results based on students' self-reports

		Estimated coefficients in a model with mathematics performance as the dependent variable							
		Before adjusting for ESCS[1]							
		Immigrant student		Low-concentration schools vs. those without immigrant students		Medium-concentration schools vs. those without immigrant students		High-concentration schools vs. those without immigrant students	
		Score dif.	S.E.	Score dif.	S.E.	Score dif.	S.E.	Score dif.	S.E.
OECD	Australia	**14**	(3.2)	**17**	(5.2)	**25**	(4.3)	**37**	(4.9)
	Austria	**-44**	(4.3)	26	(14.1)	25	(14.2)	-17	(14.3)
	Belgium	**-45**	(4.4)	-20	(10.7)	**-48**	(11.0)	**-72**	(12.6)
	Canada	**-9**	(3.4)	7	(6.1)	5	(6.8)	**16**	(5.3)
	Chile	-5	(10.3)	7	(9.2)	c	c	c	c
	Czech Republic	**-22**	(8.5)	**28**	(9.6)	-15	(16.0)	c	c
	Denmark	**-60**	(3.2)	3	(5.5)	4	(6.4)	**-17**	(6.1)
	Estonia	**-15**	(5.5)	3	(4.1)	**-32**	(6.5)	**-21**	(7.9)
	Finland	**-80**	(4.3)	**12**	(3.9)	0	(5.1)	**-34**	(16.2)
	France	w	w	w	w	w	w	w	w
	Germany	**-32**	(4.2)	18	(12.8)	-6	(13.5)	**-49**	(14.1)
	Greece	**-20**	(5.0)	-7	(11.3)	**-33**	(11.5)	**-80**	(15.4)
	Hungary	16	(10.2)	**48**	(12.9)	c	c	c	c
	Iceland	**-47**	(9.3)	**10**	(3.1)	-13	(7.3)	c	c
	Ireland	4	(4.7)	-9	(8.6)	-11	(9.6)	**-33**	(14.2)
	Israel	**-12**	(3.6)	**59**	(15.1)	**78**	(12.0)	**75**	(12.1)
	Italy	**-31**	(2.7)	**20**	(6.4)	-2	(6.8)	**-50**	(8.8)
	Japan	c	c	-16	(22.2)	c	c	c	c
	Korea	c	c	c	c	c	c	c	c
	Luxembourg	**-31**	(3.2)	c	c	**57**	(2.7)	-14	(11.8)
	Mexico	**-52**	(4.1)	**-15**	(4.0)	**-68**	(7.0)	-14	(40.1)
	Netherlands	**-35**	(5.5)	-11	(16.1)	-9	(16.4)	**-60**	(19.5)
	New Zealand	-10	(5.2)	23	(14.7)	**42**	(13.4)	**48**	(15.5)
	Norway	**-46**	(5.8)	-4	(6.6)	-5	(7.7)	-1	(11.2)
	Poland	c	c	**14**	(24.2)	c	c	c	c
	Portugal	**-31**	(7.4)	11	(9.5)	-16	(12.0)	-26	(16.6)
	Slovak Republic	-19	(16.1)	**31**	(18.2)	c	c	c	c
	Slovenia	**-33**	(5.4)	**12**	(3.6)	**16**	(4.9)	**-53**	(5.9)
	Spain	**-45**	(3.7)	8	(5.5)	-7	(7.2)	-14	(7.7)
	Sweden	**-57**	(4.6)	-4	(6.1)	6	(7.3)	-5	(8.2)
	Switzerland	**-49**	(2.5)	**35**	(15.0)	**34**	(14.8)	-11	(13.2)
	Turkey	-20	(15.0)	23	(19.7)	c	c	c	c
	United Kingdom	-9	(6.2)	8	(6.3)	14	(13.1)	1	(9.0)
	United States	-5	(4.3)	**23**	(9.6)	**24**	(9.4)	-1	(10.9)
	OECD average	**-28**	(1.2)	**12**	(2.1)	2	(2.0)	**-18**	(2.9)
Partners	Albania	c	c	c	c	c	c	c	c
	Argentina	**-12**	(6.2)	-7	(8.2)	**-40**	(9.5)	**-52**	(11.6)
	Brazil	**-39**	(8.4)	-7	(9.6)	-33	(19.0)	c	c
	Bulgaria	c	c	**-33**	(14.6)	c	c	c	c
	Colombia	**-37**	(12.0)	**-35**	(9.6)	c	c	c	c
	Costa Rica	**-19**	(5.2)	9	(7.4)	-6	(7.2)	**-42**	(11.8)
	Croatia	**-13**	(4.2)	21	(16.7)	5	(15.4)	-12	(16.5)
	Cyprus*	**-16**	(5.8)	**14**	(3.5)	-1	(4.1)	-6	(6.2)
	Hong Kong-China	1	(3.7)	**47**	(16.3)	**33**	(14.1)	**-47**	(16.3)
	Indonesia	c	c	19	(14.1)	c	c	c	c
	Jordan	**13**	(3.4)	**14**	(6.8)	**19**	(9.1)	**31**	(11.7)
	Kazakhstan	-4	(4.1)	1	(10.5)	-4	(9.8)	-5	(13.3)
	Latvia	-5	(7.4)	**16**	(7.6)	2	(10.1)	-10	(9.0)
	Liechtenstein	-17	(9.4)	c	c	c	c	c	c
	Lithuania	0	(10.2)	4	(7.8)	-29	(15.1)	c	c
	Macao-China	**16**	(2.8)	c	c	c	c	c	c
	Malaysia	-11	(8.6)	-3	(7.2)	**-20**	(8.4)	c	c
	Montenegro	**19**	(6.6)	39	(21.3)	**45**	(21.4)	c	c
	Peru	**-75**	(17.1)	3	(14.1)	c	c	c	c
	Qatar	**81**	(1.9)	**-10**	(4.0)	**-27**	(2.2)	**10**	(4.0)
	Romania	c	c	28	(22.4)	c	c	c	c
	Russian Federation	**-19**	(4.0)	**22**	(8.7)	7	(8.6)	1	(12.5)
	Serbia	**8**	(3.9)	13	(12.0)	**38**	(12.8)	-2	(19.0)
	Shanghai-China	**-65**	(14.1)	**-67**	(11.5)	c	c	c	c
	Singapore	**9**	(4.3)	20	(11.2)	**34**	(10.9)	**99**	(12.8)
	Chinese Taipei	-11	(17.0)	-24	(16.1)	c	c	c	c
	Thailand	-35	(23.4)	23	(19.9)	c	c	c	c
	Tunisia	c	c	6	(18.1)	c	c	c	c
	United Arab Emirates	**64**	(3.4)	17	(11.7)	9	(11.1)	16	(10.9)
	Uruguay	c	c	32	(17.2)	c	c	c	c
	Viet Nam	c	c	c	c	c	c	c	c

Notes: This table was calculated considering only students with data on the PISA *index of economic, social and cultural status*. Values that are statistically significant are indicated in bold.

The OECD average is computed considering also the value for countries for which data have been withdrawn at the request of the country concerned.

1. The PISA *index of economic, social and cultural status* (ESCS).

*See note at the beginning of this Annex.

Source: OECD, PISA 2012 Database.

Underlying data for the tables can be found at www.oecd.org/edu/school/Immigrant-Students-Tables.xlsx.

[Part 3/4]

Concentration of immigrant students in school

Table 4.1 ***Results based on students' self-reports***

		Estimated coefficients in a model with mathematics performance as the dependent variable							
		After adjusting for student ESCS[1]							
		Immigrant student		Low-concentration schools vs. those without immigrant students		Medium-concentration schools vs. those without immigrant students		High-concentration schools vs. those without immigrant students	
		Score dif.	S.E.	Score dif.	S.E.	Score dif.	S.E.	Score dif.	S.E.
OECD	Australia	**19**	(3.2)	**9**	(4.3)	**12**	(3.7)	**25**	(3.9)
	Austria	**-22**	(4.1)	17	(12.1)	12	(12.4)	-17	(11.8)
	Belgium	**-28**	(3.6)	**-22**	(8.2)	**-48**	(8.6)	**-61**	(9.1)
	Canada	0	(3.2)	2	(5.6)	-5	(6.3)	3	(4.9)
	Chile	-4	(8.8)	-7	(6.3)	c	c	c	c
	Czech Republic	-14	(9.2)	**17**	(8.3)	-18	(12.1)	c	c
	Denmark	**-37**	(3.1)	2	(4.3)	4	(4.9)	-10	(5.2)
	Estonia	**-15**	(5.2)	-3	(3.7)	**-31**	(6.4)	**-23**	(6.7)
	Finland	**-59**	(4.0)	5	(3.7)	-5	(4.4)	**-33**	(16.1)
	France	w	w	w	w	w	w	w	w
	Germany	**-9**	(4.6)	14	(10.6)	-4	(11.0)	**-39**	(12.0)
	Greece	-5	(5.3)	-7	(8.3)	**-28**	(9.1)	**-66**	(14.3)
	Hungary	11	(12.4)	**29**	(9.7)	c	c	c	c
	Iceland	**-28**	(8.9)	5	(3.1)	-7	(7.1)	c	c
	Ireland	0	(4.4)	-4	(6.3)	-7	(6.8)	**-24**	(10.5)
	Israel	-2	(3.4)	**41**	(11.4)	**58**	(9.6)	**62**	(9.0)
	Italy	**-21**	(2.7)	**19**	(5.4)	2	(5.9)	**-38**	(7.1)
	Japan	c	c	-13	(17.4)	c	c	c	c
	Korea	c	c	c	c	c	c	c	c
	Luxembourg	-4	(3.3)	c	c	**43**	(2.7)	**-43**	(2.7)
	Mexico	**-48**	(4.0)	**-14**	(3.2)	**-49**	(7.9)	-23	(24.5)
	Netherlands	**-16**	(5.8)	-13	(13.7)	-12	(15.3)	**-54**	(17.2)
	New Zealand	-4	(4.4)	14	(14.6)	22	(14.2)	27	(14.8)
	Norway	**-27**	(5.8)	-4	(6.0)	-7	(7.1)	-3	(10.0)
	Poland	c	c	-7	(19.7)	c	c	c	c
	Portugal	**-25**	(8.6)	0	(6.8)	**-26**	(8.4)	**-27**	(13.1)
	Slovak Republic	-10	(19.3)	16	(13.5)	c	c	c	c
	Slovenia	**-13**	(4.9)	**7**	(3.3)	9	(4.9)	**-42**	(5.2)
	Spain	**-33**	(3.7)	**7**	(3.8)	-3	(5.9)	-7	(6.8)
	Sweden	**-40**	(4.7)	-5	(5.2)	4	(6.2)	-4	(6.8)
	Switzerland	**-30**	(2.6)	27	(13.8)	22	(13.0)	-17	(11.4)
	Turkey	-24	(15.2)	18	(15.9)	c	c	c	c
	United Kingdom	-7	(5.9)	5	(5.6)	14	(9.6)	2	(7.0)
	United States	**19**	(4.5)	12	(7.7)	**19**	(7.3)	-1	(9.0)
	OECD average	**-16**	(1.3)	**5**	(1.7)	-1	(1.7)	**-19**	(2.2)
Partners	Albania	c	c	c	c	c	c	c	c
	Argentina	-1	(6.1)	-5	(6.6)	**-27**	(8.9)	**-36**	(11.0)
	Brazil	**-40**	(8.2)	-9	(7.1)	**-43**	(8.8)	c	c
	Bulgaria	c	c	**-24**	(8.3)	c	c	c	c
	Colombia	**-43**	(11.5)	**-26**	(7.6)	c	c	c	c
	Costa Rica	-6	(4.8)	5	(5.9)	-5	(5.4)	**-34**	(6.1)
	Croatia	-3	(4.0)	15	(13.3)	1	(12.3)	-14	(13.6)
	Cyprus*	-9	(5.3)	6	(3.6)	-4	(4.3)	-6	(6.2)
	Hong Kong-China	**14**	(3.6)	19	(15.6)	21	(12.1)	-21	(12.1)
	Indonesia	c	c	15	(12.8)	c	c	c	c
	Jordan	**10**	(3.3)	10	(6.6)	12	(8.0)	19	(10.7)
	Kazakhstan	-1	(3.8)	-5	(10.2)	-10	(9.4)	-6	(12.8)
	Latvia	-8	(7.7)	9	(6.1)	-1	(8.2)	-10	(6.1)
	Liechtenstein	-13	(9.4)	c	c	c	c	c	c
	Lithuania	3	(10.5)	0	(6.9)	**-28**	(10.6)	c	c
	Macao-China	**22**	(2.8)	c	c	c	c	c	c
	Malaysia	5	(10.3)	-5	(6.0)	-15	(7.9)	c	c
	Montenegro	**16**	(6.2)	20	(19.0)	22	(19.1)	c	c
	Peru	**-74**	(18.2)	-1	(8.8)	c	c	c	c
	Qatar	**80**	(1.9)	**-14**	(4.1)	**-27**	(2.3)	**27**	(2.3)
	Romania	c	c	12	(14.7)	c	c	c	c
	Russian Federation	**-16**	(4.3)	3	(8.1)	-7	(7.4)	-7	(11.1)
	Serbia	**8**	(3.9)	12	(10.0)	**30**	(10.4)	6	(16.7)
	Shanghai-China	**-55**	(15.6)	**-51**	(9.6)	c	c	c	c
	Singapore	-4	(4.4)	**23**	(10.9)	**34**	(10.5)	**80**	(13.3)
	Chinese Taipei	18	(17.8)	-22	(12.5)	c	c	c	c
	Thailand	-14	(29.5)	24	(19.2)	c	c	c	c
	Tunisia	c	c	4	(13.9)	c	c	c	c
	United Arab Emirates	**62**	(3.2)	10	(10.1)	2	(9.0)	7	(8.6)
	Uruguay	c	c	13	(9.8)	c	c	c	c
	Viet Nam	c	c	c	c	c	c	c	c

Notes: This table was calculated considering only students with data on the PISA *index of economic, social and cultural status*. Values that are statistically significant are indicated in bold.

The OECD average is computed considering also the value for countries for which data have been withdrawn at the request of the country concerned.

1. The PISA *index of economic, social and cultural status* (ESCS).

*See note at the beginning of this Annex.

Source: OECD, PISA 2012 Database.

Underlying data for the tables can be found at www.oecd.org/edu/school/Immigrant-Students-Tables.xlsx.

[Part 4/4]

Table 4.1 Concentration of immigrant students in school
Results based on students' self-reports

		Estimated coefficients in a model with mathematics performance as the dependent variable							
		After adjusting for student and school ESCS[1]							
		Immigrant student		Low-concentration schools vs. those without immigrant students		Medium-concentration schools vs. those without immigrant students		High-concentration schools vs. those without immigrant students	
		Score dif.	S.E.	Score dif.	S.E.	Score dif.	S.E.	Score dif.	S.E.
OECD	Australia	**20**	(2.9)	0	(4.6)	-3	(4.2)	**14**	(4.0)
	Austria	**-33**	(3.9)	5	(10.7)	0	(11.2)	4	(9.6)
	Belgium	**-31**	(3.9)	**-23**	(6.4)	**-43**	(6.7)	**-30**	(6.5)
	Canada	2	(3.3)	-2	(5.2)	**-14**	(6.0)	-4	(4.9)
	Chile	-4	(9.4)	**-15**	(5.6)	c	c	c	c
	Czech Republic	**-19**	(7.9)	-3	(8.0)	**-21**	(9.0)	c	c
	Denmark	**-40**	(3.2)	2	(3.8)	8	(4.4)	7	(5.7)
	Estonia	**-14**	(5.4)	**-10**	(3.8)	**-31**	(6.9)	**-25**	(5.9)
	Finland	**-61**	(4.0)	1	(3.7)	-6	(4.2)	-25	(15.8)
	France	w	w	w	w	w	w	w	w
	Germany	**-23**	(3.9)	10	(9.2)	10	(8.2)	1	(9.9)
	Greece	-7	(5.1)	-6	(6.7)	**-20**	(8.1)	**-40**	(14.8)
	Hungary	11	(9.6)	3	(7.2)	c	c	c	c
	Iceland	**-29**	(9.0)	1	(3.2)	3	(7.2)	c	c
	Ireland	3	(4.3)	-1	(5.1)	-4	(5.4)	-16	(9.0)
	Israel	-5	(3.5)	**18**	(8.9)	**34**	(9.0)	**51**	(7.6)
	Italy	**-25**	(2.5)	**18**	(4.3)	**14**	(5.1)	-2	(5.2)
	Japan	c	c	-4	(9.2)	c	c	c	c
	Korea	c	c	c	c	c	c	c	c
	Luxembourg	**-14**	(3.1)	c	c	**7**	(2.8)	-12	(12.0)
	Mexico	**-50**	(3.7)	**-13**	(2.9)	**-34**	(9.0)	**-30**	(14.9)
	Netherlands	**-30**	(5.2)	-13	(9.3)	-8	(14.5)	0	(12.8)
	New Zealand	-2	(4.0)	6	(15.2)	2	(15.4)	9	(14.3)
	Norway	**-30**	(5.7)	-3	(5.8)	-6	(6.9)	9	(9.9)
	Poland	c	c	-22	(18.4)	c	c	c	c
	Portugal	**-25**	(8.1)	-7	(7.0)	**-32**	(7.1)	**-26**	(11.3)
	Slovak Republic	-8	(17.9)	3	(10.7)	c	c	c	c
	Slovenia	**-26**	(4.9)	1	(3.2)	1	(4.0)	8	(6.5)
	Spain	**-34**	(3.7)	**7**	(3.4)	1	(5.6)	1	(6.7)
	Sweden	**-43**	(4.6)	-5	(5.1)	5	(5.9)	6	(6.3)
	Switzerland	**-36**	(2.7)	16	(14.9)	10	(12.9)	-14	(11.8)
	Turkey	-19	(13.1)	8	(11.8)	c	c	c	c
	United Kingdom	-9	(5.1)	2	(5.4)	**16**	(6.3)	6	(6.4)
	United States	**18**	(4.6)	4	(6.8)	**19**	(6.7)	11	(8.5)
	OECD average	**-19**	(1.2)	-1	(1.4)	**-4**	(1.5)	**-5**	(2.0)
Partners	Albania	c	c	c	c	c	c	c	c
	Argentina	-8	(6.3)	-2	(5.5)	-9	(9.9)	-8	(12.1)
	Brazil	**-39**	(8.4)	**-11**	(5.1)	**-53**	(10.9)	c	c
	Bulgaria	c	c	**-19**	(7.6)	c	c	c	c
	Colombia	**-40**	(11.1)	**-19**	(6.7)	c	c	c	c
	Costa Rica	**-13**	(4.6)	4	(5.6)	-1	(5.4)	**-21**	(9.3)
	Croatia	**-8**	(3.8)	5	(10.6)	-2	(9.6)	-10	(12.3)
	Cyprus*	**-17**	(4.8)	-4	(3.6)	-7	(4.1)	-6	(5.8)
	Hong Kong-China	**8**	(3.4)	**-62**	(17.2)	-19	(12.2)	**62**	(17.2)
	Indonesia	c	c	9	(12.8)	c	c	c	c
	Jordan	**10**	(3.0)	4	(7.6)	0	(7.4)	-2	(11.7)
	Kazakhstan	0	(3.6)	-14	(10.7)	-19	(10.3)	-5	(13.1)
	Latvia	-7	(7.6)	3	(5.8)	-3	(7.6)	-12	(8.1)
	Liechtenstein	-14	(9.6)	c	c	c	c	c	c
	Lithuania	3	(10.1)	-6	(6.7)	**-25**	(8.2)	c	c
	Macao-China	**26**	(2.7)	c	c	c	c	c	c
	Malaysia	-2	(9.1)	-6	(5.8)	-6	(9.5)	c	c
	Montenegro	**14**	(5.5)	-27	(16.1)	**-34**	(16.2)	c	c
	Peru	**-71**	(17.0)	-4	(6.2)	c	c	c	c
	Qatar	**74**	(1.9)	**-24**	(3.8)	**-30**	(2.3)	**24**	(3.8)
	Romania	c	c	-5	(8.5)	c	c	c	c
	Russian Federation	**-16**	(4.2)	-14	(9.2)	**-20**	(7.8)	-13	(12.3)
	Serbia	**7**	(3.7)	9	(7.2)	12	(7.2)	24	(13.8)
	Shanghai-China	**-57**	(14.3)	**-27**	(8.3)	c	c	c	c
	Singapore	-4	(4.8)	**25**	(9.8)	**33**	(9.3)	**41**	(11.7)
	Chinese Taipei	4	(16.6)	-17	(9.5)	c	c	c	c
	Thailand	-28	(26.1)	26	(19.3)	c	c	c	c
	Tunisia	c	c	1	(9.6)	c	c	c	c
	United Arab Emirates	**53**	(3.4)	2	(10.8)	-6	(9.5)	1	(8.7)
	Uruguay	c	c	-3	(6.6)	c	c	c	c
	Viet Nam	c	c	c	c	c	c	c	c

Notes: This table was calculated considering only students with data on the PISA *index of economic, social and cultural status*. Values that are statistically significant are indicated in bold.

The OECD average is computed considering also the value for countries for which data have been withdrawn at the request of the country concerned.

1. The PISA *index of economic, social and cultural status* (ESCS).

*See note at the beginning of this Annex.

Source: OECD, PISA 2012 Database.

Underlying data for the tables can be found at www.oecd.org/edu/school/Immigrant-Students-Tables.xlsx.

[Part 1/1]

Table 4.2 **Percentage of immigrant students who do not speak the language of assessment at home**

		Second-generation immigrants		First-generation immigrants	
		%	S.E.	%	S.E.
OECD	Australia	31.9	(1.8)	34.0	(1.9)
	Austria	73.8	(2.4)	71.3	(3.2)
	Belgium	50.2	(2.8)	52.1	(4.7)
	Canada	37.9	(1.9)	62.3	(1.6)
	Chile	c	c	5.0	(2.9)
	Czech Republic	49.4	(7.7)	85.2	(4.5)
	Denmark	45.7	(2.2)	66.1	(3.1)
	Finland	71.7	(3.2)	88.8	(1.8)
	France	31.5	(2.7)	58.5	(3.5)
	Germany	35.3	(2.5)	70.6	(5.9)
	Greece	15.7	(2.3)	56.8	(3.5)
	Iceland	c	c	87.9	(3.1)
	Ireland	7.2	(3.1)	54.9	(3.2)
	Israel	29.6	(3.2)	81.5	(2.8)
	Italy	35.4	(3.0)	72.3	(2.0)
	Luxembourg	77.9	(1.2)	66.8	(1.6)
	Mexico	9.9	(3.3)	21.8	(4.4)
	Netherlands	45.0	(3.2)	66.2	(5.1)
	New Zealand	40.5	(2.9)	55.3	(2.4)
	Norway	55.2	(3.7)	77.0	(2.7)
	Portugal	6.9	(2.3)	46.4	(5.3)
	Slovenia	50.2	(3.9)	85.2	(4.0)
	Spain	51.4	(4.8)	48.3	(2.4)
	Sweden	56.4	(2.5)	83.1	(2.6)
	Switzerland	52.1	(1.8)	58.0	(2.7)
	United Kingdom	23.7	(2.6)	64.9	(3.8)
	United States	51.1	(2.8)	71.6	(3.6)
	OECD average (25)	41.4	(0.6)	64.0	(0.7)
Partners	Argentina	14.2	(4.2)	18.3	(4.2)
	Brazil	12.3	(5.9)	29.4	(10.4)
	Costa Rica	3.6	(2.0)	5.0	(2.3)
	Croatia	1.1	(0.4)	4.5	(1.7)
	Hong Kong-China	5.0	(1.0)	19.3	(1.7)
	Jordan	4.8	(0.7)	11.3	(3.1)
	Kazakhstan	10.0	(1.9)	6.9	(2.2)
	Liechtenstein	32.2	(6.6)	35.8	(7.9)
	Macao-China	11.0	(0.6)	9.9	(1.0)
	Montenegro	1.6	(1.1)	4.8	(1.7)
	Qatar	36.7	(1.1)	56.4	(0.8)
	Russian Federation	13.2	(3.5)	16.0	(3.2)
	Serbia	9.0	(3.7)	7.3	(3.7)
	Shanghai-China	c	c	42.5	(9.8)
	Singapore	67.3	(2.8)	77.1	(1.9)
	United Arab Emirates	35.8	(1.6)	50.8	(1.7)

Note: OECD average (25) includes only countries with valid data on first- and second-generation immigrant students.
Source: OECD, PISA 2012 Database.
Underlying data for the tables can be found at www.oecd.org/edu/school/Immigrant-Students-Tables.xlsx.

[Part 1/1]

Table 4.3 **Reduction in performance gap after accounting for students' characteristics**

		Difference in mathematics performance between non-immigrant and immigrant students				Difference in reading performance between non-immigrant and immigrant students			
		Before accounting for students' socio-economic status		After accounting for students' socio-economic status		Before accounting for differences in language spoken at home		After accounting for differences in language spoken at home	
		Score dif.	S.E.	Score dif.	S.E.	Score dif.	S.E.	Score dif.	S.E.
OECD	Australia	**-26**	(3.6)	**-29**	(3.4)	**-19**	(3.0)	**-26**	(3.0)
	Austria	**59**	(5.2)	**33**	(4.9)	**51**	(5.8)	**17**	(8.5)
	Belgium	**75**	(5.0)	**52**	(3.9)	**66**	(5.8)	**53**	(5.7)
	Canada	2	(4.4)	-2	(3.9)	-3	(4.2)	**-10**	(4.8)
	Chile	1	(13.3)	12	(11.1)	-9	(14.2)	-8	(14.6)
	Czech Republic	**26**	(11.8)	20	(11.4)	20	(10.4)	4	(22.6)
	Denmark	**66**	(3.6)	**40**	(3.2)	**59**	(3.5)	**41**	(4.6)
	Estonia	**30**	(5.8)	**30**	(5.2)	**35**	(5.2)	**32**	(5.4)
	Finland	**85**	(5.0)	**65**	(4.6)	**93**	(5.1)	**72**	(6.6)
	France	**67**	(6.9)	**37**	(6.4)	**67**	(8.5)	**51**	(9.0)
	Germany	**54**	(6.0)	**25**	(5.6)	**49**	(5.7)	**29**	(6.7)
	Greece	**51**	(6.4)	**28**	(6.4)	**53**	(8.0)	**30**	(9.0)
	Hungary	**-31**	(13.3)	-13	(13.2)	-16	(14.0)	-21	(14.6)
	Iceland	**52**	(8.6)	**31**	(8.4)	**80**	(10.3)	30	(16.8)
	Ireland	2	(4.8)	4	(4.5)	**11**	(4.9)	-3	(6.6)
	Israel	-7	(5.7)	**-16**	(4.8)	-8	(6.2)	**-15**	(6.5)
	Italy	**48**	(3.5)	**32**	(3.3)	**65**	(4.2)	**39**	(4.8)
	Japan	c	c	c	c	c	c	c	c
	Korea	c	c	c	c	c	c	c	c
	Luxembourg	**40**	(3.3)	**10**	(3.3)	**47**	(3.0)	**54**	(3.1)
	Mexico	**73**	(5.5)	**66**	(4.3)	**76**	(6.0)	**69**	(6.2)
	Netherlands	**57**	(7.1)	**35**	(7.2)	**56**	(7.8)	**33**	(9.0)
	New Zealand	0	(5.4)	-2	(4.4)	**13**	(5.7)	**-14**	(5.4)
	Norway	**46**	(6.6)	**29**	(6.6)	**50**	(6.5)	**25**	(9.0)
	Poland	c	c	c	c	c	c	c	c
	Portugal	**44**	(7.2)	**39**	(7.8)	**38**	(7.8)	**34**	(7.7)
	Slovak Republic	-5	(21.1)	-6	(18.8)	-7	(20.3)	-34	(28.5)
	Slovenia	**51**	(5.0)	**26**	(4.6)	**46**	(4.8)	**15**	(6.4)
	Spain	**52**	(4.3)	**36**	(4.3)	**48**	(4.4)	**44**	(4.5)
	Sweden	**58**	(5.1)	**40**	(4.9)	**63**	(5.8)	**41**	(8.9)
	Switzerland	**63**	(3.2)	**42**	(3.0)	**55**	(3.3)	**38**	(3.9)
	Turkey	-3	(31.1)	5	(27.3)	12	(26.9)	6	(26.2)
	United Kingdom	9	(7.9)	6	(6.2)	11	(7.5)	4	(7.1)
	United States	**13**	(5.9)	**-15**	(4.9)	7	(5.2)	-10	(6.3)
	OECD average (31)	**34**	(1.7)	**21**	(1.5)	**36**	(1.6)	**20**	(2.0)
Partners	Albania	c	c	m	m	c	c	c	c
	Argentina	**37**	(6.7)	**17**	(6.3)	**43**	(11.0)	**36**	(11.2)
	Brazil	**56**	(11.0)	**63**	(11.7)	**59**	(11.4)	**59**	(11.7)
	Bulgaria	c	c	c	c	c	c	c	c
	Colombia	**69**	(13.0)	**67**	(13.0)	**92**	(21.7)	**90**	(22.6)
	Costa Rica	**29**	(9.6)	**14**	(6.7)	**25**	(9.2)	**24**	(9.5)
	Croatia	**19**	(5.2)	9	(4.8)	**19**	(6.4)	**17**	(6.5)
	Hong Kong-China	8	(4.4)	**-11**	(3.8)	0	(4.3)	-3	(4.1)
	Indonesia	c	c	c	c	c	c	c	c
	Jordan	**-22**	(4.4)	**-15**	(3.9)	**-24**	(4.5)	**-25**	(4.4)
	Kazakhstan	7	(5.8)	2	(5.3)	**15**	(5.4)	**14**	(5.3)
	Latvia	6	(7.8)	10	(7.7)	2	(8.5)	-2	(8.0)
	Liechtenstein	**50**	(11.5)	**40**	(11.9)	**53**	(12.1)	**35**	(15.5)
	Lithuania	1	(9.8)	2	(9.3)	17	(12.5)	-1	(12.3)
	Macao-China	**-16**	(2.8)	**-22**	(2.8)	**-22**	(2.2)	**-19**	(2.3)
	Malaysia	**21**	(8.9)	2	(9.9)	-2	(11.8)	-1	(11.6)
	Montenegro	**-21**	(6.5)	**-16**	(6.0)	-3	(7.1)	-3	(6.9)
	Peru	**90**	(22.5)	**86**	(20.8)	c	c	c	c
	Qatar	**-89**	(1.7)	**-88**	(1.6)	**-88**	(1.8)	**-79**	(2.0)
	Romania	c	c	c	c	c	c	c	c
	Russian Federation	**22**	(4.5)	**19**	(4.4)	**29**	(4.7)	**26**	(4.3)
	Serbia	**-15**	(6.2)	**-14**	(5.6)	**-24**	(6.8)	**-25**	(6.9)
	Shanghai-China	**126**	(14.6)	**98**	(14.7)	**90**	(13.8)	**63**	(16.0)
	Singapore	**-26**	(4.3)	-7	(4.6)	**-18**	(4.1)	**-28**	(4.5)
	Chinese Taipei	32	(23.1)	1	(20.1)	c	c	c	c
	Thailand	17	(56.4)	-26	(53.6)	50	(36.4)	44	(36.4)
	Tunisia	c	c	c	c	c	c	c	c
	United Arab Emirates	**-66**	(3.1)	**-63**	(3.1)	**-63**	(3.1)	**-61**	(3.3)
	Uruguay	c	c	c	c	c	c	c	c
	Viet Nam	c	c	c	c	c	c	c	c

Notes: Values that are statistically significant are indicated in bold.
OECD average (31) includes only countries with valid data on immigrant students.
Source: OECD, PISA 2012 Database.
Underlying data for the tables can be found at www.oecd.org/edu/school/Immigrant-Students-Tables.xlsx.

[Part 1/1]

Table 4.4 **Attendance at pre-primary education and immigrant background**

		Mathematics performance of immigrant students						Reading performance of immigrant students						Increased likelihood of first-generation immigrant students having attended pre-primary education compared to non-immigrant students			
		Had not attended pre-primary education		Had attended pre-primary education		Difference between students who had attended and those who had not attended pre-primary education		Had not attended pre-primary education		Had attended pre-primary education		Difference between students who had attended and those who had not attended pre-primary education		Before accounting for students' socio-economic status		After accounting for students' socio-economic status	
		Mean score	S.E.	Mean score	S.E.	Score dif.	S.E.	Mean score	S.E.	Mean score	S.E.	Score dif.	S.E.	Odd-ratios	S.E.	Odd-ratios	S.E.
OECD	**Australia**	496	(15.4)	540	(4.9)	**44**	(15.2)	487	(15.7)	541	(4.0)	**54**	(15.3)	0.77	(0.11)	0.80	(0.12)
	Austria	c	c	c	c	c	c	c	c	c	c	c	c	0.74	(0.30)	1.45	(0.50)
	Belgium	c	c	c	c	c	c	c	c	c	c	c	c	0.96	(0.31)	1.25	(0.42)
	Canada	490	(9.4)	517	(4.5)	**27**	(9.5)	487	(8.8)	532	(4.2)	**45**	(9.8)	1.74	(0.21)	1.94	(0.23)
	Czech Republic	c	c	c	c	c	c	c	c	c	c	c	c	0.16	(0.09)	0.16	(0.09)
	Denmark	c	c	c	c	c	c	c	c	c	c	c	c	0.31	(0.10)	0.31	(0.11)
	Estonia	c	c	c	c	c	c	c	c	c	c	c	c	1.64	(0.57)	1.67	(0.59)
	Finland	c	c	c	c	c	c	c	c	c	c	c	c	0.69	(0.25)	0.97	(0.37)
	France	c	c	c	c	c	c	c	c	c	c	c	c	0.41	(0.18)	0.58	(0.30)
	Germany	c	c	c	c	c	c	c	c	c	c	c	c	0.42	(0.10)	0.50	(0.13)
	Greece	405	(22.6)	417	(5.7)	13	(22.4)	417	(23.3)	450	(7.2)	33	(20.9)	0.29	(0.08)	0.41	(0.11)
	Iceland	c	c	c	c	c	c	c	c	c	c	c	c	0.68	(1.02)	1.00	(1.52)
	Ireland	507	(19.3)	506	(8.6)	-1	(19.7)	513	(21.8)	524	(9.7)	11	(22.2)	0.56	(0.11)	0.51	(0.11)
	Israel	c	c	c	c	c	c	c	c	c	c	c	c	1.39	(0.57)	1.59	(0.68)
	Italy	391	(25.8)	461	(4.7)	**70**	(25.3)	369	(21.7)	457	(5.8)	**88**	(21.5)	0.27	(0.05)	0.30	(0.06)
	Luxembourg	444	(17.9)	471	(2.4)	27	(17.9)	425	(19.0)	465	(2.7)	**40**	(19.6)	0.70	(0.19)	0.87	(0.28)
	Mexico	307	(11.2)	351	(8.2)	**44**	(14.4)	326	(13.1)	361	(8.9)	**35**	(15.7)	0.43	(0.09)	0.49	(0.11)
	Netherlands	c	c	c	c	c	c	c	c	c	c	c	c	0.38	(0.17)	0.46	(0.18)
	New Zealand	432	(13.8)	504	(7.0)	**72**	(14.0)	423	(18.6)	513	(7.1)	**90**	(17.8)	0.43	(0.07)	0.48	(0.09)
	Norway	c	c	c	c	c	c	c	c	c	c	c	c	1.56	(0.44)	2.22	(0.66)
	Portugal	403	(14.7)	452	(11.2)	**49**	(18.0)	416	(15.7)	465	(13.2)	**49**	(17.1)	0.85	(0.18)	0.88	(0.19)
	Slovenia	448	(12.2)	464	(5.7)	16	(14.3)	433	(14.5)	452	(5.4)	19	(16.7)	1.36	(0.36)	1.91	(0.55)
	Spain	426	(24.7)	459	(6.1)	33	(25.1)	401	(22.5)	454	(6.5)	**52**	(22.0)	0.55	(0.20)	0.60	(0.21)
	Sweden	389	(21.4)	445	(5.6)	**56**	(21.2)	389	(25.6)	456	(6.2)	**67**	(25.1)	0.82	(0.17)	0.97	(0.22)
	Switzerland	422	(34.9)	489	(3.6)	67	(35.2)	415	(33.4)	473	(3.8)	57	(33.8)	0.45	(0.13)	0.49	(0.15)
	Turkey	c	c	c	c	c	c	c	c	c	c	c	c	3.10	(1.41)	2.67	(1.34)
	United Kingdom	c	c	c	c	c	c	c	c	c	c	c	c	0.75	(0.30)	0.80	(0.33)
	United States	c	c	c	c	c	c	c	c	c	c	c	c	0.72	(0.31)	0.89	(0.34)
	OECD average[1]	428	(5.5)	467	(1.8)	**40**	(5.7)	423	(5.7)	473	(2.0)	**49**	(5.7)	0.83	(0.08)	0.97	(0.09)
Partners	**Argentina**	c	c	c	c	c	c	c	c	c	c	c	c	0.29	(0.08)	0.39	(0.12)
	Brazil	333	(13.6)	332	(16.4)	-1	(21.0)	356	(24.3)	350	(18.6)	-6	(31.7)	0.46	(0.25)	0.38	(0.24)
	Costa Rica	352	(16.6)	382	(11.1)	**30**	(12.8)	402	(11.9)	414	(11.8)	12	(13.4)	0.55	(0.09)	0.75	(0.13)
	Croatia	455	(7.9)	459	(6.0)	4	(9.4)	464	(9.1)	475	(6.3)	11	(9.1)	0.75	(0.07)	0.91	(0.10)
	Hong Kong-China	c	c	c	c	c	c	c	c	c	c	c	c	1.24	(0.63)	1.53	(0.82)
	Jordan	386	(7.2)	417	(5.5)	**30**	(8.5)	404	(8.3)	438	(5.5)	**34**	(8.9)	1.16	(0.14)	1.04	(0.13)
	Kazakhstan	430	(9.7)	455	(8.2)	**24**	(11.5)	380	(8.0)	416	(7.5)	**36**	(9.8)	0.89	(0.13)	0.90	(0.12)
	Latvia	c	c	c	c	c	c	c	c	c	c	c	c	0.80	(0.18)	0.75	(0.17)
	Lithuania	c	c	c	c	c	c	c	c	c	c	c	c	1.87	(0.46)	1.96	(0.42)
	Macao-China	499	(14.1)	546	(1.7)	**48**	(14.2)	438	(13.6)	519	(1.4)	**81**	(13.3)	1.41	(0.29)	1.29	(0.27)
	Malaysia	396	(15.6)	408	(11.7)	11	(20.0)	411	(19.1)	406	(14.4)	-5	(22.7)	0.53	(0.16)	0.67	(0.20)
	Montenegro	418	(12.9)	440	(8.4)	23	(14.8)	417	(11.7)	440	(9.7)	23	(14.9)	1.69	(0.34)	1.45	(0.31)
	Qatar	370	(2.9)	419	(2.1)	**49**	(3.8)	384	(3.2)	432	(2.4)	**48**	(4.1)	1.09	(0.05)	1.15	(0.06)
	Russian Federation	441	(10.3)	473	(4.5)	**32**	(10.1)	417	(10.1)	459	(5.5)	**42**	(10.4)	0.77	(0.11)	0.80	(0.12)
	Serbia	457	(14.9)	470	(7.8)	13	(16.3)	456	(17.9)	476	(7.9)	20	(19.4)	1.45	(0.26)	1.46	(0.27)
	Singapore	c	c	c	c	c	c	c	c	c	c	c	c	0.78	(0.29)	0.62	(0.23)
	Thailand	c	c	c	c	c	c	c	c	c	c	c	c	0.12	(0.10)	0.18	(0.17)
	United Arab Emirates	417	(4.3)	470	(2.9)	**53**	(4.7)	432	(4.4)	479	(3.1)	**47**	(4.8)	0.86	(0.07)	0.83	(0.07)

Note: Values that are statistically significant are indicated in bold.

1. OECD average includes only countries with valid data on immigrant students.

Source: OECD, PISA 2012 Database.

Underlying data for the tables can be found at www.oecd.org/edu/school/Immigrant-Students-Tables.xlsx.

[Part 1/1]

Table 5.1 **Students' expectations to work as professionals and managers, by immigrant background**
PISA 2006

		Percentage of students who expect to work in professional and managerial occupations									
		Non-immigrants		Immigrants		Gap between immigrant and non-immigrant students		Gap between immigrant and non-immigrant students, after accounting for socio-economic status		Gap between immigrant and non-immigrant students, after accounting for socio-economic status and performance	
		%	S.E.	%	S.E.	% dif.	S.E.	% dif.	S.E.	% dif.	S.E.
OECD	Australia	50.7	(0.8)	67.6	(1.3)	**16.9**	(1.4)	**17.1**	(1.4)	**14.8**	(1.4)
	Austria	35.4	(1.6)	42.0	(3.1)	**6.6**	(3.3)	**19.2**	(3.0)	**18.4**	(3.3)
	Belgium	57.8	(1.1)	57.2	(2.8)	-0.6	(2.8)	**8.7**	(3.1)	**15.7**	(2.6)
	Canada	55.5	(0.7)	72.8	(1.5)	**17.3**	(1.6)	**17.5**	(1.6)	**18.0**	(1.6)
	Czech Republic	45.4	(1.5)	40.2	(7.2)	-5.2	(7.4)	1.2	(6.0)	4.2	(6.8)
	Denmark	41.0	(1.1)	48.2	(3.6)	**7.2**	(3.5)	**20.3**	(3.6)	**22.4**	(3.1)
	Estonia	53.4	(1.1)	48.8	(2.7)	-4.6	(3.0)	-3.5	(2.9)	0.2	(2.8)
	Finland	41.2	(1.0)	55.8	(7.1)	**14.6**	(7.0)	**22.0**	(7.9)	**29.3**	(7.8)
	France	41.6	(1.5)	51.8	(3.3)	**10.2**	(3.3)	**20.1**	(3.2)	**17.8**	(2.9)
	Germany	33.9	(1.2)	30.8	(2.5)	-3.0	(2.4)	**9.1**	(2.5)	**11.5**	(2.5)
	Greece	60.7	(1.2)	55.1	(3.9)	-5.6	(4.1)	0.9	(3.5)	1.2	(3.5)
	Hungary	46.1	(1.5)	36.9	(6.6)	-9.2	(6.4)	-7.9	(5.8)	-9.7	(6.4)
	Iceland	61.1	(0.9)	50.9	(7.8)	-10.2	(7.8)	-4.1	(8.0)	-0.9	(7.6)
	Ireland	59.0	(1.2)	73.1	(3.4)	**14.2**	(3.3)	**12.4**	(3.5)	**16.3**	(3.6)
	Italy	59.9	(0.8)	50.2	(3.3)	**-9.6**	(3.2)	-4.2	(3.2)	-4.5	(2.9)
	Israel	73.1	(1.4)	75.0	(2.3)	1.8	(2.2)	2.4	(2.2)	1.6	(2.2)
	Luxembourg	62.6	(0.9)	55.1	(1.4)	**-7.6**	(1.7)	1.7	(1.9)	0.2	(1.7)
	Mexico	80.6	(0.6)	80.5	(5.3)	0.0	(5.5)	1.4	(5.6)	1.5	(5.7)
	Netherlands	44.8	(1.1)	52.4	(4.3)	7.7	(4.4)	**19.0**	(3.6)	**21.8**	(3.1)
	New Zealand	51.6	(0.9)	66.6	(1.5)	**15.0**	(1.7)	**14.5**	(1.8)	**14.8**	(1.8)
	Norway	50.9	(1.1)	62.3	(3.3)	**11.4**	(3.4)	**20.3**	(3.5)	**19.8**	(3.6)
	Portugal	60.0	(1.2)	64.5	(4.6)	4.5	(4.6)	3.3	(4.9)	**12.7**	(5.1)
	Slovenia	58.1	(0.9)	49.3	(2.7)	**-8.7**	(3.0)	0.7	(2.8)	-0.9	(2.6)
	Spain	61.2	(0.9)	66.9	(2.9)	5.7	(3.1)	**8.6**	(3.1)	**14.1**	(3.0)
	Sweden	38.0	(0.9)	51.7	(2.5)	**13.7**	(2.7)	**18.1**	(2.8)	**20.6**	(3.1)
	Switzerland	32.4	(0.9)	37.5	(1.5)	**5.0**	(1.7)	**12.9**	(1.6)	**16.3**	(1.4)
	Turkey	82.5	(1.1)	79.3	(5.6)	-3.1	(5.7)	-4.6	(5.7)	-5.7	(5.6)
	United Kingdom	49.9	(0.8)	73.0	(2.4)	**23.1**	(2.6)	**25.3**	(2.7)	**26.5**	(2.6)
	United States	62.6	(1.0)	70.9	(2.1)	**8.4**	(2.1)	**13.2**	(2.1)	**11.4**	(2.1)
	OECD average (29)	53.5	(0.2)	57.5	(0.7)	**4.0**	(0.7)	**9.2**	(0.7)	**10.7**	(0.7)
Partners	Azerbaijan	82.6	(1.0)	85.3	(3.3)	2.7	(3.3)	1.8	(3.2)	2.7	(3.2)
	Argentina	69.1	(1.5)	71.7	(4.8)	2.6	(4.6)	6.3	(4.5)	4.4	(4.9)
	Brazil	61.9	(0.9)	59.1	(5.6)	-2.8	(5.7)	-2.8	(5.7)	-3.6	(5.8)
	Croatia	41.0	(1.3)	35.5	(2.5)	**-5.5**	(2.6)	0.5	(2.5)	-2.4	(2.4)
	Hong Kong-China	55.6	(1.2)	54.5	(1.4)	-1.1	(1.6)	**4.2**	(1.6)	0.1	(1.6)
	Jordan	84.0	(0.8)	87.5	(1.4)	**3.5**	(1.5)	2.0	(1.5)	1.5	(1.5)
	Kyrgyzstan	71.1	(1.1)	63.6	(5.0)	-7.5	(5.1)	-9.8	(5.1)	**-12.5**	(5.1)
	Latvia	56.9	(1.1)	58.4	(2.8)	1.5	(2.7)	-0.4	(2.5)	1.8	(2.4)
	Liechtenstein	31.2	(3.5)	31.7	(4.5)	0.5	(6.0)	5.6	(5.5)	7.9	(5.6)
	Lithuania	62.7	(1.1)	76.6	(5.0)	**13.9**	(4.9)	**13.5**	(5.2)	**10.9**	(5.5)
	Macao-China	64.2	(1.6)	64.3	(1.1)	0.1	(1.9)	2.3	(2.0)	-0.6	(1.9)
	Montenegro	53.7	(1.0)	55.0	(4.4)	1.3	(4.4)	0.2	(4.5)	0.3	(4.5)
	Russian Federation	65.5	(1.4)	61.1	(3.0)	-4.4	(3.2)	-3.8	(3.2)	-2.2	(3.3)
	Serbia	52.1	(1.7)	49.2	(3.5)	-2.9	(3.5)	-1.6	(3.2)	-4.8	(2.9)
	Chinese Taipei	64.3	(0.9)	64.8	(11.3)	0.5	(11.2)	1.7	(10.7)	2.7	(9.9)

Notes: Values that are statistically significant are indicated in bold.
OECD average (29) includes only countries with valid data for immigrant students.
Source: OECD, PISA 2012 Database.
Underlying data for the tables can be found at www.oecd.org/edu/school/Immigrant-Students-Tables.xlsx.

[Part 1/1]

Table 5.2 **Openness to problem solving, by immigrant background**

		Percentage of students who reported that they like solving complex problems							
		Non-immigrants		Second-generation immigrants		First-generation immigrants		Difference between first-generation and non-immigrant students	
		%	S.E.	%	S.E.	%	S.E.	% dif.	S.E.
OECD	Australia	29.4	(0.6)	33.6	(1.6)	36.8	(2.0)	**7.4**	(2.0)
	Austria	27.1	(0.9)	24.7	(2.4)	21.4	(3.2)	-5.7	(3.4)
	Belgium	23.4	(0.8)	24.8	(2.9)	27.0	(2.7)	3.6	(2.7)
	Canada	35.7	(0.7)	35.2	(1.5)	47.7	(2.3)	**12.0**	(2.5)
	Chile	37.6	(0.9)	c	c	54.5	(9.1)	16.9	(9.2)
	Czech Republic	27.8	(0.9)	29.3	(8.1)	33.4	(8.2)	5.7	(8.3)
	Denmark	33.4	(1.0)	36.5	(2.8)	41.1	(3.7)	**7.7**	(3.8)
	Finland	33.5	(0.8)	32.2	(3.4)	35.5	(4.1)	1.9	(3.9)
	France	25.3	(1.0)	22.8	(2.9)	33.3	(4.3)	8.0	(4.4)
	Germany	32.2	(1.1)	29.7	(2.5)	35.4	(5.8)	3.2	(5.8)
	Greece	34.4	(1.0)	24.0	(4.0)	26.6	(3.4)	**-7.9**	(3.5)
	Iceland	34.6	(1.1)	c	c	41.7	(6.6)	7.2	(6.7)
	Ireland	29.0	(0.7)	33.8	(5.9)	36.8	(3.6)	**7.8**	(3.6)
	Israel	45.5	(1.1)	36.8	(2.1)	38.2	(3.7)	-7.3	(3.9)
	Italy	26.2	(0.4)	23.9	(3.0)	31.1	(1.8)	**4.9**	(1.8)
	Luxembourg	33.6	(1.2)	29.9	(1.3)	34.5	(1.9)	0.9	(2.3)
	Mexico	32.8	(0.5)	44.0	(6.8)	40.2	(5.6)	7.3	(5.6)
	Netherlands	30.8	(1.0)	38.2	(2.8)	36.7	(5.8)	5.8	(6.0)
	New Zealand	26.9	(1.2)	33.6	(2.9)	43.6	(1.9)	**16.7**	(2.3)
	Norway	42.3	(1.0)	46.7	(4.1)	48.2	(4.0)	5.9	(4.1)
	Portugal	40.3	(1.1)	38.3	(6.9)	34.2	(3.5)	-6.1	(3.9)
	Slovenia	34.2	(1.0)	34.5	(4.3)	30.8	(5.8)	-3.4	(5.8)
	Spain	31.1	(0.8)	21.1	(4.6)	29.4	(2.2)	-1.7	(2.3)
	Sweden	35.1	(0.9)	39.2	(3.3)	38.6	(3.6)	3.5	(3.5)
	Switzerland	29.2	(1.0)	27.8	(1.9)	30.7	(2.7)	1.5	(2.8)
	United Kingdom	35.3	(0.9)	45.5	(3.4)	50.9	(3.6)	**15.6**	(3.7)
	United States	39.5	(1.0)	36.1	(2.3)	47.5	(5.0)	8.0	(4.9)
	OECD average (25)	32.6	(0.2)	32.9	(0.8)	36.4	(0.8)	**3.8**	(0.8)
Partners	Argentina	28.6	(0.9)	25.0	(5.5)	34.3	(5.4)	5.6	(5.8)
	Brazil	39.6	(0.7)	41.8	(12.6)	48.2	(9.8)	8.5	(9.8)
	Costa Rica	40.0	(1.0)	28.8	(7.3)	33.4	(6.1)	-6.6	(6.4)
	Croatia	32.8	(0.9)	26.8	(3.1)	35.2	(4.1)	2.5	(4.0)
	Hong Kong-China	31.7	(1.3)	27.9	(1.9)	30.9	(2.1)	-0.8	(2.6)
	Jordan	57.3	(1.1)	56.1	(3.0)	59.3	(4.9)	2.0	(4.9)
	Kazakhstan	54.7	(1.3)	58.0	(3.0)	68.4	(3.9)	**13.7**	(4.1)
	Macao-China	24.5	(1.2)	25.4	(1.1)	27.4	(2.1)	2.8	(2.3)
	Montenegro	57.4	(0.9)	53.4	(4.7)	51.4	(5.8)	-5.9	(5.8)
	Qatar	47.8	(0.9)	53.9	(1.4)	51.6	(1.2)	**3.9**	(1.5)
	Russian Federation	40.7	(1.1)	45.9	(3.2)	38.8	(4.9)	-1.9	(5.4)
	Serbia	46.8	(0.9)	46.7	(3.6)	45.0	(6.2)	-1.9	(6.3)
	Singapore	37.0	(1.0)	42.0	(3.9)	50.3	(2.4)	**13.3**	(2.6)
	United Arab Emirates	46.6	(1.3)	48.3	(1.7)	52.0	(1.4)	**5.4**	(1.8)

Notes: Values that are statistically significant are indicated in bold.
OECD average (25) includes only countries with valid data for first- and second-generation immigrants.
Source: OECD, PISA 2012 Database.
Underlying data for the tables can be found at www.oecd.org/edu/school/Immigrant-Students-Tables.xlsx.

[Part 1/1]

Table 5.3 **Resilience of immigrant students**

		Percentage of resilient[1] students					
		Non-immigrants		Immigrants		Difference between immigrants and non-immigrant students	
		%	S.E.	%	S.E.	%	S.E.
OECD	**Australia**	29.3	(1.3)	43.7	(2.4)	**14.4**	(2.6)
	Austria	34.8	(2.9)	24.0	(3.1)	**-10.9**	(3.9)
	Belgium	39.2	(1.5)	24.3	(3.3)	**-14.9**	(3.6)
	Canada	40.3	(1.3)	41.1	(2.5)	0.8	(3.0)
	Czech Republic	29.9	(1.8)	33.0	(8.8)	3.1	(8.6)
	Denmark	28.7	(2.2)	16.6	(2.1)	**-12.2**	(2.9)
	Estonia	48.9	(2.2)	39.7	(8.4)	-9.2	(8.9)
	Finland	42.3	(1.9)	18.7	(3.0)	**-23.6**	(3.6)
	France	29.1	(2.4)	23.8	(2.9)	-5.3	(4.1)
	Germany	37.6	(2.5)	31.2	(3.3)	-6.4	(4.1)
	Greece	19.3	(1.8)	13.3	(2.6)	-6.1	(3.3)
	Iceland	27.8	(1.9)	13.5	(5.2)	**-14.3**	(5.0)
	Ireland	31.9	(1.9)	41.3	(7.1)	9.5	(6.9)
	Israel	14.7	(1.6)	24.6	(3.1)	**9.9**	(3.3)
	Italy	33.7	(1.3)	25.4	(2.5)	**-8.4**	(2.6)
	Luxembourg	32.7	(3.5)	30.2	(1.7)	-2.6	(3.5)
	Mexico	20.4	(1.1)	2.4	(1.4)	**-18.0**	(2.0)
	Netherlands	43.4	(3.2)	36.5	(4.7)	-6.9	(4.5)
	New Zealand	28.6	(2.1)	21.9	(3.0)	-6.6	(3.8)
	Norway	28.4	(2.4)	18.5	(3.3)	**-9.9**	(3.8)
	Portugal	39.2	(2.6)	16.5	(5.3)	**-22.7**	(6.2)
	Slovenia	31.9	(2.0)	25.1	(3.9)	-6.7	(4.3)
	Spain	35.1	(1.4)	19.3	(3.0)	**-15.8**	(2.8)
	Sweden	25.5	(1.7)	17.3	(3.1)	**-8.1**	(3.3)
	Switzerland	55.5	(2.3)	38.8	(2.2)	**-16.7**	(2.5)
	United Kingdom	29.9	(1.8)	28.7	(4.7)	-1.2	(4.8)
	United States	23.7	(2.3)	30.9	(2.8)	**7.2**	(3.6)
	OECD average (27)	32.7	(0.4)	25.9	(0.8)	**-6.7**	(0.9)
Partners	**Argentina**	7.1	(1.4)	4.3	(2.3)	-2.9	(2.5)
	Costa Rica	11.0	(1.4)	4.3	(2.7)	**-6.6**	(3.1)
	Croatia	26.5	(1.7)	26.9	(3.8)	0.4	(4.1)
	Hong Kong-China	76.2	(2.5)	79.1	(2.3)	2.9	(2.9)
	Jordan	5.1	(0.9)	6.5	(3.6)	1.4	(3.8)
	Kazakhstan	11.2	(1.9)	12.3	(4.0)	1.1	(4.1)
	Latvia	33.1	(2.2)	25.2	(8.4)	-7.9	(8.9)
	Liechtenstein	54.6	(8.1)	36.0	(8.5)	-18.6	(12.0)
	Macao-China	64.7	(3.0)	76.7	(1.4)	**12.0**	(3.5)
	Malaysia	14.7	(1.4)	16.6	(7.1)	2.0	(6.8)
	Montenegro	7.5	(1.0)	14.3	(5.8)	6.8	(6.0)
	Qatar	0.5	(0.3)	5.2	(0.7)	**4.8**	(0.7)
	Russian Federation	27.6	(2.5)	21.4	(4.3)	-6.2	(4.2)
	Serbia	19.4	(1.7)	27.0	(5.7)	7.6	(5.6)
	Singapore	65.4	(1.5)	74.0	(4.5)	8.6	(4.6)
	United Arab Emirates	4.2	(0.7)	11.7	(1.5)	**7.6**	(1.6)

Notes: Values that are statistically significant are indicated in bold.

OECD average (27) includes only countries with valid data on immigrant students.

1. Resilient students are those who are in the bottom quarter of the PISA *index of economic, social and cultural status* in the country of assessment, and who perform among the top quarter of students in all countries, after accounting for socio-economic status.

Source: OECD, PISA 2012 Database.

Underlying data for the tables can be found at www.oecd.org/edu/school/Immigrant-Students-Tables.xlsx.

[Part 1/1]

Table 5.4 **Parents' expectations for their child's education, by immigrant status**

	Difference in expectations (immigrants – non-immigrants)		Difference in expectations (immigrants – non-immigrants), after accounting for socio-economic status		Difference in expectations (immigrants – non-immigrants), after accounting for socio-economic status and performance in mathematics	
	Percentage-point difference	S.E.	Percentage-point difference	S.E.	Percentage-point difference	S.E.
Belgium	**8.88**	(3.38)	**23.23**	(3.65)	**37.47**	(3.60)
Chile	0.02	(7.57)	-4.17	(7.51)	-2.35	(6.82)
Croatia	**-10.23**	(2.30)	-3.31	(2.07)	-1.26	(1.86)
Germany	**6.19**	(3.12)	**20.89**	(3.27)	**23.90**	(3.05)
Hong Kong-China	**-6.11**	(2.41)	**6.49**	(1.80)	**4.47**	(1.71)
Hungary	**22.14**	(5.14)	**13.76**	(5.29)	**10.49**	(4.08)
Italy	**-18.66**	(1.85)	**-9.15**	(1.72)	**-3.60**	(1.71)
Macao China	**-3.86**	(1.42)	0.82	(1.41)	-1.76	(1.35)
Mexico	**-13.49**	(3.32)	**-9.61**	(3.09)	-1.84	(3.09)
Portugal	-1.64	(3.43)	0.41	(3.56)	5.11	(3.36)

	Difference in expectations (immigrants – non-immigrants)				Difference in expectations (immigrants – non-immigrants), after accounting for socio-economic status				Difference in expectations (immigrants – non-immigrants), after accounting for socio-economic status and performance in mathematics			
	First-generation		Second-generation		First-generation		Second-generation		First-generation		Second-generation	
	Percentage-point difference	S.E.	Percentage-point difference	S.E.	Percentage-point difference	S.E.	Percentage-point difference	S.E.	Percentage-point difference	S.E.	Percentage-point difference	S.E.
Belgium	**10.21**	(5.02)	**7.76**	(3.95)	**22.66**	(5.62)	**23.71**	(4.08)	**39.17**	(6.11)	**36.07**	(3.25)
Chile	0.49	(8.00)			-5.45	(8.09)			-3.25	(7.48)	0.00	(0.00)
Croatia	**-9.44**	(4.11)	**-10.58**	(2.53)	0.59	(4.01)	**-5.04**	(2.34)	2.03	(3.07)	-2.73	(2.19)
Germany	0.72	(6.10)	**7.59**	(3.69)	**14.93**	(6.26)	**22.32**	(3.71)	**22.03**	(5.82)	**24.35**	(3.40)
Hong Kong-China	**-12.89**	(3.22)	-1.40	(2.37)	1.84	(2.61)	**9.55**	(1.88)	1.92	(2.18)	**6.16**	(1.91)
Hungary			**30.37**	(4.99)			**19.70**	(4.60)			**13.95**	(4.06)
Italy	**-21.43**	(2.27)	**-10.67**	(2.91)	**-11.20**	(2.14)	-3.30	(2.53)	**-4.68**	(2.18)	-0.53	(2.32)
Macao China	**-5.80**	(1.82)	**-3.26**	(1.58)	-2.48	(1.86)	1.87	(1.53)	**-4.42**	(1.76)	-0.90	(1.49)
Mexico	**-15.08**	(4.15)	-10.44	(5.49)	**-10.19**	(3.79)	-8.50	(5.16)	-1.54	(3.84)	-2.41	(4.92)
Portugal	1.67	(4.56)	-5.34	(5.62)	3.21	(4.73)	-2.68	(4.86)	6.56	(4.66)	3.49	(4.46)

Note: Values that are statistically significant are indicated in bold.
Source: OECD, PISA 2012 Database.
Underlying data for the tables can be found at www.oecd.org/edu/school/Immigrant-Students-Tables.xlsx.

ORGANISATION FOR ECONOMIC CO-OPERATION AND DEVELOPMENT

The OECD is a unique forum where governments work together to address the economic, social and environmental challenges of globalisation. The OECD is also at the forefront of efforts to understand and to help governments respond to new developments and concerns, such as corporate governance, the information economy and the challenges of an ageing population. The Organisation provides a setting where governments can compare policy experiences, seek answers to common problems, identify good practice and work to co-ordinate domestic and international policies.

The OECD member countries are: Australia, Austria, Belgium, Canada, Chile, the Czech Republic, Denmark, Estonia, Finland, France, Germany, Greece, Hungary, Iceland, Ireland, Israel, Italy, Japan, Korea, Luxembourg, Mexico, the Netherlands, New Zealand, Norway, Poland, Portugal, the Slovak Republic, Slovenia, Spain, Sweden, Switzerland, Turkey, the United Kingdom and the United States. The European Union takes part in the work of the OECD.

OECD Publishing disseminates widely the results of the Organisation's statistics gathering and research on economic, social and environmental issues, as well as the conventions, guidelines and standards agreed by its members.

OECD PUBLISHING, 2, rue André-Pascal, 75775 PARIS CEDEX 16
(91 2015 11 1P) ISBN 978-92-64-24949-3 – 2015

www.ingramcontent.com/pod-product-compliance
Lightning Source LLC
LaVergne TN
LVHW081408110826
845149LV00010B/1670

* 9 7 8 9 2 6 4 2 4 9 4 9 3 *